PC Toys
14 Cool Projects for Home, Office, and Entertainment

Barry Press and Marcia Press

WILEY

Wiley Publishing, Inc.

PC Toys
14 Cool Projects for Home, Office, and Entertainment

Published by
Wiley Publishing, Inc.
10475 Crosspoint Boulevard
Indianapolis, IN 46256
www.wiley.com

Published simultaneously in Canada

ISBN: 0-7645-4229-X

Manufactured in the United States of America

10 9 8 7 6 5 4 3 2 1

1B/ST/RQ/QT/IN

For general information on our other products and services or to obtain technical support, please contact our Customer Care Department within the U.S. at (800) 762-2974, outside the U.S. at (317) 572-3993 or fax (317) 572-4002.

Wiley also publishes its books in a variety of electronic formats. Some content that appears in print may not be available in electronic books.

Library of Congress Cataloging-in-Publication Data

Press, Barry, 1950–
  PC toys : 14 cool projects for home, office, and entertainment / Barry
Press and Marcia Press.
    p. cm.
  ISBN 0-7645-4229-X (PAPER/CD-ROM)
  1. Home automation. 2. Home computer networks. 3. Household
electronics. 4. Home entertainment systems. I. Press, Marcia, 1950–
II. Title.
 TK7881.25.P74 2003
 004.16--dc22

                                                    2003017922

WILEY is a trademark of Wiley Publishing, Inc.

Credits

Executive Editor
Chris Webb

Development Editor
Emilie Herman

Production Editor
Gabrielle Nabi

Technical Editor
Bill Karow

Copy Editor
Jennifer Ashley

Editorial Manager
Kathryn A. Malm

Vice President & Executive Group Publisher
Richard Swadley

Vice President and Executive Publisher
Bob Ipsen

Vice President and Publisher
Joseph B. Wikert

Executive Editorial Director
Mary Bednarek

Project Coordinator
Maridee Ennis

Graphics and Production Specialists
Jennifer Click
Sean Decker
LeAndra Hosier
Mary Gillot Virgin

Quality Control Technicians
John Tyler Connoley
John Greenough
Susan Moritz
Brian Walls

Permissions Editor
Carmen Krikorian

Media Development Specialist
Greg Stafford

Cover Designer
Anthony Bunyan

Proofreading and Indexing
TECHBOOKS Production Services

This book is dedicated to Eve and Cain.

Acknowledgments

We gratefully acknowledge the assistance of the following people and companies in the development of this book:

George Alfs, Armin Bacher, Steve Bisque, Mike Braun, Melody Chalaban, Albert Chang, Kaiwen Cheng, Donna Durant, Craig Ecclestone, Tom Ehrensperger, Mark Espenshied, Karen Franz, Juergen Freiwald, Kelly Gordon, Russ Heilig, Emilie Herman, Bill Karow, Brett Kikawa, Reed Little, Gayle McDonnell, Jake McKee, Niko Mak, Nathan Papadopulos, John Paulsen, Jonah Peskin, Joan Peterson, Jen Press, Kate Press, Paulien Ruijssenaars, Carolyn Schmidt, Ken Schulz, John Swinimer, Sam Tingey, Manny Vara, Dr. Gilbert Verghese, Matt Wagner, Chris Webb, and Al Wijoyo.

ATI Technologies Incorporated, Belkin Corporation, Data Harvest Educational Incorporated, Davis Instruments Corporation, DeLorme, Digitrax Incorporated, Eagletron Incorporated, Epic Games Incorporated, Freiwald Software, Homeseer Technologies LLC, Intel Corporation, LEGO Systems Incorporated, Logitech Incorporated, Meade Instruments Corporation, Pinnacle Systems Incorporated, RadioShack Corporation, Seagate Technology LLC, Shuttle Computer Group Incorporated, Software Bisque, Soltek Computer Incorporated, Streamzap Incorporated, VGPS, Webcam Corporation, Winland Electronics, Incorporated, and X10.

Wiley's *Toys* series of books for hardcore technology enthusiasts was inspired by Chris Negus, author of *Linux Toys* and the *Red Hat Linux Bible*.

Contents at a Glance

Contents

Introduction

I think there is a world market for maybe five computers.

~IBM Chairman Thomas Watson, 1943

Life with and near computers has changed dramatically in the few decades they've been around. From mechanical devices to highly secret electronic machines used for breaking cryptographic codes, computers evolved from crude calculation assistants to systems capable of independent operation. In the transformation from expensive, room-filling monsters to laptop computers, each with perhaps more power than the sum of all the computers built in the 1960s, computers have become indispensable assets in business and in our personal lives.

The next transformation for computers, the one happening now, is from being distinct objects to commonplace tools. Our parents had no concept of a personal computer. We had the advantage of learning the science and technology of computers in universities and in business. Many adults, however, have had to train themselves, and have ended up seeing their computers as things set apart from life, foes in an endless struggle. Our children are different. They were born into a world where computers always existed, and indeed we've made a point of giving our own children free access to their own computers from the time they could walk. They didn't do much with them as toddlers, but they did enough to learn their computers would respond to them and were every bit as much a commonplace part of life as the telephone, television, and dogs. Computers, for them, aren't something to be in awe or fear of. Computers are simply instruments to be coerced into doing what they want.

In that change of worldview is power. Your computer isn't some monolithic entity capable of only the magic someone else imbues it with; it's an appliance—a minion, really—available to be part of anything you can imagine and create.

What Are PC Toys?

PC Toys fit the mold of electronic minions, in that none of them are computers for their own sake. Instead, all the projects in Table I-1 are interesting devices that happen to contain a PC as a core component because it was easier or more useful to build each project around a computer.

Table I-1   PC Toys

Chapter	Description
1	Create your own TiVo-like digital video recorder
2	Build a jukebox for your home stereo
3	Have hot, fresh coffee whenever you get up
4	Build a telescope tracking station
5	Monitor your workout
6	Home surveillance with Internet remote access
7	Monitor your refrigerator and freezer
8	Monitor your fish tank
9	Do your own automotive diagnostics
10	Build your own in-car navigation system
11	Build a weather station
12	Create and control your own robots
13	Throw a networked head-to head video gaming party
14	Set up a computerized control center for model trains

Nearly every PC Toy has a commercial equivalent, be it a literal TiVo digital video recorder, a DVD MP3 player, your automated treadmill, one of the Hertz Neverlost GPS navigators, or some other product. Depending on what you build, and how much work you put into building it, a commercial product might be better than your version, might be inferior, or might simply not be available in pre-assembled form you can go out and buy. What's unique to the PC Toys you build yourself is that your having built them equips you to modify and customize them to be what you want, not a one-size-fits-all generic answer designed by someone else.

What's Required to Build the PC Toys

You can build every one of the PC Toys using nothing but the parts lists and directions you'll find in this book, you can take that information as a baseline and veer off in your own direction, or you can follow a middle course. Whichever path you take, here are the assumptions we've made about you and the components that go into the PC Toys.

Some Skills and Experience

First off, we're assuming you're interested in the PC Toys premise to begin with, which implies you're not intimidated by the common view of computers as monsters from the office automation swamp. Instead, you know your computer is just a machine, one you can twist to your whim.

People with that view invariably obtained it from a sound knowledge of what makes up a computer and how it works. We're not expecting readers to be trained engineers or computer scientists, although some will be, and those people are the best candidates to be extending the PC Toys with their own designs. To build what we've described in the book, however, we're simply expecting you to be comfortable modifying and operating a Windows personal computer using equipment and software you can buy and install.

Equipment

Very few of the PC Toys require a next-generation, expensive computer to run. You may want such a machine for the LAN gaming chapter, depending on the kind of game you'll play, but if you're already playing the fast action games that exploit that kind of power, then you probably already have the machine you need. Adding the gaming network doesn't significantly increase the power required, and you'll see that even a relatively modest machine works as a game server.

The rest of the PC Toys can use what many people would call obsolete computers, ones in the 350 MHz and faster range. A reasonable amount of memory will help performance—we put at least 256 MB into our machines, with 512 MB or more in ones we use intensively. As cheap as quality memory is now, it's an effective upgrade. The modest computing demands for the PC Toys gives you a lot of choices for what computers to use, which fits in nicely with the fact that many of the projects run constantly on the PC and therefore need the computer to be reliable. The most reliable computer is one nobody touches, which lets out the computer you use yourself—get one you can stick in a corner and ignore.

Unless your PC is shockingly well equipped, the PC Toys will likely require you to add hardware to your computer. Some of the hardware is quite inexpensive, while some is not. We've used the more expensive parts in as many of the projects as possible to keep down the overall cost of building multiple PC Toys, but sometimes there were no readily-available inexpensive designs to be found.

We've included some recommendations for how to work with hardware in Appendix B in case you need some guidance or a refresher. If you're after more in-depth information and guidance, look for our *PC Upgrade and Repair Bible*. The fourth edition will be available some time after *PC Toys* arrives in stores, updated for all the new developments since the third edition was published in 2000.

Software

We designed all the PC Toys to run under Windows. We're aware of the religious wars surrounding the choice of operating system, but since computers running our personal favorite (the Symbolics Corporation Lisp language and Genera operating system—http://kogs-www.informatik.uni-hamburg.de/~moeller/symbolics-info/symbolics.html) are in tragically short supply, we chose to use the operating system the largest number of people are familiar with. Like Microsoft or not, that operating system is Windows.

We're not, however, unmitigated fans of Windows. Older, by now sclerotic versions (Windows 3.1, 95, 98, and Me) have warts, high cholesterol, and an unfortunate tendency towards epileptic seizures. We strongly recommend you use the sturdier, younger versions whenever possible. Windows 2000 is what we use most often, but Windows XP is technically even better so long as you're willing to put up with Microsoft's invasions of privacy masquerading under the name Windows Product Activation. Install the service packs and critical security updates from Windows Update (`http://windowsupdate.microsoft.com`; be *exceedingly* careful configuring the automatic updater if you install it) and stick with the device drivers that come with Windows unless you have no options, and you can make either version quite stable.

Appendix A includes more detail on these recommendations.

Internet

We think access to the Internet is essential for building the PC Toys. It's your best source for the hardware and software you'll need, and a rich source of ideas. We've included web links for nearly everything we've used in the projects in the parts lists and accompanying text, but a simpler way to use the links in the book is to find them online at `http://www.wiley.com/compbooks/extremetech`. Bookmark the links page and you've got fast access to any of the sites we suggest in the book.

If you have a choice, you're also better off with a broadband connection to the Internet. Not only will broadband give you faster access to the software you're likely to want to download, most broadband services give you "always-on" access, meaning you don't have to go through the ritual of dialing the modem, waiting for it to connect, waiting for it to authenticate, checking the speed of the connection, and redialing when you discover the telephone company helped you out again with a lousy connection. Always-on access means if your computer is on, you're connected to the Internet. Run the programs you need (PC Toys use a lot of different software to work over the Internet) whenever you need them, regardless of who wants the telephone.

Imagination

A little bit of effort will let you replicate the PC Toys described in this book just the way we built them, and we expect you'll do a lot of interesting things with them just as they are. Stop there, though, and you'll miss what we most hope readers take from the book: a better understanding of how to think about computers as tools to solve everyday problems, not just do work, play games, and surf the Internet.

What you need to take that last step is your imagination and the ability to observe yourself throughout the day, culling out those times when things could be more convenient or when you can't do something the way you want. Learning to think from the point of view that your PC can help solve those problems, learning to see what's possible, can be difficult even with the best imagination. We've included a chapter to help you see your way, a chapter that sketches concepts and approaches for a whole other set of PC Toys:

- Grandparents' screen saver
- Camera as handy copier
- Automated lawn watering
- Running indoor/outdoor Christmas decorations
- Running outdoor/indoor lights while you're on vacation

- Telephone answering machine/Caller ID
- Track cell phone minutes used
- Watch for eBay auctions

We haven't written down the details of how to build each one of these projects, just the idea and a short analysis of an approach. Filling in the details is your work for that chapter, using your imagination and what you'll learn building the other projects in the book.

How Chapters for Each Toy Are Organized

Every chapter in this book, with the exception of this introduction and Chapter 15 (Inventing Your Own PC Toys) follows the same basic structure — you'll read what the project is about and how it works, what's on the parts list, how to build the basic project, and ways you might extend the basic project.

Building from Kits

Every PC Toys project includes a section with a parts list and description of how to build the project from those parts. We're not going to bore you with the details of hardware or software installation in those sections — we assume you've done your share and there are no big mysteries left. We've focused on what's new and different in building the project.

If you get into trouble, find your local experts and tell them what you're building — you'll get all the help you can stand.

The word "kit" is a misnomer if it's leading you to expect you can go to the store and buy a single box with everything you need for one of the PC Toys projects. To begin with, you'll likely have to get the parts you need from several places, some local and some mail order. What we intend to convey by calling these versions of the projects "kits" is that (along with some extras you'll find discussed in the text) the parts lists detail what you need to duplicate the version of the project we built and tested.

You don't have to build your version our way. Indeed, differences between your computer or goals and ours may cause our design not to work for you. You'll use our version as a guideline in that case, combining different parts in a different design.

Building Your Own Design

In addition to the kit instructions that let you replicate the project as we built it, every project includes a section of ideas for how you could extend or modify the design to improve it or add different capabilities. Some of the suggestions are relatively straightforward applications of the design for other purposes, while others suggest you perform your own software development or hardware modifications to make the implementation more sophisticated. Our build-your-own-design suggestions aren't the only ways to extend the projects — you'll undoubtedly think of your own extensions and modifications too.

Where to Find Information and Equipment

Each chapter in *PC Toys* describes the equipment we used and provides web links to the equipment manufacturer. In many cases, the manufacturer's web site lets you order products or links you to retailers, both online and local. Nevertheless, finding parts (particularly if you're as impatient as we are) can be a challenge, so we've listed some of the ways we did it to get you started.

Searching the Internet

If something you need for your project exists, be it parts or information, you can probably get it on the Internet. There are so many people and companies offering so many things on the Internet that your success is almost assured.

Finding what you want is another matter. You have to dig out the ones that have what you need, sometimes without knowing what's available, and when you're searching for something, the sheer numbers of suppliers can work against you to mask what you need to find.

Searching the Internet effectively is therefore a key skill. We search in several ways, ranging from very direct to general, based on how well what you want is defined:

- *Go directly to the manufacturer's web site and search there.* If you know the company that makes what you need, it's most efficient to find their web site and look up the product. Company web sites are often of the form `http://www.company.com`; if that doesn't work, you can typically use a search engine to find the site. Surprisingly few companies we've looked for don't have a web site.

- *Search on a specialized web site.* More general searches you do will frequently turn up web sites focused on specific ideas, technologies, or types of products. Good sites like that are worth bookmarking, because they're good places to search for later needs. You'll find a variety of them, ranging from pure information sites such as `http://gpsinformation.net` to specialized retailers like `http://www.smarthome.com`.

- *Search by make and model, or with key words.* Internet search engines wade through billions of pages for you, and will turn up pure gold if you can invent the right set of search terms. We've used many of them, but Google (`http://www.google.com`) is the one we prefer and the one that was the most useful writing this book. You'll be doing a lot of searching, which you can make much more convenient by loading the Google toolbar and/or making Google the default search engine in your web browser. Instructions for doing that are on the Google web site on their tools page.

- A particularly effective way to find retailers once you know the make and model of what you need is to search for the make and model using Google. The web pages that turn up will be either users of the product (useful in their own right) or sites listing the product for sale.

- Take the time to learn how to use the facilities the search engine offers. Google normally treats words you type as independent search entities, but looks for a phrase if you enclose it in quotes. You can require a word or phrase *not* appear by prefixing it with a minus sign, and can refer to specific web hosts using modifiers listed on the Google site.

- Google isn't limited to searching the entire web. If you install the Google toolbar, you'll find you have buttons available to search just the site containing the page you're looking at, which makes up for sites that lack their own search engines. Sites whose listings are driven from a data base may not index well under Google, but it's worth a try if there's no site-specific alternative.

- *Ask a question.* You don't always know a good set of keywords, causing search engines to return either nothing or too many irrelevant results. Ask Jeeves (http://www.ask.com) is useful in those circumstances — you can ask a question, such as "What is the average annual temperature in Atlanta?" and get back a selection of relevant places to look. The technology underlying Ask Jeeves is different than keyword-based search engines, something that becomes evident if you enter the same question as keywords into Google.

There are yet other places to look for what you need on the Internet. You can often find equipment on eBay, sometimes at a discount and sometimes not. Information and opinions are nearly always available in the Internet newsgroups (also searchable with Google — pick the newsgroups tab on the Google main page). Good newsgroups can be rich in important information, and offer you the ability to ask your own questions and get answers back from well-informed contributors, but they can also be homes for idiots with no idea what they're talking about who nevertheless talk to the exclusion of seemingly anyone else. Differentiating one from the other can be hard if you're not reasonably well informed yourself.

Local and National Sources

We buy parts for projects at both local stores and national chains. Radio Shack, Best Buy, CompUSA, Costco, and Home Depot all have stores near us, and have all been sources of equipment, but so have local merchants with only one or a few locations. The local stores sometimes have better informed staff than what we find in the chains.

We've also found web sites for what looked to be good sources in England and Canada. There's likely to be good sources worldwide, but unfortunately we can't read many of their sites.

Computer Upgrades

Where we buy computer parts depends a lot on what we're looking for and how much of a hurry we're in. We rarely buy memory anywhere but from Crucial (http://www.crucial.com). We've regularly bought motherboards, processors, cases, and power supplies from ESC Technologies (http://www.esctech.com). They can get the Intel motherboards we typically put into computers. The Intel boards are hard to find in local stores, having been pushed out by less expensive motherboard brands that, unfortunately, have usually cost us more time and trouble than we saved buying the board.

We've done well several times at http://www.allstarshop.com, and inevitably buy cables from Cables N Mor (http://www.cablesnmor.com).

The downside to all of the Internet-only stores is that you'll wait several days for shipping, longer if you need to order on a weekend. The big computer chains — Best Buy and CompUSA particularly — have coordinated their web sites with their stores, so you can find what you need on the site and check if the store near you has it in stock. They don't always get it right, but it's every bit as good as waiting on hold for someone who doesn't check for the right item anyhow, and far faster.

We also watch the ads the big stores put in the newspaper. Sales on disk drives are common, and sometimes offer huge 7200 RPM drives for a dollar a gigabyte or less. (We like Seagate and Maxtor, and don't often use Western Digital.)

Sensors

A Google search for *sensors* returns over 1,850,000 pages, which indicates that there's a lot of people involved in building and using sensors but is fundamentally useless. We've found sensors we needed at times using direct searches, such as *temperature sensors*, but typically go looking for sites that catalog and list sensors. A search on *sensors catalog* returns about 250,000 pages, a far smaller number, but one that still needs some pruning. You could keep adding keywords to narrow the search, or could bookmark sites that seem to have collections of what you're looking for. Scrolling through the hits on *sensors catalog*, we found a number of those, including:

- www.measureanything.com
- www.temperatures.com
- www.thomasregister.com (search for *sensor*)
- www.findasensor.com
- www.sensorsportal.com

Home Automation

Most of the home automation and surveillance equipment we used in the book is based on the X-10 power line signaling and control technology. The equipment is no longer available at retail as extensively as it once was, but some simple modules can be found at Radio Shack stores (there's a wider selection on their web site). Your best sources will be online, including www.x10.com and www.smarthome.com. Don't ignore these projects if you happen to live in an area with 220 volt power—versions of some of the X-10 equipment adapted for 220 volts are available.

Data Loggers

Data loggers are modules capable of recording data from sensors independent of a supporting computer. A Google search for *data logger* returns over 94,000 hits, but often the equipment you'll find is too expensive for all but the most serious projects. The one we used in the book, from Data Harvest, isn't inexpensive, but we've used it in three different projects, spreading the cost. You can find the equipment, including sensors, in both the U.S. (www.dataharvest.com) and England (www.data-harvest.co.uk).

Subsystems

You'll need some independent subsystems (telescopes, LEGOs, a CarChip, model trains, and such) to build the PC Toys. The individual chapters include web links to sites where we obtained the equipment, but you'll want to search the web before you buy anything, looking for the best prices and alternative equipment that might better suit your interests.

You'll need some miscellaneous hardware, too, including magnets (try a hardware store; we found them at Home Depot), computer cables (we get them at Cables n Mor, www. cablesnmor.com), and networking equipment (try the same places as above for computer upgrades).

Software

Some of the software we used in the book is on the CD; the rest is either available on the web — there are links in the individual chapters — or comes with products you'll use building the toys. See Appendix C for a description of the CD-ROM.

Enjoy the book!

Entertainment

Create Your Own TiVo-Like Digital Video Recorder

The sky above the port was the color of television, tuned to a dead channel.

~William Gibson, *Neuromancer*

I surf, therefore I am.

~Anonymous

There are more jokes about men and channel surfing than you'd ever want to hear (probably more learned academic studies, too). For all of that, we claim channel surfing stems from just one thing: boredom, caused by not having anything interesting to watch. Not that there's a lack of interesting shows to watch, just that there's a lack of interesting shows *at that particular time.*

Enter the VCR. Literally everyone we know with a TV set, and probably most people you know, have a VCR. Far fewer actually record with them anymore.

The VCR Is Dead. Long Live the VCR!

Jay Leno got a lot of laughs at the Windows 95 launch party ribbing Bill Gates that his VCR flashes 12:00. No one really believes Bill Gates can't set his VCR, but the idea is funny. It's interesting to speculate *why* his and so many other people's VCRs don't have the time set; the likely answer is that he and these other people don't care, because they don't use the timers, which, in turn, is because they're not recording shows.

Most likely, people don't use VCRs to record because it's too much of a pain. There's other evidence that setting up timers is a nuisance, including the existence of VCR Plus codes, which encode into a short number the channel and times for programs. You enter the code into your recorder and it sets up the timer, but for most people it's too much bother—they have to look up the code in the newspaper, *TV Guide*, or another source, then key it into the VCR and make sure a blank tape is loaded. Once it's set up, you can't use the VCR until the recording is done.

Until a few years ago, that was the limit of what was practical in home video recording. You could record what you wanted, but there were lots of little things to set up, and you wouldn't want to set it up for very far in the future. For most people television meant either scheduled TV shows or rental tapes and DVDs.

TiVo, ReplayTV, and UltimateTV (collectively called *personal video recorders*, or *PVRs*) changed everything simply by adding a PC—albeit in disguise—to the process. That one innovation eliminates all the nuisance involved in home video recording, and makes a lot of other features possible. Although we're not as fanatic as some whose posts we've read on the TiVo Community forums at www.tivocommunity.com, TiVo has very much changed the way we watch TV. We tell our TiVo what shows we want to make sure are available for us to see, and it records them whenever they're on. We watch the shows we want to see at the time we choose, not the time the networks choose.

How PVRs Work

MPEG compression and huge increases in disk capacity were the key to PVRs, because together they made it possible to store relatively large amounts of video at a reasonable cost. Figure 1-1 shows the basic design of a PVR and how those elements work together.

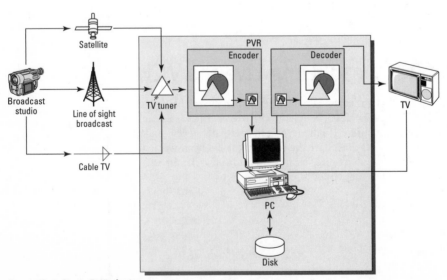

FIGURE 1-1: Basic PVR design

A PVR is a PC with TV display output, a TV tuner, an MPEG compressor, and an MPEG decompressor. Analog video signals, whether from a satellite receiver, antenna, cable network, or cable set top box, come into a tuner in the PVR. The tuner chooses the specific channel and passes the audio/video (AV) signal to the encoder, which digitizes the signal and compresses it. The PC records the compressed AV stream and, if desired, passes a copy to the decoder which decompresses the stream and outputs it to the TV.

PVR magic comes from the fact that the decoder isn't fed directly from the live stream coming from the encoder, it's fed from the disk. Anything on disk is immediately accessible, so you can slow playback down, speed it up, pause, play a prerecorded show, or watch an instant replay. You can do any of these actions simply by repositioning the access point in a file.

Digitizing, Compressing, and Recording Television

Your PVR converts the signal to digits before it records to disk. The television signal output from the tuner delivers 30 pictures every second, each about 720 x 480 pixels. Using 8 bits per pixel for each of red, green, and blue (that is, 24 bits per pixel total), the video alone converts to more than 30 megabytes per second (MBps). That's equivalent to nearly 107GB per hour of recorded video. Desktop computer disk drives — which may not sustain 30 megabits per second (Mbps), much less 30 MBps — cost roughly $1 per gigabyte at retail. Without compression, storage for one hour's recording would cost over $100 and PVRs would not exist.

MPEG-1 and MPEG-2 compression change the cost equation. MPEG-1 compression gives you video quality on playback equivalent to that of a VCR, and requires only 1.5 Mbps (200 kilobytes per second, KBps). MPEG-2 compression, used on DVDs, is very high quality and requires 6–8 Mbps (0.8–1.0 MBps). Using MPEG-2 compression at a full 9 Mbps, even a 40GB drive can hold 11 hours of recordings; a 120GB drive holds over 33 hours.

The PVR has to complete MPEG compression in real time to store compressed video on disk, consuming pictures from the video signal as fast as they arrive. Current-generation X86 processors, including the latest and best from Intel and AMD, cannot quite keep up using software for MPEG encoding — a hardware assist or a complete hardware encoder is required.

The hardware MPEG encoder is the one weak spot in PVRs. The broadcast-quality digitizers and encoders used by satellite television providers are very expensive, impractically so for use in consumer electronics. The versions used in consumer electronics are much less expensive, but sacrifice some video quality. (Interestingly, DirecTV subscribers get broadcast quality compression *and* consumer-priced PVRs, because the DirecTV TiVo receivers get a compressed stream off the satellite they record straight to disk — there's no encoder in the PVR, because the encoding is done in the studio.)

The final step in the PVR encoding path is recording the compressed stream to disk. Even DVD-quality MPEG-2 compressed streams only need about 1 MBps, a sustained transfer rate readily achievable by even the least expensive disk drive now in production. You'll need an aggregate of more than 2 MBps to cover simultaneous record, playback, program access, and swapping, but unless the PC has less memory than the average gnat, even that workload won't keep a drive very busy.

Never Bet Against Silicon

More than a few companies have gone broke betting against advances in microprocessor price and performance. The first examples we saw of this shortsightedness were companies in the mid-eighties that bet that their proprietary designs running the LISP programming language would always be faster than generic microprocessors running LISP in software. Today you can find the Symbolics Lisp machine in an online museum (`kogs-www.informatik.uni-hamburg.de/~moeller/symbolics-info/symbolics.html`), the Lisp Machine Incorporated K-machine in an online retrospective (`fare.tunes.org/tmp/emergent/kmachine.htm`), and the Texas Instruments Explorer in even more obscure places (`lemonodor.com/archives/000242.html`). Even the magnificent, then massively parallel Thinking Machines computers (`www.inc.com/articles/finance/fin_manage/bankrupt/2622.html`) have been completely eclipsed by distributed computing over the Internet (see `www.grid.org/projects` or `www.seti.org`).

All these companies shared one fatal problem: they could never keep up with the massive investment in research and development companies like Intel and AMD focus on general purpose microprocessors. No elegance of architecture and design could outpace the brute force of faster clocks and deeper pipelining.

Precisely the same effect is guaranteed to eclipse the custom chips now used for real-time MPEG compression. Software *will* be able to encode real-time video on your desktop computer within a few years.

Today, for example, the 933 MHz Pentium III we use to encode DVDs runs nearly seven times slower than real time, requiring ten hours to encode the 86 minutes of video making up two one-hour television broadcasts. However, Intel tests (see www.intel.com/performance/resources/desktop/charts.htm) suggest that the fastest Pentium 4 processors—3.06 GHz with hyperthreading as of the writing of this chapter—are nearly six times faster than a 500 MHz Pentium III when encoding video, so they're homing in on the target. Digital signal processors from Texas Instruments can already encode some versions of the MPEG-4 standard in real time. The days of the special-purpose compression chip are definitely numbered.

Playback and Special Effects

At the simplest level, a PVR mimics a VCR. You record a show to disk, and then play it back linearly from beginning to end. Inside the PC, recording creates a large file, and playback reads it. Pausing during playback stops reading the file and remembers the last position. Rewinding skips backwards in the file, grabs a frame and displays it, skips backwards some more, and so on. Fast forwarding skips a bunch of frames, plays one, skips some more, and repeats.

Playback doesn't need to wait until recording is complete. As soon as the PC has any recorded data to play, it can start feeding the compressed stream to the decoder and can make all the special effects available. TiVo PVRs use that idea, for example, to maintain a running 30-minute history for the current channel (it's cleared whenever you change channels), letting you replay events or skip commercials. The 30-minute buffer always contains the most recent 30 minutes because the file is used as a circular buffer (see Figure 1-2). The encoder fills the file at whatever point in the file is the "front," wrapping around from the physical end of the file space to the beginning when necessary. The decoder empties the file from the "back," which is the oldest data in the file. If the front passes the back, the oldest data gets erased and replaced with new data, and the "back" moves forward to always stay properly positioned.

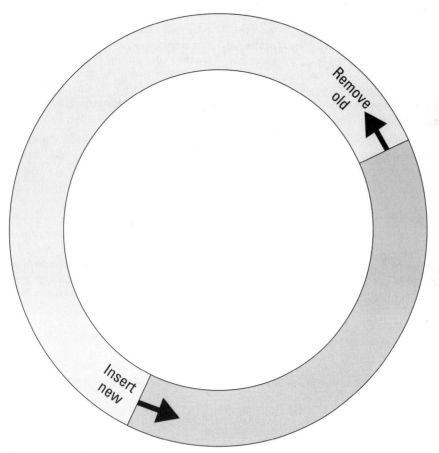

FIGURE 1-2: Circular buffer operation

A PVR can do all its special effects tricks over the data held in the circular buffer file just as it does over a complete file for a prerecorded show, which is how you implement the ability to replay the past 30 minutes.

Program Guides

There's more to a PVR than a VCR on steroids. Giving your PC information about what's coming up on each channel — a *program guide* (sometimes called an *interactive program guide*) — lets you simply tell the PC what you want to see, then have it search the listings and figure out what to record and when. If the program guide delivers information beyond show titles, times, and channels, your PC can search on that added information. Knowing who's in the show, what its story line and content rating are, whether it's a rerun or first run, when it first aired, or whether there are secondary audio channels can all help you decide what to record.

Program guides must be tailored to your specific broadcast area, cable system, or satellite provider. A useful program guide includes not only the data itself, but also a delivery mechanism and a user interface for display, search, and control. The Gemstar program guide you'll see later in this chapter downloads its data over the Internet; other program guide services download through satellite TV channels, and downloads embedded in TV channels are possible. The program guide update frequency depends on how much advance information can be stored; less information stored means more frequent updates are necessary.

A basic program guide grid looks a lot like the listings you find in the newspaper, giving you a matrix of shows sorted by time and channel. Other program guide views typically filter and sort by station, actor, and category.

Building and Using Your PVR from Kits

Although your PC provides the processing and control for the entire PVR, you need a TV tuner in the PC to make all the processing possible. A Google search on *windows tv tuner* led us to the page at www.techadvice.com/help/Products/T/tvTunerCards.htm, which says Windows-compatible tuners are available from eight different companies. We used a tuner integrated with a graphics board from ATI, their All-In-Wonder product line. ATI offers a range of All-In-Wonder boards, from the lower-end All-In-Wonder VE (mirror. ati.com/products/pc/aiwve/index.html) to the gamer quality All-In-Wonder 9700 Pro (mirror.ati.com/products/pc/aiw9700pro/index.html). If you want only the tuner, ATI has the TV Wonder VE and TV Wonder Pro boards. You'll likely want an add-on remote control (mirror.ati.com/products/pc/remotewonder/index.html) with the VE; it's included in the 9700 Pro version.

If you don't want to open the case to install a tuner on a PCI or AGP card, Hauppage Computer Works offers their WinTV-USB module (www.hauppauge.com/html/usb_data.htm).

Parts List

We used the All-In-Wonder VE combined with the Remote Wonder for our project, removing the old video board from the computer before installing the new card. Table 1-1 shows the parts we used in this chapter. You need only a TV tuner with software for a bare-bones PVR; everything else in the list is optional.

Table 1-1   PC PVR Parts List

Part	Manufacturer and Model Number
TV Tuner and Graphics Card	ATI All-In-Wonder VE ($103.79 and up at www.shopper.com) mirror.ati.com/products/pc/aiwve/index.html
Remote Control	ATI Remote Wonder ($49.99 list) mirror.ati.com/products/pc/remotewonder/index.html
DVD Writer	Memorex DVD+R/RW Drive ($299.99 list; $199.99 at BestBuy) www.memorex.com/products/product_display.php?cid=161&pid=496&oid=573
Video Editing and DVD Authoring Software	Pinnacle Studio ($61.60 and up at www.shopper.com) www.pinnaclesys.com/ProductPage.asp?Product_ID=577
	We also use Pinnacle Expression to do the compression and write DVDs, leaving Studio free for editing ($27 and up at www.shopper.com) www.pinnaclesys.com/productpage.asp?product_id=603

The minimum PC requirements for your PVR are really basic, although if you're going to be doing DVDs you'll want a much beefier machine (see the sidebar "Never Bet Against Silicon" for some estimates of how long MPEG compression for DVDs can take on different processors). We used a 600 MHz Pentium III with 128MB of RAM running Windows 2000 to host the PVR. The only display on the machine was the TV next to it; we used no computer monitor. The machine we use for DVD creation is a 933 MHz Pentium III with 512MB RAM also running Windows 2000.

Disk storage is another matter altogether. We found that recording directly in MPEG format from the All-In-Wonder VE required about 800 KBps, while recording uncompressed video through a Pinnacle Studio AV (www.pinnaclesys.com/docloader.asp?templ=1070&doclink=/WebVideo/studioversion8/English(US)/doc/comparison.htm&product_id=577), which we use to digitize analog video, requires about 4 MBps. Table 1-2 shows the implications of those rates — if you're doing much recording at all, you're going to want an enormous disk. Not several disks adding up to a large total, but one enormous disk, because if the space is spread across multiple disks you'll have to keep fiddling with dialog boxes to tell your PVR where to put recordings.

Table 1-2   Video Recording Storage Requirements

Duration (Hours)	MPEG at 800 KBps	MPEG-like compression at 4,096 KBps
	Required Storage (GBps)	
0.5	1.373	7.031
1.0	2.747	14.063
1.5	4.120	21.094
2.0	5.493	28.125
2.5	6.866	35.156
3.0	8.240	42.188
3.5	9.613	49.219
4.0	10.986	56.250

A useful comparison is that a first-generation DirecTV TiVo (DirecTiVo) stores up to 35 hours of video on a 40GB drive, implying compressed data rates less than 320 KBps. The compression rate coming from the DirecTV satellite is variable, though, and we've found the average capacity of a DirecTiVo to be closer to 25 hours, which at times is severely constraining. If you assume you want at least 20 hours of storage using the MPEG compression provided by the All-In-Wonder VE, you'll need around 60GB of available disk space.

Table 1-3 summarizes the MPEG-1 and MPEG-2 compression formats predefined in the All-In-Wonder software. The table is sorted by compression type and then by video data rate. The DVD Low and Video CD formats are close to VCR quality, although not as good; the DVD High format is comparable to what you'll find on a commercial DVD. The Good format is the basis for Table 1-2 (the discrepancy between the 6.0 Mbps video rate in Table 1-3 and the 6.4 Mbps overall rate implied by the 800 KBps rate in Table 1-2 covers the audio channel).

Table 1-3   All-In-Wonder Video Recording Storage Requirements

Name	Type	Width	Height	Video Rate (Mbps)
Low Res QCIF	MPEG 1	176	144	0.8
DVD Low	MPEG 1	352	240	1.0
Video CD	MPEG 1	352	240	1.1
Quarter VGA	MPEG 1	320	240	1.6

Name	Type	Width	Height	Video Rate (Mbps)
Quarter CIF	MPEG 1	352	240	2.4
Longer	MPEG-2	480	480	2.0
Super Video CD	MPEG-2	480	480	2.3
DVD Medium	MPEG-2	352	480	3.0
Medium	MPEG-2	320	480	4.0
Half Horizontal	MPEG-2	352	480	4.8
VGA	MPEG-2	640	480	6.0
Good	MPEG-2	640	480	6.0
Full Res CCIR-601	MPEG-2	720	480	7.2
DVD	MPEG-2	352	480	8.0
DVD High	MPEG-2	720	480	8.0

Later in this chapter you'll see how to make DVDs from your PVR recordings using a DVD writer. We've used the Memorex writer listed in the table, but implicit in that choice is that we happen to record using the DVD+R format. There are, unfortunately, two DVD recordable formats—the other one, incompatible with DVD+R, is DVD-R. Both formats are compatible with about 80 to 85 percent of the available DVD players, although not the same 80 to 85 percent. The DVD Player Compatibility List at www.dvdrhelp.com/dvdplayers is a good (but not infallible) way to see which formats your DVD player can handle. If you're willing to pay a little more, however, you don't have to choose between the two formats, because the Sony DRU500AX (www.sonystyle.com/is-bin/INTERSHOP.enfinity/eCS/Store/en/-/USD/SY_DisplayProductInformation-Start;sid=JgBMcCAOGI9MWx6 DKMNGe28fMKtyFaxSTg4=?CatalogCategoryID=mbsKC0%2eNSUMAAAD0ge4Xh0jm& ProductID=PuwKC0%2eNT9IAAAD0XlAXh0jr&Dept=cpu) will write both DVD+R and DVD-R formats.

If you're a PC video gamer with an aging video card, don't underestimate the benefits of the combination of the very high performance Radeon 9700 Pro with a TV tuner in the All-In-Wonder 9700 Pro. The latest generation of games, such as Id Software's Doom III, requires more horsepower than an aging video card can deliver, so the combined card is a good way to serve both needs. John Carmack of Id Software, who leads much of what the PC gaming industry does in the area of computer graphics, often comments on video cards and performance in his .plan file (available at www.bluesnews.com/plans/1/). He's made it clear there that even cards as recent as the nVidia GeForce won't be fast enough to run Doom III, and that a GeForce 2 will need a very fast processor behind it to give minimally acceptable performance. The Pinnacle Studio software is included with the All-In-Wonder 9700 Pro, reducing your total costs if you'll be writing DVDs.

How the ATI All-In-Wonder VE Works

The All-In-Wonder 9700 Pro board (Figure 1-3) includes little on the card besides the TV tuner and the graphics chip (which is under the surprisingly large fan).

FIGURE 1-3: All-In-Wonder 9700 Pro

ALL-IN-WONDER, ALL-IN-WONDER 9700 PRO, and REMOTE WONDER are trademarks of ATI Technologies.

More interesting from a functional point of view is Figure 1-4, which shows what's *inside* an All-In-Wonder board. The left half of the drawing shows the functions required to pull in the TV signal, while the right half shows the TV and graphics output. The connection between the AV digitizer and the graphics frame buffer provides an efficient way to display video on screen without bogging down the PC.

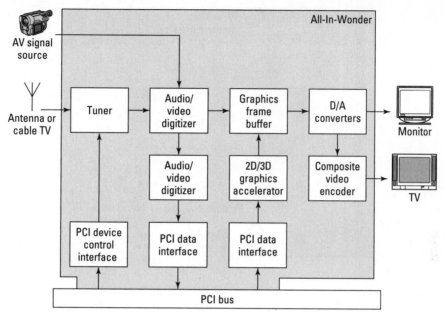

FIGURE 1-4: All-In-Wonder VE block diagram

Hooking Up Your Computer and Television

Figure 1-5 expands on the interfaces in Figure 1-4 to show you the essential connections required to connect your All-In-Wonder equipped computer to a television. You'll use a 75-ohm coaxial cable to bring the television signal to the tuner on the All-In-Wonder, whether from an antenna or a cable system. You're better off avoiding the flat, 300-ohm cable sometimes used for TV signals, because good coaxial cable has lower loss, is more resistant to interference, and the matching transformers (called *baluns*) you need to adapt 300-ohm line to a 75-ohm input introduce loss themselves.

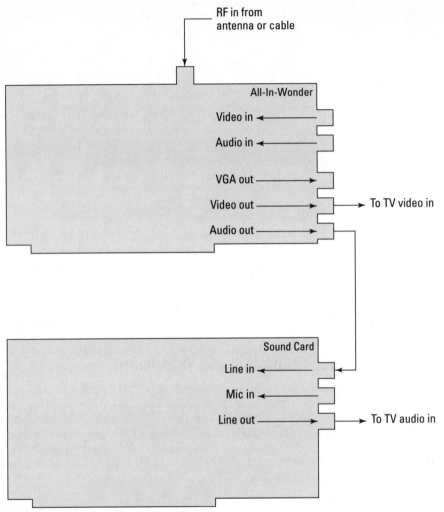

FIGURE 1-5: Key All-In-Wonder connections

Splitters, Amplifiers, and the Accessories Rack

A TV hook-up isn't always available conveniently near the back of your computer, and if not, you've got some cabling to do. That means a trip to Home Depot, Radio Shack, or their equivalent, where you'll poke your way through a wall of connectors, cables, adapters, amplifiers, and other accessories, all of which proclaim to be the key to a sharp, crisp picture. Keep just a few things in mind, though, and you'll be able to sort through your situation and figure out what you need.

- **Signal strength.** The input to any *radio frequency* (RF) device has a range of signal strength it's designed to handle. Too weak a signal gets overpowered by noise, but too strong a signal overpowers the device and gets distorted.

- **Noise.** Noise that combines with your RF signal is literally everywhere, coming both from radio and television transmissions and from electronic equipment with less than perfect shielding (that would be essentially all of them). You can't get rid of noise; you can only knock it down with good shielding or overpower it with a strong signal.

- **Loss.** Cables, connectors, splitters, switches, and almost everything else you put in the signal path introduce loss, reducing the signal strength. A good-quality cable introduces less loss than a poor one or than one abused by weather for years. Clean, tight connectors introduce less loss and tend to keep water and corrosion out. Splitters are evil, knocking the signal down by a factor greater than the number of ports (yes, a four-port splitter reduces your signal by a factor of more than four).

Once a signal is too weak to overpower the noise, you'll never separate the two again. That means you want to amplify signals at the start of a long cable run, or near the middle, rather than at the end, because at the end of the cable the signal is weak and the amplifier builds up both the signal and the noise. Amplify at the beginning or in the middle, and the signal remains strong compared to the noise. Similarly, you should amplify before a splitter, not after it.

It's not as easy as tossing in amplifiers after every 20 or 30 feet, though, because too much amplification creates too strong a signal and can overload the sensitive inputs of the tuner or downstream amplifiers. RF engineers calculate the loss across a signal distribution system, evaluate signal strength along the way, and then systematically introduce gain blocks (amplifiers) where the signal is in danger of getting too weak. Those calculations are difficult for home situations, because you typically don't know the incoming signal strength to begin with, and because you often don't have the specifications for what signal levels the tuner or amplifiers you're using can accept.

If you're on a cable system, the cable provider wants to provide a good signal at the entrance to your home, but they lose control at that point. If you're using an antenna, you need a way to gauge the strength of the signal the antenna sees and how powerful an antenna you need. Fortunately, you're not at the mercy of people who sell both plywood and antennas—the Consumer Electronics Association maintains a Web site at www.antennaweb.org that will both help you calculate how powerful an antenna you need and figure out which way to point it. The calculator itself is at www.antennaweb.org/aw/Address.asp. Pretending that Wiley Technical Publishing headquarters was a single-family residence with no local obstructions, we obtained the map in this figure:

Continued

Continued

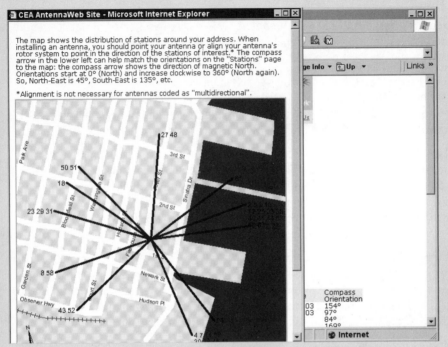

AntennaWeb.org map of available TV stations (numbers are channel numbers)

A corresponding table shows the antenna power required for each station according to a color code commonly used by antenna manufacturers in rating their products. Don't fall into the trap of buying the most powerful antenna available—if it's too strong, you could overload the tuner and distort the picture.

Because you're reduced to trial and error, a small TV you can carry with you to test the signal along the line is the best test equipment you can have.

You can use either S-Video or composite video for the connection from the graphics port on the All-In-Wonder to the TV. You'll get better color using S-Video, although in our case we decided we'd rather use the one S-Video port our television has for a direct connection from the DVD player.

The stereo sound connection from the All-In-Wonder does *not* connect to the TV; it connects to the line input on your sound card. The TV connection is the line output (where you'd normally connect speakers) from the sound card, because your computer has other sounds and noises to make besides the audio from TV programs. Piping the television sound into the line input sound card port lets the sound card mix TV and computer sound together before they're output to the TV.

Running Your PVR

Setting aside the usual media player start/stop controls, the focus for choosing what you watch with your PVR is the program guide. Figures 1-6 through 1-10 show most of what's available from the Gemstar Guide Plus program guide shipped with the All-In-Wonder. Figure 1-6 shows the basic channel-and-time grid, which tells you both what's currently playing and what's coming up later. The black rectangle in the upper left of the figure will show live video for the show you've selected on your computer. Once you pick a show, you can click on *Watch* to view the show in real time or on *Record* to save the show to disk and have all the PVR controls available.

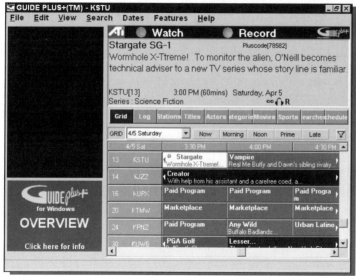

FIGURE 1-6: Guide Plus grid view

ALL-IN-WONDER, ALL-IN-WONDER 9700 PRO, and REMOTE WONDER are trademarks of ATI Technologies.

The log view (see Figure 1-7) expands what you see for each show, listing shows in order by time and channel. You also get three new options in the row for each show that, left to right, let you choose to watch the show, record the show, or identify that the show is a favorite and should show up in the favorites list. Choosing to watch a future show adds it to the schedule, while choosing to watch a show that's currently playing simply puts it on screen.

The station view (see Figure 1-8) works much like the log view, but lets you filter the listing to just the shows of a specific channel. The station view retains the options to watch, record, and select a show as a favorite.

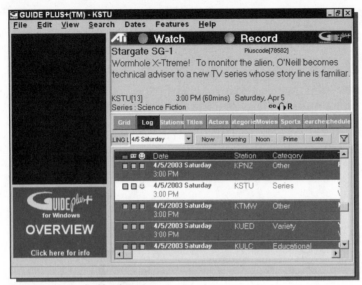

Figure 1-7: Guide Plus log view

ALL-IN-WONDER, ALL-IN-WONDER 9700 PRO, and REMOTE WONDER are trademarks of ATI Technologies.

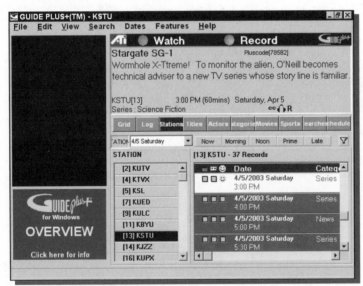

Figure 1-8: Guide Plus station view

ALL-IN-WONDER, ALL-IN-WONDER 9700 PRO, and REMOTE WONDER are trademarks of ATI Technologies.

The title view (see Figure 1-9) lists all showings of a specific show or movie, regardless of what station it's on.

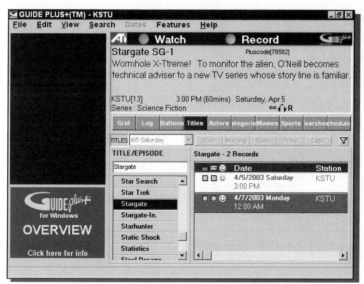

FIGURE 1-9: Guide Plus title view

ALL-IN-WONDER, ALL-IN-WONDER 9700 PRO, and REMOTE WONDER are trademarks of
ATI Technologies.

Finally, the favorites view (see Figure 1-10) lets you see all the upcoming showings for shows you've flagged as favorites, making it convenient to then schedule them for viewing or recording.

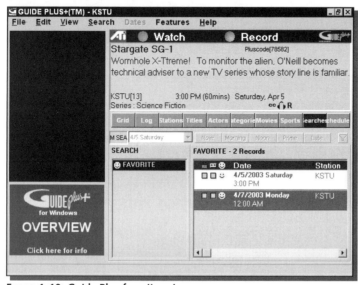

FIGURE 1-10: Guide Plus favorites view

ALL-IN-WONDER, ALL-IN-WONDER 9700 PRO, and REMOTE WONDER are trademarks of
ATI Technologies.

Adding a Remote Control

For your PC PVR setup to really be an integrated, useful installation, you'll need a remote control. We used the ATI Remote Wonder simply because it's already integrated with ATI's Catalyst PVR software. The Remote Wonder (see Figure 1-11) is a USB device, using radio waves instead of the more common infrared beam to communicate with the PC. The control works as a mouse with other Windows applications.

FIGURE 1-11: Remote Wonder RF remote control

ALL-IN-WONDER, ALL-IN-WONDER 9700 PRO, and REMOTE WONDER are trademarks of ATI Technologies.

If you're using a different remote control, such as the Streamzap, you'll see in Chapter 2 for control of the MusicMatch MP3 player, you'll need to program some of its buttons for unique functions of the PVR software, including a button to start the software running.

Using a DVD Writer to Save Recorded Programs

The disadvantage of using your PC to replace your VCR is that most PCs have no equivalent of the removable tape in a VCR. When the hard disk fills, you have to delete something to make room for other recordings. If you're willing to settle for a VCR-quality recording, you can fit 60 minutes of video on a CD using the *VCD* (Video CD) format. That's a low-cost option, because blank CD media are almost free and CD/RW writers are very common.

If you want top quality DVD video, though, you're going to need almost 2.8GB per 60 minutes of video, and while software exists that can span a recording across multiple CDs, it's a nuisance. Instead, you can install a DVD writer to replace the CD/RW drive and burn disks up to 4.7GB. Using MPEG-2 compression at a 6.4 Mbps data rate, you can fit 2 hours of raw video, edited down to 86 minutes by taking out the commercials, into just under 4GB, fitting the video plus a set of DVD menus onto a single disk.

An internal DVD writer with an IDE interface is nearly indistinguishable from the ubiquitous CD/RW drive. Set the DVD writer to the same IDE master/slave configuration as the CD/RW and you can mount it in the same chassis drive bay and plug it right in to the same cables.

Software, however, is a different matter. You may have some work to do.

- **Data disks.** You may need to update the software you use to get drivers compatible with the DVD writer, or even to get capabilities to write disks as large as fit on DVDs. We used Ahead Software's Nero (www.nero.com), and had all the drivers we needed, but noticed that an old version of Roxio's EZ-CD Creator we now rarely use needed updates before it would operate.

- **Video capture and edit.** You'll want video editing software to edit and assemble material from the files you make, and you will need video capture software if you're bringing in material from analog sources such as an older camcorder or a VCR.

- **DVD authoring.** DVDs you can watch with a DVD player have more than the compressed audio and video streams — they include files that define the menus that let you pick what you want to see. DVD authoring software provides the tools to build those menus, combine them with the audio/video streams, and write the disk.

We once used Adobe Premiere for video capture and editing, which is very capable but very expensive ($488.95 and up at www.shopper.com, and over $132 for upgrades). Microsoft MovieMaker is bundled with Windows XP (upgrade to MovieMaker 2 on Windows Update), but lacks the tools to capture or output at DVD quality.

You're likely to get DVD authoring software along with your DVD writer from Pinnacle, Ulead, Sonic, or another publisher. We're using a combination of Pinnacle Studio and Expression, using Studio for capture and editing, and Expression for authoring. Version 8 added the ability to author from within Studio, eliminating the requirement for Expression, but having both tools means it's possible to edit files while running the relatively long compression part of authoring.

Although the inability to resize the panes in the Studio window irritates us beyond redemption, we've found that Studio has nearly all the features of Premiere we need, so for cost reasons we keep using it. Figure 1-12 shows the capture window view in Studio. The frame in the upper-right corner shows the live video preview, while the controls on the bottom let you adjust the video and audio input characteristics.

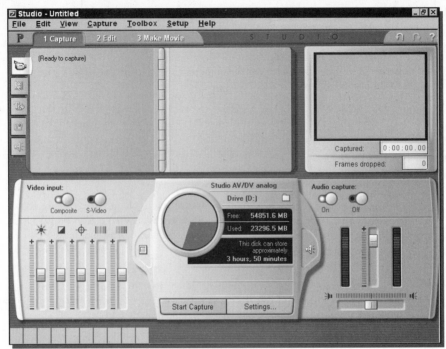

FIGURE 1-12: Pinnacle Studio video capture window

You'll want to make a test disk and run the process from beginning to end before recording anything you want to keep. You're likely to get different results with different output formats — VCD versus DVD, for example — so you must check the settings. (We didn't know that to begin with, and after adjusting the brightness for VCDs, made a DVD some months later. The DVD was relatively bright and washed out, an effect we fixed by returning the brightness to its zero setting.)

The middle pane on the bottom of Figure 1-12 lets you choose where to store capture files (the button at the upper right of the pane) and the capture parameters (the settings button). Once you're ready, click Start Capture, enter the file name you want, and start the recording. The Pinnacle AV capture board, together with the Studio software, will detect scene changes in the incoming analog video and record scene thumbnails in the album image in the upper-left corner.

Figure 1-13 shows Studio in its edit mode. The upper-right corner remains the video preview, but now shows the image at the current edit point. The upper-left pane provides the edit controls for the scene selected in the timeline, which itself is displayed in the bottom half of the figure.

You can select multiple scenes in the timeline by selecting the first one, then holding down the Shift key and clicking on the last one. If you right-click in the selected area, you can then choose a command to combine all the selected scenes into a single one.

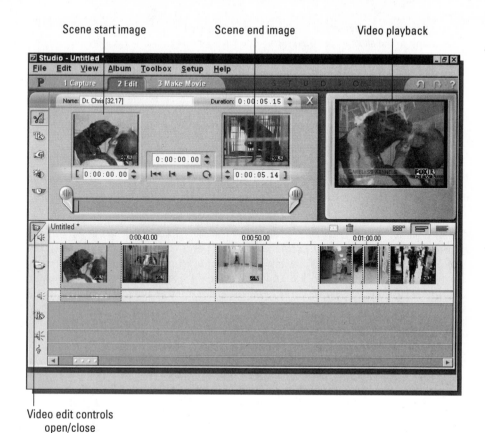

FIGURE 1-13: Pinnacle Studio video edit window

Our routine to edit out scenes we don't want goes like this:

Editing Unwanted Scenes Out of a Video File

1. Start Studio, open the edit view, and open the video file you want to edit. We capture in AVI format, so we look for those files.

2. Select all the scenes (Ctrl-A is convenient) and drag them into the timeline.

3. Open the video edit controls with the button at the middle of the left edge.

4. Select the first scene containing frames you want to eliminate, and position the slider in the video edit controls just before the first frame to be eliminated.

5. Click on the "]" button near the right of the edit controls to trim the scene, eliminating all frames in the scene later than the slider position.

6. Select the next sequential scene, which is (presumably) part of the material to eliminate. Look to the right in the timeline to find the last scene entirely composed of frames you want to discard.

7. Hold down the Shift key and click on that last full scene, then press the delete key to delete all the selected scenes.

8. Select the next scene; then position the slider in the edit controls at the first frame you want to keep. Click on the "[" button (on the left of the controls) to eliminate all the frames to the left of the current one.

9. Repeat Steps 4 through 8 until you've removed all unwanted scenes and frames.

Once that's done, we write a new AVI file through the Make Movie tab at the top of the Studio window.

We then author the DVD with Expression. You can drag edited video files into the Edit Video dialog box (see Figure 1-14; the button to open it is next to the menu image in the edit mode, which is step two at the top of the window), then choose the frame you want to represent the file in the playback window. Click the button next to the bottom to choose that frame for use in the menu. Figure 1-15 shows how Expression previews the result you'll see when you play the disk. Once you've loaded all the files that will make up your disk, close the dialog box, select the third step at the top of the window, load a blank disk, and click on Start.

FIGURE 1-14: The Edit Video dialog box in Pinnacle Expression lets you both load video files and select the frame that will represent each file in the disk menu.

FIGURE 1-15: Pinnacle Expression shows you the main menu for your DVD once you complete the Edit Video dialog box.

Building Your PVR to Your Own Design

A PVR is simple hardware — the tuner and video compression hardware — tied to relatively sophisticated software and a source of upcoming TV listings. Even if you're willing to write your own software, you'll either have to feed commands to software like Gemstar's Guide Plus (so you can continue to use their guide), clip listing information from Web pages like www. tvguide.com, or type in your own data from the newspaper. None of those are easy, so in this section we've limited the variants you might take on.

Alternative PVR Equipment: Snapstream

One design option is to use different hardware and software. Snapstream offers their Personal Video Station PVR software (www.snapstream.com/products/sspvs/PVS3.htm), including a program guide and remote control support. Supported TV tuners include ones from ATI, AVerMedia, Hauppage, Matrix Marvel, and a number of others.

If you're a programmer, Snapstream gives you the tools with which you can build additions to the basic system. Their Web site highlights existing third party add-ons for these functions:

- TV listings integration

- SnapStream-DigiGuide (a program guide) integration

- Pinnacle Systems PCTV tuner integration

- Digital Satellite System Serial Port tuning for Sony or RCA satellite tuner boxes using a simple serial port cable

- IRTuner (`sourceforge.net/projects/irtuner/`) to support infrared devices as remote controls for things like VCRs, TVs, and cable boxes, with support for the RedRat tuner coming

You're Going to Need a Lot More Disk Space

Unless you plan to record to DVD, VCD, or tape, you're going to run out of disk space in a hurry.

You can get single disk drives in the 200MB and up range, so it *is* possible to put an enormous amount of disk storage in a PC. More than that requires multiple disks, but because you still want all the disks to appear in one place, you're going to want a *Redundant Array of Inexpensive Disks* (RAID array) to join them together. Adaptec has a variety of RAID controllers you can add to your PC, including ones that support SCSI, ATA (IDE), and the new Serial ATA. Rack up a terabyte or so of storage and you'll be able to surf for quite some time.

However, don't get carried away looking for speed. Even a single 5400 RPM disk has ample speed to run a PVR—you're just after more space, with adequate speed for large files. The RAID array doesn't have to boost disk access speed.

Summary

The PC has forever changed the idea of a VCR from a relatively dumb, passive recorder to an active device—the PVR—that can learn what you want and work to get it for you. Hardware and software now available for Windows makes adding PVR capabilities to your PC simple.

Build a Jukebox for Your Home Stereo

Music is your own experience, your own thoughts, your wisdom. If you don't live it, it won't come out of your horn.

~Charlie Parker in *Children of Albion: Poetry of the Underground in Britain*

Across the street from the university near where we live is a wonderful pizza place called The Pie, a tiny room in a basement under a pharmacy. In the very back of The Pie, in a dark corridor off the main room, sits an ancient-looking box replete with flashing lights and rafts of buttons. A jukebox, one of a dying breed, loaded with CDs and ready to exchange tunes for money. College pizza places being what they are, it's probably no accident that Pink Floyd's *Money* is number 42.

Radio Is Boring

Jukeboxes have a long history, as electronics goes. The Wurlitzer Web site (www.wurlitzer.de/index.php/article/archive/519/) shows the first jukebox, the 1933 invention of Homer Capehart and Paul Fuller, filled with shellac records spun at 78 RPM (see Figure 2-1). The automation provided by the jukebox let people choose the songs they wanted to hear, not a repetition of songs chosen by someone else.

That one simple characteristic — the ability to choose your own music — survives today in CD changers, in the thriving practice of burning collections of songs to CD to play in your car, and with millions of office workers playing songs through headphones on desktop PCs.

Oddly, having a wide variety of music at home over the course of hours is a different and more difficult story. You can play CDs and other files through the speakers on your PC, but the sound quality of the usual cheap PC speakers is horrible. You can play CDs or radio through your stereo, but you have to get up to change CDs, and the constant repetition of the same few songs on most radio stations is enough to drive a saint to drink. You can get a CD changer for your stereo — Kenwood's 200 disc CD changer, for example — but it's pretty expensive at $400.

FIGURE 2-1: The first jukebox, the
Wurlitzer P10

Alternatively, you can combine the best capabilities of your computer and stereo, using your computer to store and play songs, with the controls at your fingertips, and using your stereo amplifier and speakers to give you rich, full sound. That's this chapter's project — turning your computer and stereo into a high-fidelity jukebox.

The minimum PC you'll need for this project is pretty basic. The MusicMatch software we've recommended lists these minimum requirements:

- Intel Pentium II processor at 300 MHz
- 96MB of RAM (32MB of RAM for Win 98)
- 50MB hard drive space
- Windows-compatible sound card
- Video display card (minimum resolution 800x600)
- Microsoft Windows 98/2000/NT/XP
- Microsoft Internet Explorer 5.0 or later

In practice, you'll want a CD-ROM drive and an Internet connection, as well. A faster processor and faster CD-ROM drive will speed up file conversions to MP3, and you'll definitely want a bigger hard drive to store your converted files. You'll see how to compute the amount of disk space you will need later in the chapter.

You can do this project in stages, starting out simply and expanding as you see fit.

Building Up Your Jukebox

1. Play songs on your PC using a file library on disk.

2. Cable your PC to your stereo and use the quality speakers there.

3. Use a wireless link to eliminate the wires across the floor.

4. Control a small PC next to your stereo with a wireless remote.

5. Retrieve music files from a server on your local area network.

The first step in building your PC jukebox is to get lots of songs in one place, which is the subject of the next section.

Sound, Compact Discs, and MP3 Compression

High-quality, uncompressed sound files are big. A CD holds about 650MB of data, equivalent to a little more than an hour of music. If your jukebox were as modest as the equivalent of ten CDs, you'd need close to 7GB of disk space to store those files directly. Our collection of CDs — a small one at that — numbers well over 300, so we'd need nearly 200GB to store the entire collection in uncompressed files. People who are really *serious* about their music collections are likely to have thousands of discs. Given those figures, you have two practical choices for how you store music:

- Store uncompressed sound files, using lots of hard disk storage
- Store compressed sound files on CD, DVD, or hard disk

Storing uncompressed sound files, eliminating the time and work to compress the files, isn't as absurd as it would have been a few years ago because hard drives have become ridiculously large and cheap. When we wrote this chapter in early 2003, for example, CompUSA ran a promotion offering a 200GB drive for $200. That was an amazing price at the time — about half the normal value — but the example shows how dramatically prices are coming down for large drives.

MP3 Compression and File Sizes

Huge disk farms aren't yet practical for large music collections, so the best option for most people will be to compress raw sound files from CD using MP3 or another algorithm, getting huge reductions in size in exchange for relatively small reductions in sound quality. You measure the severity of the compression applied to an MP3 sound file by the average bit rate at which player software consumes the file on playback, with higher-quality sound corresponding to higher data rates.

Table 2-1 shows some of the higher rates used in MP3 files. The 128 Kbps (kilobits per second) rate is the most commonly used of those shown, but you'll hear a noticeable degradation in quality. The higher rates, which still give file sizes better than four times smaller than the raw, uncompressed files you can extract from CD, significantly improve the quality. You'll want to experiment with different compressed file bit rates to discover the best choice of bit rate versus file size for your sound card and stereo system.

Table 2-1 MP3 Bit Rates and Compression Factors

File Format	Average Bit Rate (Kbps)	Compression Factor	Play Time per GB (hours)
Raw WAV (CD)	1411.2		1.57
MP3	128	11.0	17.36
MP3	160	8.8	13.89
MP3	192	7.4	11.57
MP3	256	5.5	8.68
MP3	320	4.4	6.94

In our testing, we decided that 256 Kbps offered the best compromise between sound quality and file size. Table 2-2 shows the file sizes we produced for Led Zeppelin's "Stairway to Heaven" (track 4 on the *Led Zeppelin* CD) and confirms the compression ratios shown in Table 2-1.

Table 2-2 File Sizes for Stairway to Heaven (duration 7:55)

File Format	Average Bit Rate (Kbps)	File Size (KB)	Actual Compression Factor
WAV	1411.2	82,955	
MP3	128	7,525	11.0
MP3	160	9,406	8.8
MP3	192	11,287	7.3
MP3	256	15,049	5.5
MP3	320	18,812	4.4

These are interesting results, because they show that you can put a lot of high-quality music into a relatively small space. Table 2-3 makes this conclusion explicit, showing how many hours of compressed music you can store on a CD, on a 4.7GB DVD, and in 10GB of hard disk space.

Table 2-3   MP3 Play Time Versus Storage Capacity

Bit Rate (Kbps)	Compression Factor	Play Time in Hours		
		CD	DVD	Disk
128	11.0	11.28	81.60	173.61
160	8.8	9.03	65.28	138.89
192	7.4	7.52	54.40	115.74
256	5.5	5.64	40.80	86.81
320	4.4	4.51	32.64	69.44

Making Compressed MP3 Files from CDs

The following three steps convert a CD to MP3 files. Some software, including the MusicMatch software we describe in this chapter, combines or simplifies these steps.

Create an MP3 File

1. Name each track on the audio CD. You can do this yourself, typing in the track titles manually, or you can load the names from an album database service on the Internet.

2. Copy the digital music data from the CD, putting the data for each track in a separate file on disk. For convenience, you'll want to name each file with the name of the track developed in Step 1. This step is called *ripping* the songs from the CD, and results in files with a .WAV extension.

3. Set up the conversion parameters for your MP3 compression software, which may include only the bit rate, and run the compression.

MusicMatch does this all in one step — configure its settings once, then simply insert a CD, select the tracks you want, and click Record. MusicMatch finds the album title, artist, and track title, then does the work. Converting a complete CD (Meat Loaf, *Bat Out of Hell*) took less than 12 minutes to rip from a Toshiba SD-M1212 DVD-ROM and encode at 256 Kbps on a Pentium III at 933 MHz running Windows 2000 Professional. CPU utilization ran 10 to 15 percent, so the drive speed was the limiting factor rather than the processor. Overall, the drive ran at about 4.8X while we did the conversion; when we later upgraded the software to the paid version, MusicMatch Plus, which advertises faster conversions, we saw drive speeds as high as 5.9X, reducing the conversion time correspondingly.

You should think about how you'll organize the MP3s on your disk before you start ripping and compressing with MusicMatch. A mere few hundred CDs will turn into thousands of MP3 files, and if you simply give them random names and throw them all in one directory, it's going to get hard to find anything at all. We've typically organized all the files for one album in their own directory; with MusicMatch, it's easy to collect album directories themselves into directories grouped by artist. You don't have to follow that scheme, of course, but you'll want some organization.

Here's how MusicMatch works. Download and install the free version from the MusicMatch Web site at www.MusicMatch.com/download/free. Once you complete the installation, start MusicMatch, click Options, and then click on Settings (see Figure 2-2).

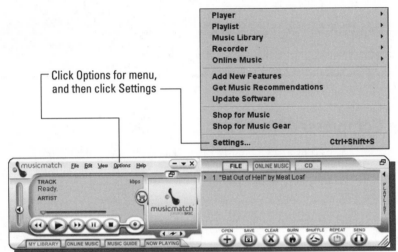

FIGURE 2-2: Bring up the MusicMatch Settings dialog box to set up the MP3 conversion.

The Recorder tab settings in the dialog box (see Figure 2-3) control what you get when you rip a CD and convert its tracks to MP3 files. Figure 2-3 shows how we set it up, including how we set the custom quality settings to convert to MP3 at the 256 Kbps rate. The MP3Pro format (available in the recording format dropdown) gives you better sound for the same data rate, and can be played back by MusicMatch and WinAmp, but isn't likely to work if you want to record an MP3 CD or DVD for playback away from your computer.

The Tracks Directory button gives you a dialog box (see Figure 2-4) that lets you automate creating a well-organized directory structure with fully descriptive file names. Figure 2-4 shows that we've set up MusicMatch to put all the automatically created directories under two subdirectories, and shows at the bottom a sample of what a complete path with file name looks like. If you set up the directory storing all the subdirectories and files to be shared to the other computers on your LAN, each computer can play songs from the library.

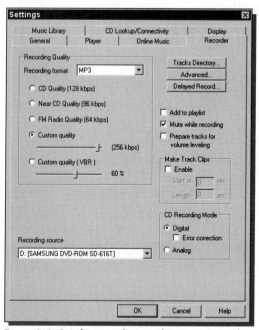

FIGURE 2-3: Set the recording quality to custom; then choose the bit rate you want.

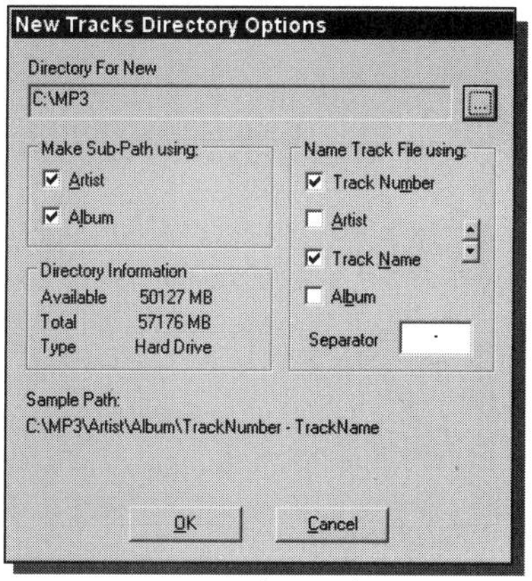

FIGURE 2-4: Set up the Tracks Directory dialog box to make directories and file names that organize your MP3 library effectively.

Security May Be a Nuisance, but Don't Ignore It

Sharing MP3 files across your LAN is a wonderful idea, because it's easy for your music library to eat up a lot of disk space. However, one of the most common attacks from the Internet onto your computers will be directed at unprotected or badly protected file shares, so it's important you think about and ensure your systems' security before you open up file sharing. You also should not assume that you're invulnerable simply because you're on a dial-up connection that you only use infrequently. The odds of attack are less, but not zero.

There are several ways to protect your systems. Our favorite approach is a hardware router running *Network Address Translation (NAT)* between modem and LAN, because no matter what you do (or forget to do) you're reasonably secure. NAT, as usually configured in hardware routers, by default prevents incoming probes from even reaching your computers. Hardware routers run $40 and up, and combined with such outgoing security as Zone Alarm provides (free version at `www.zonelabs.com/store/content/catalog/products/zonealarm/znalm_details.jsp`), are enough to make sure most people can sleep at night. Hardware routers are even available with embedded 56K modems if you don't have broadband (for example, see the 3Com Web site at `www.3com.com/products/en_US/prodlist.jsp?tab=cat&pathtype=purchase&cat=32&selcat=Internet+Gateway+Routers+%26+LAN+Modems&family=178`).

You can set up an old PC to do much the same thing as a hardware router using a modem, Ethernet card, and Microsoft Internet Connection Sharing, but we guarantee that Windows is more complicated to make secure than a dedicated hardware router.

Once you have the setup done, the actual conversion is trivial — simply put the CD in the drive, let the song titles download from the Internet, click on Record, let the recorder window open, and click on Record in the recorder window (see Figure 2-5). If you want to convert the good tracks only (yes, we know, they're all good), just uncheck the ones you don't want before clicking the final record.

With that, building your MP3 file library is just a matter of feeding CDs into your computer any time you think of it. You can even play back already-converted files while converting new ones.

After you've converted a useful number of CDs, you'll want to start building *playlists*, which are simply lists of songs selected from your library. MusicMatch lets you sort your library display by many more features than we've shown in Figure 2-6 (album, artist, artist Web page, audio file Web page, bit rate, commercial info, data added to library, genre, mood, preference, situation, file name, file type, track title, tempo, time, track number, and release year), giving you good tools to find and select specific songs. Once you select the songs you want in your playlist, empty the playlist window with the Clear button, then right-click in one of the selected items in My Library and add the songs to the playlist window. Continue adding songs to the playlist window. When you're done, right-click on the top of the playlist window and save the playlist.

FIGURE 2-5: Insert a CD and click two buttons, and you'll convert an entire album to MP3s neatly organized in your file system.

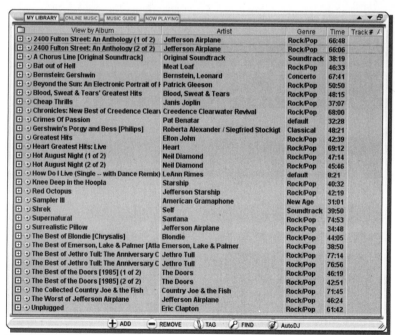

FIGURE 2-6: The MusicMatch My Library window lets you sort and select by a variety of features, and then add songs to the playlist window.

Your Copyright Rights Are Under Attack for a Reason

If you've spent any time at all reading the news, you probably know about the peer-to-peer file sharing networks, including Napster, Kazaa, Gnutella, and Morpheus. If so, you're well aware of the controversy surrounding sharing copyrighted songs and other files on those networks. The record companies believe file sharing is costing them billions in sales, so they are doing everything they can to stop file sharing, including sponsoring legislation that will impose severe controls and restrictions on what you can do with the data on your computer and also give them the right to break into or otherwise interfere with your computer.

Although he wrote it in March 2002, we suggest you take the time to read Dan Gillmor's editorial "Bleak Future Looms if You Don't Take a Stand" (www.siliconvalley.com/mld/siliconvalley/2922052.htm). Our view is that, scary as his future is, he's not exaggerating what could happen.

Our practice is to store only MP3s we've made from CDs we own on our computers, and to not share them with anyone else. We don't download music from the Internet, specifically because most of what we've seen for download is copyrighted. After you read Gillmor's editorial, you'll want to think about the issues and decide what your policy will be.

Building and Using Your Jukebox from Kits

With your MP3 library well underway, let's turn to the hardware you'll need. Table 2-4 lists all the parts we used setting up the jukebox that weren't part of the PC we used (so, for example, we haven't listed the DVD drive). Every part we list in Table 2-4 has competitive equivalents; for example, WinAmp is a great MP3 player, the Creative Labs SoundBlaster Audigy sound cards get good reviews, and the ATI Remote Wonder remote control we used in Chapter 1 for the personal video recorder could be used here too. We chose MusicMatch because it makes ripping and filing MP3s easier, the Turtle Beach sound card because it's very good and lesser known, and the Streamzap remote control because it uses infrared rather than radio waves.

Table 2-4   MP3 Jukebox Parts List

Part	Manufacturer and Model Number
MP3 Player	MusicMatch (free version) www.MusicMatch.com/download/free
	MusicMatch Plus ($10–$40 depending on special offers and whether you license future versions) www.MusicMatch.com/download/plus
Sound Card	Turtle Beach Santa Cruz 6-Speaker DSP Audio Accelerator ($79.95) www.turtle-beach.com/site/products/santacruz

Part	Manufacturer and Model Number
Remote Control	Streamzap PC Remote ($39.95) www.streamzap.com/products/pcremote
Wireless Audio / Video	Radio Shack 2.4GHZ Wireless Room-to-Room Audio/Video Sender (Catalog No. 15-1972, $79.99) www.radioshack.com/product.asp?catalog%5Fname=CTLG&category%5Fname=CTLG%5F002%5F004%5F004%5F000&product%5Fid=15%2D1972
Audio Cables	Cables N Mor www.cablesnmor.com/stereo-rca-y.html (Sound card to RCA, 6", $3) www.cablesnmor.com/rca-patch.html (RCA patch cables, $3–6)

The first step (assuming you've already installed MusicMatch) is to set up your PC to send MP3s to your stereo, because your stereo amplifier will have a lot more power, and your stereo speakers are likely to sound a lot better than your PC speakers. There are at least three ways to do this:

- Run cables from your sound card to the stereo preamp inputs.

- Run a wireless link from your sound card to the stereo preamp inputs.

- Burn the MP3s onto CD or DVD and play them through your CD or DVD player.

Cables

Running cables from your sound card to your stereo is probably the easiest of these options, requiring only that you get cables that are long enough and have the right connectors. The cable we like for making long connections easy—it takes much more cable when you don't run across the middle of the carpet—is the soundcard-to-RCA Y splitter from Cables N Mor shown in Figure 2-7.

What makes this splitter convenient is that is provides female RCA jacks like the ones on the backs of most stereo equipment, letting you use standard patch cables with male plugs on both ends. The Cables N Mor Web site lists patch cables up to 25 feet long.

Unless your sound card has a line out jack in addition to the speaker jack, plug the Y cable into the speaker jack on your sound card. The red and white RCA connectors on the Y cable are the right and left side audio channels from the sound card; patch them into either the AUX or TAPE IN inputs on your stereo preamp and adjust the volume on both the computer and stereo. You'll get less noise and distortion from your sound card if you keep the computer output volume in the middle of the range—too low and you'll get noise and hiss louder than the music, while too loud and the sound card will distort.

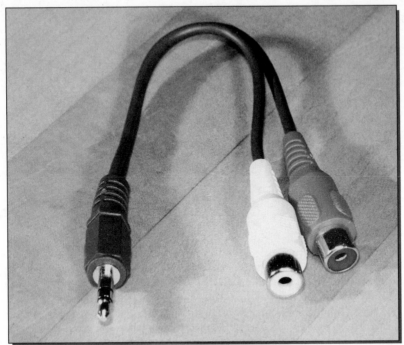

FIGURE 2-7: The female RCA connectors on this Y cable let you use any length patch cord to cable into your stereo preamp.

Wireless

Unfortunately, if your house is like ours, it wasn't built with audio, LAN, and satellite TV wiring in the walls, your PC isn't next to your stereo equipment, it's more than a bit inconvenient to have wires strewn over the carpet, and the carpentry required to string cables from PC to stereo in the walls is hard. Some years ago, cables on the carpet or a weekend of knocking walls around were your only options.

Now, however, the enormous numbers of wireless telephones being sold have prompted chip manufacturers to build chips that make small, inexpensive short range transmitters and receivers possible. The Radio Shack devices we used (see Figure 2-8) will transmit video, too; you could equally well use the X10 Sound Power System if you have no use for the video channel. The wireless links will degrade the sound a little bit, as did the MP3 compression; if you're concerned about the results, be sure to check the store's return policy before you buy.

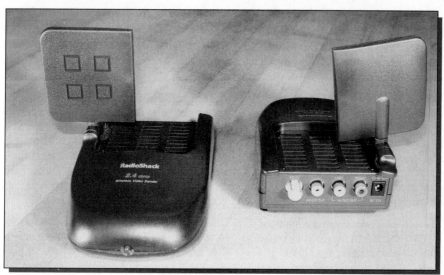

FIGURE 2-8: You can avoid running cables with a wireless connection, but you may lose some sound quality.

Photo courtesy of RadioShack Corporation.

Connecting the wireless link is easy—cable the transmitter to the line out or speaker out jack on your PC sound card (see Figure 2-10), and the receiver to the AUX or TAPE IN jacks on the stereo preamplifier.

We heard some clicks and pops at times with the Radio Shack wireless equipment. Moving the wireless equipment somewhat away from the computer, arranging for a clear line of sight between the transmitter and receiver, and pointing the faces of the antenna paddles at each other will improve the signal strength and help avoid any interference that causes that noise.

DVD Players

You still can play MP3s on your stereo, even if you can't make wireless work the way you want or can't find a way to run cables. What you'll need is a DVD player that knows how to play MP3s (newer CD players may work, too).

Manufacturers are inconsistent about building MP3 support into DVD players, and spotty about whether they advertise the feature even if it is there. Short of buying a stack of equipment and trying them all, though, you can search the DVD player compatibility listings at www.vcdhelp.com, or more specifically at www.dvdrhelp.com/dvdplayers. When we ran a search for MP3-compatible players, we found that 1,187 of 1,633 tested players had MP3 support, although most of those offered MP3 support only for files on CD. Narrowing the search to players supporting MP3s on DVD reported success for 168 of 464 tested players. Keep in mind that the reports on the site are the unqualified statements of people reporting their findings, and aren't always accurate. (For instance, the site shows that our Sony NS315 DVD player is capable of handling MP3s only up to 224 Kbps, yet we've been successful with it at 256 and 320 Kbps.)

We use Ahead Software's Nero to make data CDs and DVDs, which is what you need to make MP3 disks. You'll want to test your player's capabilities before embarking on a major burning project, because some require a pure ISO9660 file system, while others can accept the long file names available with Microsoft's Joliet format. Some players can read the ID3 information tags embedded in MP3 files (MusicMatch fills these in automatically from a database on the Internet; if your Internet connection is down, MusicMatch Plus can defer the lookup until some later time), while others don't. Some will navigate directories on the disk, while some play only files in the root of the file system.

The advantage of playing MP3s from a DVD is the DVD's 4.7GB file capacity—you'll need a DVD writer (see Chapter 1) instead of the more common CD burner—holding over 40 hours of music at 256 Kbps. Your DVD player is wired into the television, though, so you'll have to work out how to cable it into the stereo. We were able to wire audio output jacks from the television into the AUX inputs on the stereo preamp; some players have secondary audio jacks you can use directly.

Remote Control

There's always another way to do something, and wiring your PC to your stereo is no exception. Instead of stretching wires from your PC across the room to your stereo, you can always put the PC next to the stereo. This is a great application for that old, slow PC you've been storing in the basement or garage, and if you add in a video card with a TV output (the ATI All-In-Wonder VE we discussed in Chapter 1 will do that), you don't even have to clutter up the area with a monitor. Add a wireless keyboard and mouse, and you have a neat, efficient installation.

The problem with putting a PC next to the stereo is that you're generally not next to the stereo. You're in a chair, at a desk, or walking around, which means you can't reach the keyboard or mouse to change songs. Jukeboxes are supposed to give you control of what you get to hear, though, so let's add a remote control.

The Streamzap remote control (see Figure 2-9) transmits an infrared signal to a small receiver—we put it on top of the monitor. Installing the remote is embarrassingly easy, consisting of inserting the batteries and running the device driver installer. Once that's done, MusicMatch responds to the play/pause/forward/back/skip commands, and the computer itself responds to the mute and volume up/down buttons. Streamzap offers more extensive support for WinAmp, including direct access to any track and changing and scrolling the playlist. We found the Streamzap useful not only on a PC across the room with the stereo, but also on a PC playing MP3s on its local speakers when we weren't at that desk. If you add MusicMatch to the Startup group in Windows, it will launch automatically at boot and be ready for Streamzap commands.

FIGURE 2-9: The Streamzap remote control lets you access a PC from across a room.
Courtesy of Streamzap®

You can set up the colored buttons near the bottom of the Streamzap to start specific playlists in MusicMatch or whatever player you've associated with playlist files. Most commonly, you'll set each of the buttons to start a playlist file, which has an M3U file extension. Windows then runs the application associated with that extension; the application reads the playlist and loads the tracks whose names it contains. If the M3U association isn't set up the way you want, you can usually associate it with the player from within the player application. Alternatively, in Windows 2000 and Windows XP you can use Tools ➔ Folder Options, select the File Types tab, then select the file type you're interested in and edit the setup through the Change button. (You follow a similar process for older versions of Windows, but the command sequences are slightly different.) Once you get the file associations right, launching a playlist works whether MusicMatch is running or not.

Sound Quality

Most, if not all, of the PCs we've seen in the past few years had the "sound card" built into the motherboard. Integrating the sound into the motherboard chip set reduces the cost of the system, but doesn't provide the best sound quality. As a measure of how insignificant sound is to most manufacturers, the last — and maybe only — motherboard advertisement we saw extolling sound quality was for the AOpen AX4GE Tube motherboard (see `english.aopen.com.tw/products/mb/AX4GETube.htm`), which literally incorporates a vacuum tube amplifier to appeal to those who believe the sound from transistors can never equal that from a tube. With the exception of that board and a couple of related ones from AOpen, sound is simply something motherboards are expected to have, but which gets little or no attention.

Experiment with your existing sound card or motherboard by playing a CD from the computer through your stereo. If the quality is noticeably worse than when playing the CD directly in your stereo's CD player, you might want to consider adding a high-quality sound card to your computer. We chose the Turtle-Beach Santa Cruz (see Figure 2-10), featuring 20 bit digital to analog converters, specifically for its specifications, which include a frequency response from 10 to 120 kHz, and a signal-to-noise ratio greater than 96 dB. A high signal-to-noise ratio is particularly important for computer sound equipment, because the digital electronics in the computer generate high levels of high-frequency noise. If designers fail to shield and properly filter out the noise, you'll hear it as high-frequency hiss and see it in the specifications as a lower signal-to-noise ratio.

FIGURE 2-10: A high-quality sound card like this Turtle-Beach Santa Cruz will improve sound quality and reduce noise.

Installing a sound card is completely straightforward using the hardware and software techniques you'll find in the appendixes — simply plug the card into an available PCI slot and install the manufacturer's drivers. See the manufacturer's instructions to see if the driver installation should precede or follow the hardware installation, disconnect the computer from the power line before opening it, and be sure to use a ground strap to prevent damage from static electricity. The precaution about disconnecting the computer from the power line is more than a safety concern—most computers now provide standby voltages to the motherboard and card slots even when turned off, voltages you can only eliminate by disconnecting the main power line. Inserting or removing cards with those standby voltages present can cause damage to the circuits on the motherboard or card.

Finish the sound card installation by rerouting the analog and/or digital sound cables from the motherboard to the new card and turning off the old sound chips in the BIOS; then play a CD through your stereo to hear the difference.

Media Players

Media player is a horribly stilted term for the software your computer needs to play CDs, MP3s, video, and other multimedia files. We mentioned MusicMatch and WinAmp earlier; the other well-known players include Microsoft's Windows Media Player and Real Networks' RealPlayer. That's the last we'll mention the last two for reasons discussed in the sidebar "Software, Control, Ethics, and Politics."

Software, Control, Ethics, and Politics

So long as the entertainment industry continues its assault on consumers—recall, for instance, Michael Greene's rant over downloading music at the 2002 Grammy awards, or Jamie Kellner (chairman and CEO of Turner Broadcasting) stating in an interview that skipping television ads with a PVR is theft—we find it impossible to trust anything these entertainment companies say or do. For that reason, we're categorically unwilling to load any software onto our computers that permits others to remotely modify or control what happens on those computers.

That policy means we won't install Windows Media Player 9, the license for which includes these statements:

". . . the OS Components may install on your computer technological measures that are designed to prevent unlicensed use, and Microsoft may use this technology to confirm that you have a licensed copy of the OS Software . . ."

and

"You therefore agree that Microsoft may, in conjunction with such license, also download revocation lists onto your computer on behalf of Secure Content Owners."

Worse, you can't uninstall Media Player 9 once you install it, so if you inadvertently load the program before you carefully read the license, you're stuck. Consequently, you won't find any discussion of using Windows Media Player in this book.

Continued

Continued

Our reasons for rejecting Real Player are somewhat different—it's well documented that the software installs spyware that uploads information from your computer, and when the practice began the company did not disclose that characteristic during the installation (see the *New York Times* article at `www.nytimes.com/library/tech/99/11/biztech/articles/01real.html`). That's unacceptable to us, as was the testimony of Real Networks' CEO Rob Glaser to the United States Congress that Microsoft had sabotaged Real's software, when the problem was a combination of technical misunderstanding and mistakes by all concerned (see `www.wired.com/news/print/0,1294,14270,00.html`). Because of these issues, we won't load or discuss Real Networks' software either.

Windows Media Player and RealPlayer aside, the Plus version of MusicMatch has two specific features you might find useful for your jukebox—it "levels" the volume across a set of song tracks, eliminating the too loud/too soft problems common on CDs, and adds the capability to handle MP3Pro file formats. Whichever version of MusicMatch you use, notice during setup that MusicMatch asks permission to upload your music listening information, something we always turn off.

Building Your Jukebox to Your Own Design

Following the guidelines above, you'll have built the capability to feed good- to high-quality music stored in your computer to your stereo, and to control playback remotely. That's just the basics, though—take a look at some other ideas for what you can add to your jukebox.

Very Small Form Factor PCs

There's a lot of value in adding a PC to your stereo and television combination, presuming they're in the same place, even if you don't have a high-end home theater setup. Not only can you use it for the jukebox functions in this chapter, you can use the PC to implement the personal video recorder from Chapter 1, and because the machine is likely to see only light duty (and will therefore be reasonably stable) you might consider it to host your X10 controls (Chapters 3 and 7).

Of course, a large computer doesn't fit well in most entertainment center furniture, a monitor doesn't fit at all, and the wires tethering your mouse and keyboard to the computer are a pain. One way to fix those problems is to make the computer smaller, and to use a wireless keyboard and mouse. The latter items are available from Logitech (`www.logitech.com/index.cfm?page=products/details&CRID=486&CONTENTID=5060`), Microsoft (`www.microsoft.com/catalog/display.asp?subid=22&site=11247`), and others. Buying or building a small computer is harder. Laptops have the small size you want, but they're not designed to be on all the time, and lack the expansion slots for a sound card.

New motherboard form factors have reached the market, though, making small desktop machines with some limited expansion capability possible. Among the smallest are the Soltek Qbic Series EQ2000 (`www.soltekusa.com/product/showproduct.php?product id=1042221553`) shown in Figure 2-11, and the Shuttle SB52G2 (`us.shuttle.com/specs2.asp?pro_id=183`) shown in Figure 2-12. Connect the small PC to your television, possibly with a VGA to NTSC or PAL adapter, and you can eliminate the need for a separate monitor.

FIGURE 2-11: Soltek Qbic Series EQ2000
Courtesy of Soltek Computer, Inc.

The PC Power and Cooling Sleekline systems (`www.pcpowercooling.com/products/sleekline/sleekline_2000.htm`) offer another way to hide a computer near your stereo and television, packaging the electronics into a thin, flat package yet retaining a PCI expansion slot you could use for a sound card.

Standalone Audio Player

You may not need all the functionality a complete PC offers near your stereo, yet you still might want to build your jukebox so the MP3 playback is done at the stereo equipment. In that case, you could use the Turtle Beach AudioTron (`www.turtle-beach.com/site/products/audiotron/producthome.asp`), which is capable of retrieving MP3 files from your file server over your Ethernet LAN and playing into your preamplifier. It's controllable from a PC or with a remote control, and at $299.95 is significantly less expensive than a complete PC if audio playback is all you want.

FIGURE 2-12: Shuttle SB52G2

Courtesy of Shuttle Computer Group Inc. Shuttle XPC is a copyright of Shuttle Computer Group Inc. All rights reserved.

Extending Your Jukebox Through Your House

You're not always in the same room as your stereo, but that need not keep you from listening to the songs on your jukebox. One way to keep your jukebox available throughout your house is to use a set of wireless headphones, such as the Sennheiser RS-65 available on the Internet at deep discount from their list price. The RS-65 headphones use the more common (and noisier) 900 MHz band to transmit to the headset; newer units such as those from Amphony use frequencies at 2.4 GHz. The Amphony headphones also transmit sound digitally to the headset, converting back to analog sounds at your ears. The digital transmission is less prone to noise and interference, and at $129 and up, is price competitive with the older units.

Alternatively, if your house has an intercom system that offers auxiliary inputs, you could feed the audio outputs to the intercom and just pipe the sound to the remote speakers throughout the house. The resulting sound will not likely be high fidelity, but it will probably be as good as a radio, and you'll be able to control what you hear. Couple in a radio-based remote control (such as the ATI Remote Wonder we used in Chapter 1) and you should be able to control your jukebox as you walk around the house.

Summary

The essence of building a high-fidelity jukebox with your PC is no more complex than hooking the computer's audio outputs to your stereo. You have options for connecting the two, storing music in your computer and how much storage it takes, controlling the player software, and controlling the quality of the sound. The cost of your jukebox will range from free or a few dollars for cables to as high as you like if you let your imagination run wild.

Don't overlook the importance of the source of your computer's digital music. We've recommended in this chapter that you make your sound files from CDs you already own, but don't recommend that you share those files with others.

Home

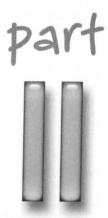

part

Have Hot, Fresh Coffee Whenever You Get Up

The morning cup of coffee has an exhilaration about it which the cheering influence of the afternoon or evening cup of tea cannot be expected to reproduce.

~Oliver Wendell Holmes, Sr., *Over the Teacups*

Web pages about coffee are far too prone to quote Johann Sebastian Bach, who once said, '"Ah! How sweet coffee tastes! Lovelier than a thousand kisses, sweeter far than muscatel wine!" *(Coffee Cantata,* 1732). We say even Starbucks won't serve coffee more than an hour old, and neither should you. Coffee that's been tortured over a hotplate for hours is bitter and revolting, not the joyous brew that leads to over 150,000 hits from a Google search for *coffee ritual.*

Engineers build gadgets to solve problems, so any store that carries electric coffee makers will have one with a built-in timer that will faithfully start making coffee at the precise time you set. If you had the same discipline for getting up as the coffee maker has for starting the brew cycle, a fresh pot of coffee would be ready just as you arrived cup in hand, and there'd be no reason for this chapter to exist.

The Day Needn't Start Until the Crack of Noon

Getting up at a fixed time may be fine for morning people, but we and millions of others judge how good a day is likely to be by how late we're able to sleep in. When the coffee maker is too stupid to do more than watch a clock, it's hard to have a fresh pot of coffee waiting when you're ready for it.

Our approach to fresh coffee, and the basis for this chapter's project, exploits the fact that we all take several minutes to get up and moving before we're looking for coffee, time enough if only the coffee maker knew what to do. What you'll build in this chapter is the smarts to let the coffee maker know you're up, using motion detectors, a remote control switch, and your PC. You'll use the motion detectors to tell the PC you've gotten out of bed, the remote control switch to turn the coffee maker on, and software in your PC to filter out the false alarms when you're simply rolling over.

Nothing Up Your Sleeve, and No Nasty Wires to Run

Remote controlled home appliances and lights are a surprisingly old idea. Early wireless television remote controls whacked tuning forks with small hammers and received the signal with a high-frequency microphone. Prior to that — during the 1950s — television remotes had wires strung across the floor, trading elegance for convenience.

X10 technology, first introduced decades ago, made it possible to control switches and plugs across the power line wiring of your home, sending small signals on top of the high voltage power. The initial X10 products, driven by small manually operated controllers, generated a cult following but were too limited in what they could do to have sustained, wide appeal. X10 became the basis for the thriving home automation industry, however, after the X10 company developed computer-based controllers to direct their remote modules. In addition to stand-alone computer controllers using embedded microcontrollers, the company had the wisdom to develop controllers that could be driven by PCs, and made available the information describing how to program them. Inserting computers into the system made low-cost sensors useful, because their outputs could be qualified by other information known to the computer, and made the modules themselves more useful because complex groups of actions could be linked.

The X10 system sends command and response messages across your home power lines. Every device sees every message, so X10 assigns an address to each device. With a few well-defined exceptions, devices listen only to messages containing their own address and ignore the rest. The simplest X10 remote control application uses a controller to send ON or OFF messages, and a switch to receive the messages and turn the controlled device on and off. A more complex application, such as you'll build in this chapter, sends messages from sensors to your PC, which, acting as an intelligent controller, then sends commands to lamps, appliances, or other devices based on the sensor information and the rules you've programmed into the PC software.

X10 Wireless Motion Sensors and RF Transceiver

The smart coffee pot project uses a motion sensor to detect that you're up and moving. We used the X10 Hawkeye motion sensor (model MS13A, shown on the left in Figure 3-1), which itself is a small battery-powered device. The Hawkeye isn't wired directly to the power line, instead transmitting commands with a radio signal. This gives you flexibility in where you can install it.

You Really Have Two Power Lines

We oversimplified a little when we said that every X10 device sees every message. In North America, residential power wiring provides 110 and 220 volts depending on how you wire to it. The following figure shows how that works — taking power from both ends of the power transformer produces 220 volts, while taking power between one end of the transformer and the center tap wire produces 110 volts.

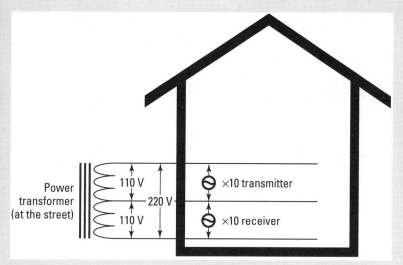

X10 signals don't propagate reliably from one side of the power transformer to the other.

X10 signals output from a command transmitter are directly visible to all other X10 devices on the same 110 volt side of the power transformer simply because they're on the same wires. The signal has to flow *through* the power transformer to reach X10 devices on the other side of the power transformer, though, and the power transformer weakens the signal drastically in the process. The weakened signals are harder or impossible to detect by X10 receivers on the opposite side of the power transformer, which leads to unreliable operation.

The fix for weak signals caused by looping through the power transformer is a *signal bridge*, such as the one by Leviton (www.smarthome.com/4815.html). Wire the bridge into an electrical utility box, connecting it to all three wires of a 110/220 volt combined circuit. The bridge provides a low loss path for X10 signals between the 110 volt sides of the house without leaking power between the two.

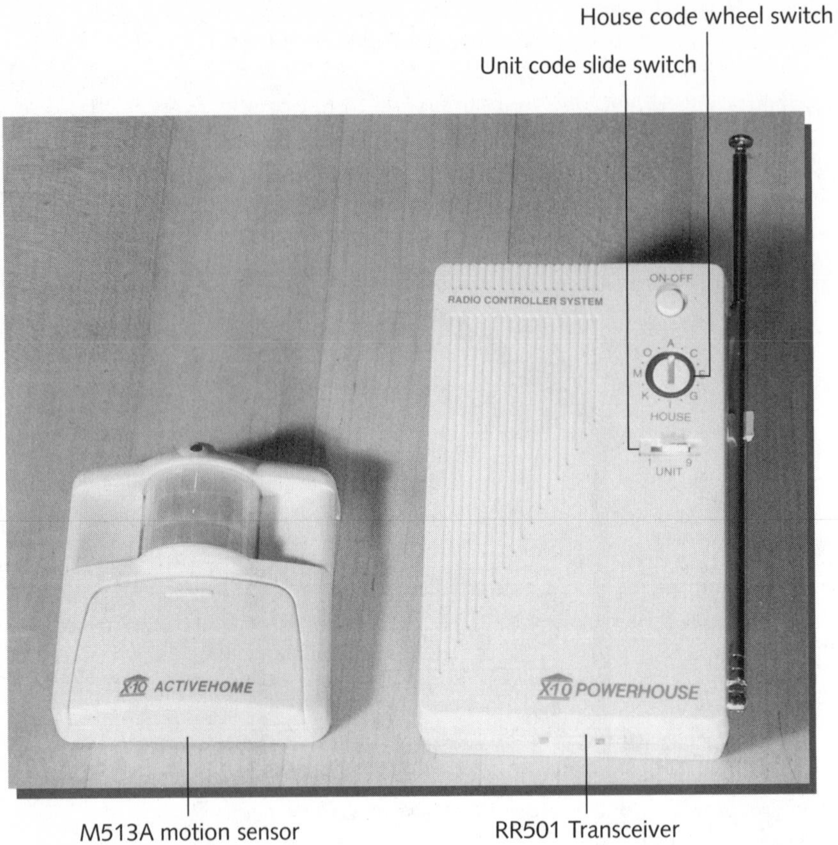

House code wheel switch

Unit code slide switch

RADIO CONTROLLER SYSTEM

ON-OFF

HOUSE

UNIT

X10 ACTIVEHOME

X10 POWERHOUSE

M513A motion sensor

RR501 Transceiver

FIGURE 3-1: The X10 MS13A Hawkeye II motion sensor and RR501 RF Transceiver
Courtesy of X10 Wireless Technology, Inc.

The radio signal from the motion sensor must be received and injected into the power line; we used the model RR501 RF Transceiver (on the right in Figure 3-1) included in the X10 ActiveHome kit. The transceiver unit contains two different functions — it not only passes the radio signal from the motion sensor to the power line, it also can function as an appliance control module. When the transceiver forwards commands from the motion sensor to the power line, those commands have the address of the motion sensor, which can (and often will be) different from that of the appliance module. The two functions are completely independent.

The radio part of the transceiver module works with more than just motion sensors—for example, you can use it with the X10 remote control or the keychain transmitter.

HomeSeer Software

It's fortunate that other companies provide software you can use with the X10 equipment, because the ActiveHome software the X10 company provides is so limited that it's useless. Free, but useless and annoying—much like the pop-under ads the X10 company insists on displaying all over the Web.

The HomeSeer software (www.homeseer.net), on the other hand, is very useful. I (Barry) worked as a programmer for a long time, and very little software gets a "wow" from me. HomeSeer got a long series of wows, because it does complicated things simply and intuitively, and because it literally could do every oddball thing I wanted.

Using HomeSeer, you think about your home automation setup in terms of devices and events:

- *Devices* are switches, plugs, sensors, and transceivers—everything in your X10 system that can either report status or take an action. HomeSeer has a library of popular devices built in, so in most cases you just select the device type, name it, and fill in its address.

- *Events* are descriptions of actions you want performed. You structure events as sets of AND/OR clauses to decide if the event should trigger, plus a set of actions to be invoked any time the event does trigger. Paraphrased into English, an event might look like this:

```
IF
   the motion sensor sees someone
OR
   it's the weekend and getting late in the morning
THEN
   turn the coffee pot on
```

You program devices and events into HomeSeer through dialog boxes such as the one shown in Figure 3-2, in which you enter a device into HomeSeer.

Although the HomeSeer dialog boxes are relatively straightforward, they're extremely powerful. You can even use them to create an event that signals you to change the batteries in the Hawkeye motion sensor!

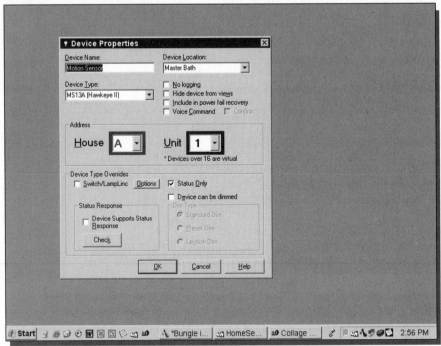

FIGURE 3-2: The HomeSeer Device Properties dialog box

Building and Using Your Coffee Controller from Kits

Here's what we want the coffee controller to do:

- Detect when you've gotten up
- Turn on the coffee pot when you get up
- Turn off the coffee pot at noon
- Turn on a light any time at night you get up
- Turn off the light after you've gone back to bed

There's no way a sensor can read your mind to know if you've gotten up for the day, so you'll have to decide what evidence the computer will look at to decide you're up for good. In our case, we sometimes get up in the middle of the night to let our dogs out and don't want the coffee pot to start brewing just because a dog woke us, so a simple check of the motion detector isn't good enough — we need to qualify the motion detector reports to eliminate signals after which we go back to bed.

There are at least two ways to qualify the motion signal:

- Require motion in specific rooms that will remain quiet until you're up
- Assume any motion late at night or too early in the morning is a false alarm

We chose the second approach, because the first one doesn't work — by the time we're moving in rooms that indicate we're really up (like the kitchen), it's too late and we might as well flip the switch manually. Either way, the coffee won't be ready when we arrive in the kitchen. The second approach works for us, though, because our dogs don't usually wake up between about 5:00 and 8:00 in the morning, but we do. You may qualify the motion signals differently, depending on the layout of your home and your habits.

Parts List

Figure 3-3 is a high-level block diagram of the coffee controller, showing all the components and the information passed among them.

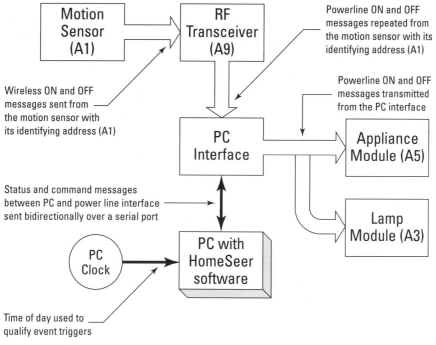

FIGURE 3-3: Coffee pot control system block diagram

The PC requirements to control the coffee pot are minimal. You'll need a 300 MHz processor running Windows if you want to use voice recognition, but a slower processor will work if you forgo voice. HomeSeer recommends 64MB of memory and 100MB of available disk space. The minimums appear to be very conservative; our installation of HomeSeer required only 16MB.

The rest of the parts we used are shown in Table 3-1.

Table 3-1   Coffee Controller Parts List

Part	Manufacturer and Model Number
Motion Sensor	X10 Model MS13A Hawkeye ($19.99) www.x10.com/automation/x10_ms13a.htm
RF Transceiver	X10 Model RR501 www.x10.com/automation/x10_rc5000.htm (This is a $39.99 kit including both the RR501 two-way transceiver and the RT504 remote control.)
Appliance Module	Radio Shack Cat. No. 61-2684B ($12.49) www.radioshack.com/product.asp?catalog%5Fname=CTLG&category%5Fname=CTLG%5F006%5F002%5F002%5F000&product%5Fid=61%2D2684
Lamp Module	X10 Model LM465 ($12.99) www.x10.com/automation/x10_lm465.htm
PC Interface	X10 Model CM11A (The CM11A is difficult to find other than packaged with several modules in the X10 ActiveHome kit, $49.99) www.x10.com/automation/x10_ck11a.htm
Control Software	HomeSeer Technologies, HomeSeer ($99.95 for unlock keys; download the 61MB application from the Web site or order a CD for $5) www.homeseer.com

What the minimum PC requirements for HomeSeer don't state is that you'll need an available serial port to connect the CM11A PC interface to the computer. Alternatively, you could substitute the SmartHome PowerLinc USB PC interface ($34.99; www.smarthome.com/1132u.html), which uses the USB port common on most computers for years now.

The X10 ActiveHome kit includes software, a UR19A remote control, CM11A PC Interface, KC674 Keychain remote control, LM465 lamp module, and RR501 transceiver module. The keychain wireless remote has some significant restrictions on how it operates with the RR501, but that's what's in the kit.

Several companies, including Radio Shack and Leviton, offer products compatible with X10 equipment. One of the largest sources on the Internet for X10-compatible equipment is at www.smarthome.com.

The key difference between a lamp module and an appliance module is that the lamp module can control only an incandescent lamp, which it can dim, while the appliance module can control lamps, heaters, motors, and other loads in exchange for loss of dimming capability on lamps. Appliance modules have limits on how much power they can control, and not all of them can handle as much power as required for a coffee maker. The Radio Shack heavy-duty appliance module (Catalog No. 61-2684B) is specifically rated at 15 amps for coffee pots (almost 1,800 watts), which is why we chose it for this project.

Installing Components

Installing the components making up the coffee controller is straightforward. You set the address for the RF transceiver, appliance module, and lamp module before you plug them in. X10 addresses have two parts, a *house code* and a *unit code*. House codes are alphabetic (A through P), while unit codes are numeric (1 through 16). The distinction between house codes and unit codes is useful when you want to use global commands like *all lights on*, which affect all devices in a specific house code regardless of unit code. There are three global commands: *all lights on*, *all lights off*, and *all units off*. Unless you run out of unit codes or need partition devices responding to global commands, there's little reason to use more than one house code.

The addressing plan you see in Figure 3-3 isn't the only one you can use. We set it up this way for these reasons:

- The motion sensor is relatively small, and doesn't have convenient switches to set the house and unit code — you have to push some buttons repeatedly and decode what the flashing LED is saying. Rather than do that, we just left the sensor at its default A1 address.

- In addition to ON and OFF messages at address A1, the motion sensor by default sends out DAWN and DUSK messages at the next higher unit code, sending at A2 by default. Putting some other device at A2 can confuse the control system, so we just left that address unassigned.

- The appliance module in the RF transceiver can be only at unit codes 1 or 9 (see the description that follows), and unit code 1 conflicts with the motion sensor. If you leave them both at the same address, the appliance module in the RF transceiver will go on when the motion sensor turns on, and go out when the motion sensor goes off. We want to control modules through the software in the PC, not directly, so we want each module at a distinct address. The only other available unit code for this module is 9, so the resulting address is A9.

- The heavy-duty appliance module and the lamp module can go at any address that doesn't conflict with other modules. We chose A5 and A3, respectively, but those choices are arbitrary.

- The PC interface doesn't have an address.

Once they're set up, you install modules simply by plugging them into the wall and plugging the controlled device into the module. Here's how to set up each of the modules you'll use.

RF Transceiver

The right-hand photo in Figure 3-1 shows the RR501 RF Transceiver. The wheel switch under the ON-OFF button sets the house code, while the slide switch below the wheel switch sets the unit code. The RR501 is unusual in that its built-in appliance module can't be set to all 16 unit codes, just to codes 1 or 9. (Don't be misled by the legend under the switch. It responds as 1 or 9.) Following the addressing plan in Figure 3-3, set the switches to address A9.

Heavy-Duty Appliance Module

Figure 3-4 shows the front of the heavy-duty appliance module you'll use to switch the coffee pot on and off. In addition to the house code wheel switch (the one on the bottom), there's a second wheel switch you use to set the unit code. Set the address to A5).

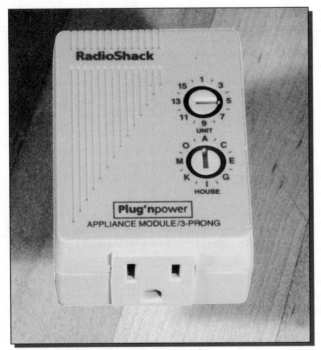

FIGURE 3-4: Heavy-duty appliance module
Photo courtesy of RadioShack Corporation.

Unlike most other X10 modules, the heavy-duty appliance module has a three-prong socket and plug, reflecting its higher power handling capabilities.

Lamp Module

You set the lamp module address in the same way you set the heavy-duty appliance module; in our plan, we set it to A3 (see Figure 3-5). The lamp module can dim lamps plugged into it, but you should never plug in anything but an incandescent lamp.

FIGURE 3-5: Lamp module
Courtesy of X10 Wireless Technology, Inc.

PC Interface

The PC interface, Figure 3-6, looks similar to the other X10 equipment but is significantly different. You don't give it an address, so there are no switches for setting the house or unit code. It doesn't contain any power control electronics — the outlet on the front simply gives you direct access to the wall socket you plugged the interface into. It doesn't connect to the telephone line; the phone jack at the bottom is the connector for the cable between the interface and the serial port on your PC.

FIGURE 3-6: PC interface
Courtesy of X10 Wireless Technology, Inc.

You can plug the interface into almost any outlet within reach of your computer, with a few restrictions:

- The outlet on the front of the interface has a limited load capability, so don't plug any high-power devices into it.

- The interface is sensitive to power surges, as are your computer, monitor, printer, and other electronics, so it's a good idea to plug the interface into the same surge protector you use with everything else. Remember that anything plugged directly into the wall and cabled to protected equipment likely exposes the equipment to damage, surge protector or not.

- The interface has to be able to transmit signals out onto the power line, so you can't plug it into a protected socket on an uninterruptible power supply (UPS) because the signals won't be able to pass back through the UPS.

Setting Up Your Motion Sensors' Field of View

The final hardware setup issues are where to put the motion sensors, how to aim them, and where to put the RF transceiver.

X10 recommends that for maximum sensitivity you place the Hawkeye II motion sensors so that traffic moves across the line of sight, not directly towards or away from the sensor. If you can't avoid having traffic moving in line with the sensor field of view, try to offset the sensor from the traffic so part of the motion vector appears as crossways traffic. Admittedly, you probably don't have to worry in an area as small as a bathroom, as in Figure 3-7 (since the range specification for the device is around 20 feet), but in larger spaces you'll want to consider sensor placement carefully.

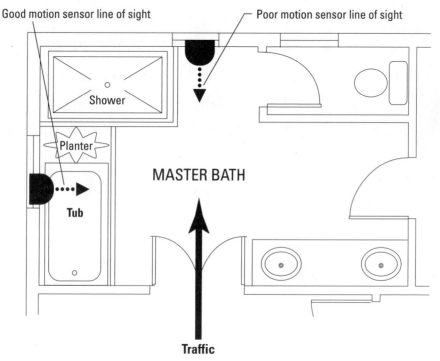

FIGURE 3-7: Position your motion sensors so traffic moves across the line of sight.

The sensor field of view is a flattened cone around the front-facing vector, extending about 45 degrees either way laterally and 15 degrees either way vertically. The passive infrared technology used in the sensor is heat sensitive, so try to keep it away from heater vents, air conditioners, and direct or reflected sunlight.

The range from the motion sensor to the RF transceiver is specified as up to 100 feet, but as with all RF equipment, the shorter the range, the better. If all your motion sensors are grouped in one area, try to put the RF transceiver near the group. If the sensors are spread out, try to put the RF transceiver near the center of a circle surrounding them all. Keep in mind that radio waves don't penetrate metal well and that they travel in a straight line.

Building Your HomeSeer Configuration

After your hardware's set up, download, install, and run HomeSeer. The startup screen includes the HomeSeer Assistant Wizard (Figure 3-8), which will walk you through some of the preliminary tasks of setting up your control configuration.

FIGURE 3-8: Use the HomeSeer Assistant Wizard for initial setup of your configuration.

The first tasks are to define your PC interface and your devices.

Configure the PC Interface and Devices

If you do the PC interface first, you can use the interface to test connections to each of the devices as you define them. The dialog box in Figure 3-9 lets you configure the interface; you need only select the Interface tab, choose the CM11A as the X10 interface device, and specify the correct serial (COM) port. In case you're unsure which port you're using for the interface, there's a "Search for CM11A" option in the list of COM ports.

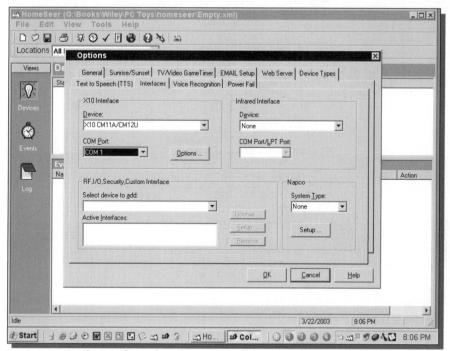

FIGURE 3-9: Use the Interface tab in the Options dialog box to tell HomeSeer what PC interface you're using and where it's connected.

The search option has the added value that, by finding the interface, it verifies correct communication.

Add a device by clicking on the light bulb in the toolbar, or by selecting Devices in the icon bar on the left, then right-clicking in the device pane and choosing Add Device. Figure 3-10 shows the Device Properties dialog box the Add Device button launches after setting up the LM465 lamp module — give the device a name, choose its location (type it in if it's not in the dropdown already), and specify the device type. Modules of the same type, such as lamp modules, differ most in whether or not they support a status readback to the PC interface. The Check button at the lower left lets you verify if a device supports a status response. The LM465 happens not to support a status response; if it did, you could choose the Lamp Module with Status type, which is more descriptive but differs only in that the Device Supports Status Response box is checked by default.

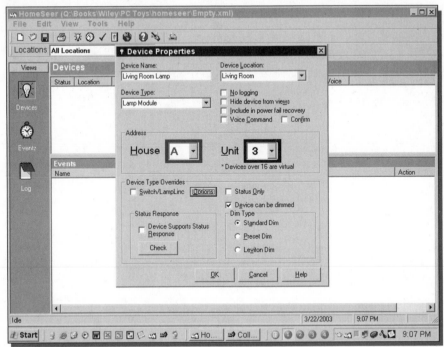

FIGURE **3-10:** The Device Properties dialog box lets you tell HomeSeer what equipment you have plugged into your house.

Similarly, the dialog box has no specific entry for the Radio Shack heavy-duty appliance module in HomeSeer, but does have a generic entry HD Appliance Module, so use that. There's a specific entry for the RR501 RF Transceiver, which will by default set up the status response. You can verify that the transceiver is working by testing that the Check button correctly determines the status response. If the transceiver doesn't work, double-check that you've plugged the transceiver into a working outlet, not one controlled by a switch. The dialog box contains a specific entry for the Hawkeye II motion sensor in addition to the generic motion sensor type; in fact, the two have exactly the same settings.

After you enter all the devices, you'll have a configuration similar to that shown in Figure 3-11.

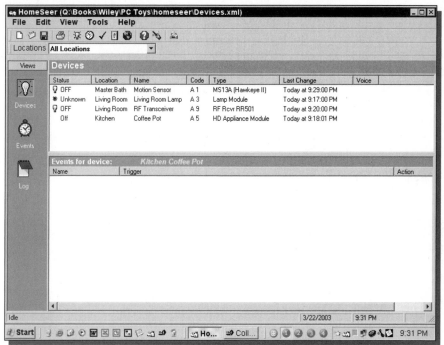

FIGURE 3-11: The completed device configuration lists all device modules, but not your PC interface.

Configure the Events

Finishing the configuration requires only that you define the events you want to occur. Events nearly always correspond to devices they're controlling, so in our version of the coffee controller, five of the six events we defined correspond to either the coffee pot or the lamp:

Coffee On. Triggered when there's motion indicating we're getting up. We defined two versions of this event, one for weekdays and one for weekends (to take into account that we get up much earlier during the week).

Coffee Off. Triggered to make sure we don't leave the coffee pot on all day.

Lamp On. Triggered when someone's walking around and needs to see.

Lamp Off. Triggered when no one needs to see any longer.

The sixth event watches the motion sensor and alerts us when the battery should be checked. You'll see how we did that in the section on building to your own design.

We decided to turn the coffee pot on whenever the motion sensor turned on within a time window, which we set for 5:00–8:00 A.M. on weekdays and 7:30–10:00 A.M. on weekends. We turned the coffee pot on at the end of the time window whether the sensor had turned on or not. All the triggers are by condition, rather than direct X10 responses or other event types offered by HomeSeer.

The following listing defines the Coffee On—Weekdays event (we added some words to what you'll see in HomeSeer to make the listing more readable). Create an empty event with the clock icon in the toolbar or with a right-click in the event window pane, then use the Event Properties dialog box (see Figure 3-12) to enter the trigger conditions. Use the Next OR Group button to add the OR condition needed for the event.

Coffee On—Weekdays (choose M–F for trigger)

```
If
  Time is after 5:00 AM and
  Time is before 8:00 AM and
  Device: Master Bath Motion Sensor changed to ON
Or
  Time is at 8:00 AM
Then
  Turn on the Coffee Pot
```

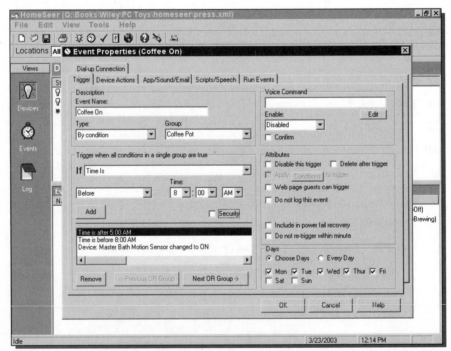

FIGURE 3-12: Use the Trigger tab in the Event Properties dialog box to select a By Condition event type and enter the necessary trigger conditions.

When you've completed the trigger conditions, move to the Device Actions tab and enter the actions as shown in Figure 3-13. You can change the displayed status text by double-clicking or right-clicking on the action line in the Selected Devices pane. (The same dialog box that pops up lets you enter a time offset to delay the action, which you'll use for the Lamp Off event.)

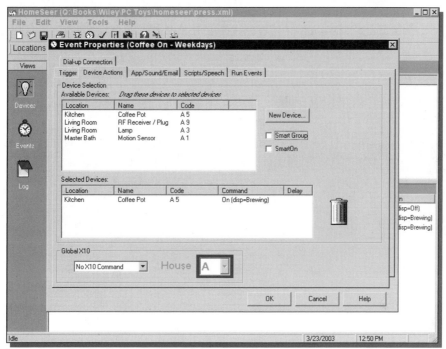

FIGURE 3-13: Use the Device Actions tab to set up what event the trigger will activate.

The Coffee On—Weekends event is much the same as for weekdays, with only the times changed.

Coffee On—Weekends (choose Sat–Sun for trigger)

```
If
  Time is after 7:30 AM and
  Time is before 10:00 AM and
  Device: Master Bath Motion Sensor changed to ON
Or
  Time is at 10:00 AM
Then
  Turn on the Coffee Pot
```

The Coffee Off event is somewhat different, triggering at noon every day to turn the pot off. Figure 3-14 shows how you use the Event Properties dialog box to set up the trigger portion of the event.

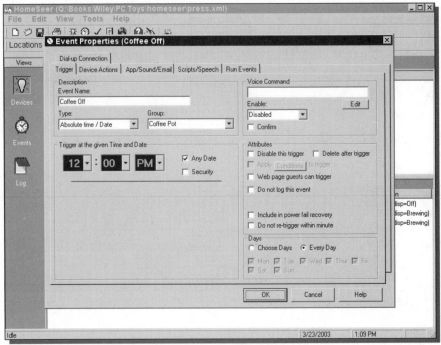

FIGURE 3-14: Use an Absolute Time/Date event type to trigger the action at a specific time or on a specific date and time.

This completes the coffee pot configuration. We added two other events to control a lamp so we could see when putting the dogs out in the middle of the night.

Lamp On (Every Day)

```
If
  Time is night time and
  Device: Master Bath Motion Sensor changed to ON
Then
  Turn on the Living Room Lamp
```

Nighttime is one of the choices in the drop down menu associated with a "time is" event, and requires you to enter your latitude and longitude (or location) in the Sunrise/Sunset tab of the Options dialog box.

Lamp Off (Every Day)

```
If
   Device: Master Bath Motion Sensor changed to OFF
Then
   Turn off the Living Room Lamp after a 5 minute delay
```

Double-click on the line defining the lamp off action in the Device Actions tab to get to the lower-level dialog box that lets you define the delay. You'll have to tell HomeSeer your latitude and longitude before the nighttime condition works properly.

We initially tested the configuration by temporarily changing the times to correspond with the time we were doing the set up, and after we had what we thought was a final configuration, we ran tests at the real times using a night light in the appliance module rather than the real coffee pot.

Building a Coffee Controller to Your Own Design

You'll constantly think of things you can do with home automation far beyond the coffee controller. In this section, though, we'd like to point out a few extensions that will make the coffee controller more useful.

Use the Universal Remote Control

The ActiveHome kit comes with a wireless remote control, which lets you issue direct X10 commands to your devices. If you keep the remote by your bed, you can turn on the coffee pot after one of those midnight calls from work when you have to go in and save the world. If you've wired lights around the house with X10 controls, you can turn all of them on if you hear noises you don't like.

E-mail Alerts

A weak link in the coffee controller is the batteries in the motion sensor, because until the system fails you might not realize the batteries are worn out and need to be replaced. You can use events in HomeSeer to detect worn batteries, and send an e-mail to yourself to report the problem.

The first step is to configure HomeSeer for e-mail. We created an e-mail account specifically for HomeSeer, and used the direct e-mail handling support in the program. (You can also operate through Outlook, Outlook Express, or another MAPI-compliant e-mail program.) Figure 3-15 shows a sample configuration; you get to the dialog box through View → Options; then select the EMAIL Setup tab.

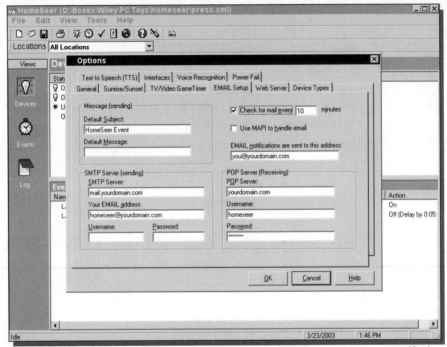

FIGURE 3-15: Configure e-mail support in HomeSeer; then send a message to yourself when an event triggers.

The event we set up to watch for worn-out batteries looks like this:

Motion Sensor Battery Check

```
If
  Device: Master Bath Motion Sensor has been off
          for at least 12 hours 59 minutes
Then
  Send a warning email
```

Internet Access

HomeSeer lets you do nearly anything the program is capable of through its Web browser interface, meaning you can check on and control your home from anywhere. Figure 3-16 shows the home page for the coffee controller system we set up. The links at the top of the page should give you an idea of what HomeSeer can do over the Web.

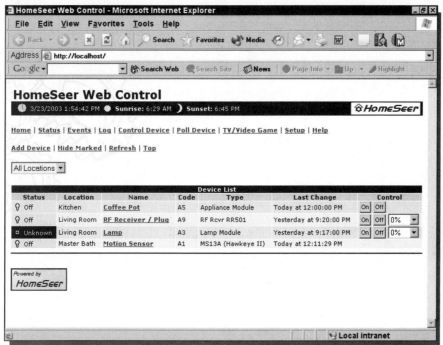

FIGURE 3-16: Check on and control your home from anywhere, but don't forget to think about attacks from the Internet.

Be sure to enable the user name and password feature if your computer running HomeSeer is accessible from the Internet, because having someone connect in and flash all your lamps in the middle of the night probably isn't what you want.

Summary

Having your PC help control your home gives you the ability to do many things automatically. The coffee controller is a simple first project; we'll expand on what you can do with X10 modules and HomeSeer later in the book.

Build a Telescope Tracking Station

The sight of a planet through a telescope is worth all the course on astronomy; the shock of the electric spark in the elbow, outvalues all the theories; the taste of the nitrous oxide, the firing of an artificial volcano, are better than volumes of chemistry.

~Ralph Waldo Emerson, *Essays*, Second Series

The truth is out there, but in the case of telescopes and astronomy we've found the truth is a little hard to find even when it's staring you in the face.

We've owned a basic telescope for years, but since a few forays into the backyard to see the craters on the moon and a few of the planets, it's been gathering dust. Not because we weren't interested, but because we never got the hang of reliably finding what we were looking for, and when we did find something, it quickly rotated out of view while the neighborhood kids took their turns.

It's Not Just Finding Them, It's Following Them Too

Astronomical chaos in the backyard is the inevitable result when you're the sort who, like us, not only knows little about practical astronomy, but has so little contact with reality that you've been known to check if it's cloudy outside by looking at the Internet, not through a window. The Earth's rotation combines with the telescope's narrow field of view to cause everything in the sky to move, so just when you get what you want to see lined up, it rotates away. Experienced observers know how to mount the telescope on its tripod to make following objects easy, but to a novice, the tripod is likely to be nothing but a confusing forest of knobs and dials.

Your PC can help you fix all these problems — knowing where you are, knowing where to look, and following objects in the sky — using nothing more than a Web connection, an interface to a motorized base under your telescope, and some software. Figure 4-1 is a block diagram that guides you through this project. The key element, besides your PC, is the base, which can independently rotate and elevate the telescope. Some telescopes have controllers to point the base and track stars, but as you'll see in this chapter, these tasks are a lot easier with a PC.

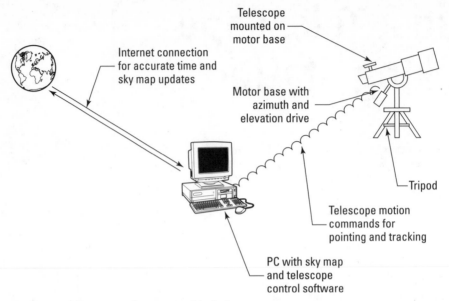

Telescope
mounted on
motor base

Internet connection
for accurate time and
sky map updates

Motor base with
azimuth and
elevation drive

Tripod

Telescope motion
commands for
pointing and tracking

PC with sky map
and telescope
control software

FIGURE 4-1: Telescope tracking station block diagram

We pointedly said *help* fix these problems, not completely fix them. Your PC can only minimally assist you in the telescope's initial setup and alignment, and until you have some practice in how to do these things, you're going to be frustrated. Nevertheless, your PC can help somewhat — we'll show you how after a few preliminaries.

A Matter of Clockwork

The first stop on the path to order in your backyard is your favorite Web browser, because you have to know where you are before you can know where to look. Our favorite way to find geographic coordinates is Terraserver, at www.terraserver.com. It's free for resolution down to 8 meters, and although a search by address requires a subscription, the free version lets you search by city, zip code, or map. Once you've homed in out of the stratosphere to your precise location in the displayed photo, a click of the mouse cues Terraserver to give you latitude and longitude to about ten significant digits — more than good enough for backyard astronomy.

The other data point you'll need to know accurately is the current time, which you can get using any of several methods. If you're running Windows XP, double-click on the time in the taskbar (see Figure 4-2); then use the Internet Time tab to keep your PC synchronized with an accurate time source on the Internet. Assuming you connect to the Internet often enough to keep your PC clock from drifting, you'll have the time accurate to within (at most) seconds.

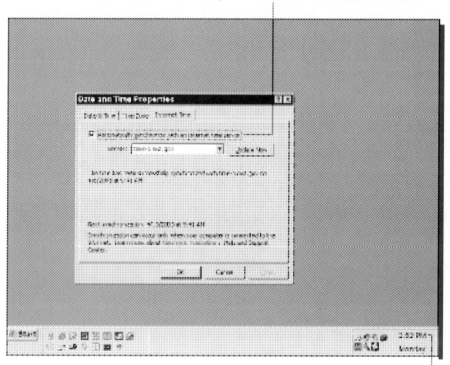

Enable automatic synchronization with an Internet time server

Double-click on the time to get the Date and Time Properties dialog

FIGURE 4-2: Use the Internet Time tab to keep your PC clock accurate.

If you're not running Windows XP, look into getting either SocketWatch ($10 from www. locutuscodeware.com/swatch.htm) or Atom Time ($12 from www.atomtime. com), which both do much the same thing. We've used SocketWatch for years with good results.

Another good way to keep accurate time is to use a clock that automatically synchronizes to the WWV radio service. We have one from Oregon Scientific that also provides a wireless outdoor temperature sensor (www.oregonscientific.com/cablefree/bar888. html). We found it on sale at Costco.

Once you have your location and the time, look up — there's a surprising amount you can see in a clear sky with just your eyes. Look at your PC first, though, using the Your Sky Web page at www.fourmilab.ch/cgi-bin/uncgi/Yoursky. Enter the precise latitude and longitude from Terraserver (or be a slacker and choose a nearby city); then click Make Sky Map. After we changed the options on the following page to use black on white colors and show constellation names and outlines, we received the image in Figure 4-3.

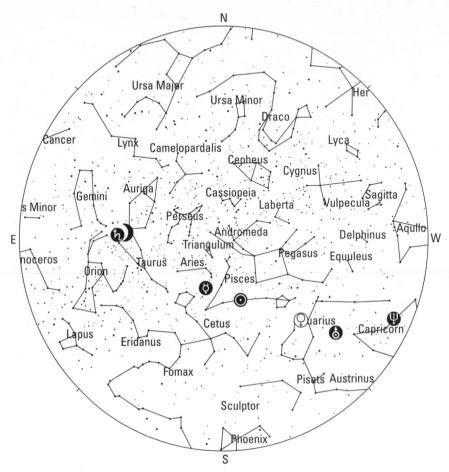

Figure 4-3: A sky map from the authors' location

The sky map doesn't show you what you'll see looking through your telescope, it shows you what you'd see if you're lying on the ground at your location staring straight up, with nothing to block your view. Picture your feet at the bottom of the map, eyes in the middle, and hands at the left and right edges, with you looking up into the map. The edges of the circle correspond to the horizon in all directions around you, but without local mountains and other geographic features. Spend a little time looking into the sky and you'll pick out the brighter stars on the star map and soon understand how the map gives you the picture of the sky.

The sky map in Figure 4-3 also shows you the positions of the sun (we captured the image during the day), moon, and five planets. All seven of those objects lie on a gently curved line, the ecliptic, which corresponds to the plane in which all the planets of our solar system orbit. Some of the planets (Venus, for example) are brighter than most stars, so when they're visible they're good points to look for to get your orientation.

A Gentle Introduction to Sky Watching and Astronomy

We've found that the more we learn about what we're looking at in the sky, the more interesting sky watching is. There were many books on astronomy at our public library, but most were not very useful. One of the books we liked the best (Wiley being the publisher of this book completely aside) was *Astronomy: A Self-Teaching Guide,* by Dinah L. Moché (Wiley Publishing, Inc., 0-471-38353-8).

The trouble is that when you're out in the backyard in the dark without much experience, you really need a guided tour to what's above you. None of the books we found worked at that level, but we found a good beginner's Web site — Bob Parvin's Beginning Urban Skywatching site, at www.sfo.com/~parvin/skywatching.html.

Building and Using Your Telescope Tracker from Kits

We based the project on a telescope and motorized base that's complete, moderately priced, and widely available. You *can* build everything yourself, though, and if that's your interest, you should immediately skip to the end of the chapter where we've identified both the Web links and the books that will get you started.

Parts List

Even assuming you're going to buy the necessary equipment rather than build it, it's important to verify that all the parts you use are compatible. Physical compatibility of the motor base with the telescope and tripod isn't the whole story — you also need to verify that your software supports the control protocol used by the motor base. Many telescopes support Meade's LX200 protocol, which has led to it being supported by most of the astronomy software we could find. If you want or need to make your own PC-to-telescope cable, there's a good discussion on the Software Bisque Web site (www.bisque.com/help/thesky/telescope/Telescope_Interface_Cables.htm#TICCables). That page is part of the overall discussion of telescope control with TheSky software (www.bisque.com/help/thesky/telescope/Telescope.htm), which is worth reading.

You'll probably want a laptop computer, not a desktop, because you'll want the computer to be right next to the telescope. Almost any Windows laptop with a serial port will have enough power to run the software.

The parts listed in Table 4-1 work together. All listed hardware is designed for the ETX-90EC, and all the software explicitly supports the LX200 protocol.

Table 4-1   Telescope Tracker Parts List

Part	Manufacturer and Model Number
Telescope	Meade ETX-90EC ($495) www.meade.com/catalog/etx/etx_mak.html
Controller	Meade Autostar #497 ($149) www.meade.com/catalog/autostar/497_autostar.html
Tripod	Meade #884 Field Tripod ($200) www.meade.com/catalog/etx/etx_tripods.html
PC Interface Cable	Meade #505 ($50 with AstroFinder software) www.meade.com/catalog/etx/etx_accy.html
Time Software	SocketWatch ($10 from www.locutuscodeware.com/swatch.htm) or Atom Time ($12 from /www.atomtime.com)
Telescope Software	Meade Epoch 2000sk ($179 at www.discovery.com) Bisque Software TheSky ($129–249 at www.bisque.com/Products/TheSky/TheSky.asp; the Level I version priced at $49 doesn't include the ability to control the telescope) Hallo Northern Sky (free) www.hnsky.org/software.htm ASCOM software to interface HNSKY to the telescope (free) ascom-standards.org

Watch for sales and special pricing. For example, in late winter-early spring of 2003, Meade ran a special offer under which you could get the Autostar controller and field tripod included in the price of the telescope. We also found discounts available on eBay — an ETX-90EC sold for less than $300, although without the Autostar controller and tripod, while complete packages tended to sell for $430 and up.

The mirrors inside the ETX-90EC (see Figure 4-4), which is a catadioptric (mirror lens) Maksutov-Cassegrain telescope, make it a compact unit that's much easier to carry around than refracting telescopes. Don't expect the small size to mean lighter weight, though — there's a lot of glass in that tube, and it feels no lighter than the 38-inch refractor we have. The electronics and batteries sit inside the circular base at the bottom, the eyepiece for the main telescope is the smaller tube pointing up and to the left, and the viewfinder, which you use to point the telescope in roughly the right direction, is located behind and parallel to the main tube.

FIGURE 4-4: Meade ETX-90EC telescope

Courtesy of Meade Instruments Corp. Meade is a registered trademark of Meade Instruments Corp. ETX-90EC is a trademark of Meade Instruments Corp.

The standard control shown in the figure simply gives you manual control over the base, using the arrow buttons to slew left, right, up, or down at variable speeds. The standard control can track motion, but only if you have a tripod that can angle the telescope base to correspond to your site's latitude to form what's called a polar mount. The reason the standard controller can track motion in this way is because a properly aligned polar mount needs only to rotate around the azimuth axis of the base at a well-known rate, eliminating the need for computations to follow planets or stars.

The microcomputer inside the Autostar controller adds significant capabilities to the ETX-90EC, including pointing, tracking, and computer-assisted alignment and calibration for the motors. Alignment is the crux of both the real value of the Autostar and your telescope's connection to your PC, but is potentially a source of a lot of frustration.

Alignment

Connected to your telescope, the Autostar controller and your PC are a lot like automated navigators sitting next to you as you drive. They can tell you just what to do to get to your destination, but only if they know exactly where you are and which way you're headed.

More specifically, when the telescope base gets a command to move to a specific azimuth, it has to know which way to go and when to stop. If the base knows its azimuth, it can compute those numbers, but the base must know where it is. The same requirement applies to the elevation away from horizontal (also called the *declination*); setting up the base so its internal azimuth and elevation estimates match reality is the essence of alignment. You have to repeat the alignment process each time you move the telescope even a little, and each time you power off the controller.

Alignment is more complex than pinning down one azimuth and elevation, though, because the base can be out of level in two directions. Even though you accurately know your location on the earth and the time, you still need to resolve three unknowns (azimuth plus offset from horizontal in two directions) to precisely align your telescope. Knowing your location on earth and sighting to one star can resolve both azimuth and elevation in one direction, but you'll need a second star to resolve horizontal position in the second direction. Moreover, you shouldn't use just any other star; you want a star approximately 90 degrees azimuth away from the first one to get the best accuracy when the computer combines the two measurements.

The Autostar controller provides routines to help you align your telescope. What it calls easy alignment consists of sighting on two stars, one at a time, centering them in the telescope eyepiece using the manual motion control arrows on the controller (see Figure 4-5). The controller looks at its database of what stars should be visible to you, and picks brighter ones you're likely to be able to see. That's where the frustration comes in.

We often didn't know what to do once the telescope finished slewing to its target, because it would point either at an empty area in space, or point at a place where there were several stars to choose from. Fail to find the star and you can tell the controller to try another one; pick the wrong star from a group and you'll misalign the telescope.

If your patience holds, you may eventually learn which stars are which. Until that time, here are our hints for less painful alignment.

Minimize the Initial Error

It's worth some time to make the initial (home) position as close to perfect as you can. The home position requires that the telescope be pivoted on the base all the way counterclockwise (loosen the azimuth lock first) and turned back clockwise so the vertical arm is centered over the control panel, and that the elevation axis be pivoted so it's at the zero mark on the calibration dial. Once you do that, you then have to physically move telescope, base, and tripod as a single assembly so that the telescope points north.

Once you set that up, the alignment routine uses sightings on two stars to compute out the error in the north alignment and in leveling the telescope tube. Unfortunately, errors in the setup will be precisely duplicated when the base points at the target stars, which is what creates the offset pointing error you see and makes alignment difficult.

Minimizing the errors means leveling the tripod the telescope is on in two directions and pointing the tube as close to north as you can. You can level the platform with a level from the hardware store (do it in two directions), but you probably don't want to use a compass to find north due to the error between magnetic north and celestial north. Instead, learn to find the Big Dipper (Ursa Major) and through it the North Star (Polaris, which won't be *too* far from magnetic North), and point the telescope north using that. Get these alignments close enough and you'll see the right star in the viewfinder when you first look.

FIGURE 4-5: Meade Autostar controller

Courtesy of Meade Instruments Corp. Meade and Autostar are registered trademarks of Meade Instruments Corp.

Use a Simplified Star Map

If you can't get the initial alignment very close, or if there are multiple stars in the viewfinder, you'll need to determine which stars are which in the night sky. Not knowing Arcturus from Aldebaran from Alderaan (that last one's very hard to find) makes lining up the telescope difficult. Your PC can help by giving you a star map tailored to what you should expect to see.

The idea is that you can't see anywhere near as much with your naked eye as you will be able to with your telescope, so a star map filtered down to just the brightest stars will correspond to what you can see, and will give you a lot less to sift through. *The Bright Star Catalogue*, 5th Revised Ed. (Preliminary Version) (Hoffleit et. al, 1991, Yale University Observatory) defines stars visible to the naked eye as those brighter than magnitude 4.5 (more negative numbers correspond to brighter stars). Figure 4-6 shows a star map limited to magnitude 6.5 and brighter, and if you live in even a reasonably large city you're not going see all those stars.

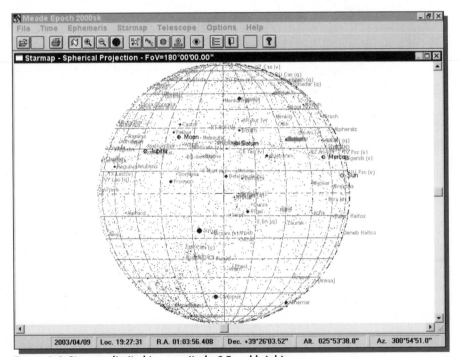

FIGURE 4-6: Star map limited to magnitude 6.5 and brighter

Courtesy of Meade Instruments Corp. Meade is a registered trademark of Meade Instruments Corp. Epoch 2000 is a trademark of Meade Instruments Corp.

You can duplicate this star map with Meade's Epoch 2000sk software by turning on the star map. Under the star map menu, change the zoom to 100 percent (180 degrees field of view) and the dimmest magnitude to 4.5. (We inverted the colors, too, simply because black images don't print as well.) You can get a similar sky map with Your Sky.

In practice, we live where the light from the city is so bright that we can't see stars much dimmer than magnitude 2.5 or 3.0. Figure 4-7 shows a star map produced by Epoch 2000sk limited to magnitude 3.0, a change that cleared away much of the clutter. The resulting sky map corresponds well to what we can actually see, so when we're trying to figure out which star in the viewfinder or telescope eyepiece is really the one we want, the view in the sky corresponds to our map and we know what to do.

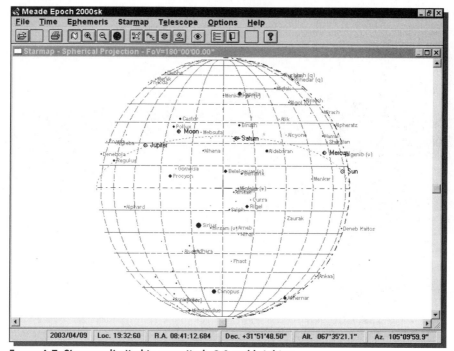

FIGURE 4-7: Star map limited to magnitude 3.0 and brighter

Courtesy of Meade Instruments Corp. Meade is a registered trademark of Meade Instruments Corp. Epoch 2000 is a trademark of Meade Instruments Corp.

Clouds only make visibility worse, but you can use the clear sky clocks at www.cleardark sky.com (and www.cleardarksky.com/csk) in particular, to find out when the best visibility will be based on location, cloud cover, darkness, and other factors.

Carefully Align the Viewfinder and Motor Tracking

The last thing you need to do is to make sure you set up the telescope properly when you first received it. That means calibrating the motors, calibrating the motor tracking, and aligning the viewfinder.

Calibrating the motors is the simplest of the three tasks — just work your way through the controller menus to the calibration command, and run it. Do this if you move the controller to another telescope, too.

Calibrating the motor tracking is somewhat harder. You need to point the telescope at a distant terrestrial object; then center the object in the eyepiece. Start the motor tracking routine, and follow its instructions to calibrate tracking in all four directions. For each direction the controller moves the telescope off center, you re-center the object. We found two tricks that help with this procedure. First, be sure the object you use is far enough away, because errors multiply when the object is close. We used a local mountaintop (see Figure 4-8) several miles distant.

Align on a distant landmark with sharp features

FIGURE 4-8: Use a distant landmark with edges to align the motor tracking and viewfinder.

If you can, pick a distant landmark with an easily seen point or edge to minimize the ambiguity of where to point. If we'd chosen a gently rounded hilltop, for example, rather than the peak in the figure, we'd have found it very hard to accurately resolve azimuth errors.

With the motors calibrated and their tracking aligned, you then need to ensure the viewfinder — the tiny telescope on the side of the main tube — accurately points to the same place as the telescope itself. If you don't, then stars in the viewfinder are likely to not be visible when you look through the telescope. Align the viewfinder using the same object used to calibrate motor tracking. Center the object in the telescope eyepiece, then adjust the rear screws on the viewfinder so the object is centered in the crosshairs.

Enjoy the Show

If you've got all the alignments down, it's time to fire up your PC — a laptop will work much better outdoors with your telescope — and load the software. We'll begin with Meade's flagship software, Epoch 2000sk. Tell the program your location, make sure the time is set properly, and then plug in your aligned telescope. Use the Telescope menu to set the protocol and communi-cations port, and the star map comes to life (see Figure 4-9). Click on an object to see the action menu shown in the figure; click on Slew Telescope to move the ETX-90EC to show you the star. A short beep from the telescope lets you know it's in position and ready for you to look.

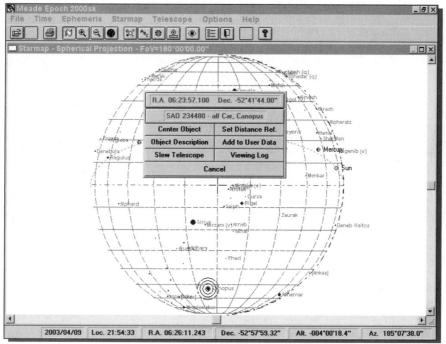

FIGURE 4-9: Click on an object (Canopus here) in the Epoch 2000sk star map for action choices.
Courtesy of Meade Instruments Corp. Meade is a registered trademark of Meade Instruments Corp. Epoch 2000 is a trademark of Meade Instruments Corp.

One of the things we liked the most about the star map in Epoch 2000sk is that it varies the size of the dot displayed for each star based on its magnitude. The PC makes finding faint stars easy (it's literally point and click), something we'd previously found difficult or impossible with our manually pointed refractor. This simple visual way to point at stars and planets, combined with the relative brightness indicators on the star map, meant we could spend our time explor-ing the sky instead of fiddling with the telescope. Add the automatic tracking so you're not constantly moving the telescope, and sky watching becomes a joy — and one free enough of hassle and delays that it remains interesting to younger children.

The software's Object Description dialog box includes a database of basic information in the program, such as magnitude, color, distance, movement, and other data (see Figure 4-10).

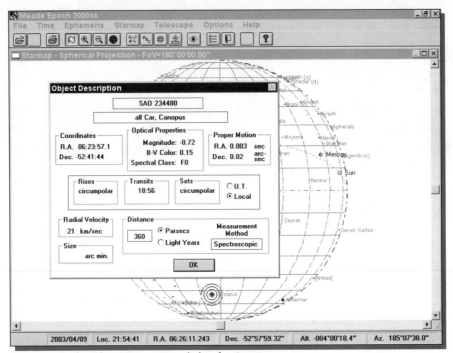

FIGURE 4-10: The Object Description dialog for Canopus

Courtesy of Meade Instruments Corp. Meade is a registered trademark of Meade Instruments Corp. Epoch 2000 is a trademark of Meade Instruments Corp.

Another commercial package you can use to control the ETX-90EC is TheSky from Software Bisque, which includes an actual printed manual with good explanations (a surprising throwback). We were even more surprised when the online help file included not only information about how to run the program, but a beginner's tutorial (see Figure 4-11) and a lot of information on astronomy.

We don't know enough about astronomy to know how Epoch 2000sk and TheSky compare with regard to the more advanced features, but as relative novices in astronomy, we have a clear preference for TheSky.

The hefty manual and tutorial alone were enough to make us ready to like TheSky; the program itself made it certain. The controls made sense to us, and the graphics conveyed what we wanted to see. Figure 4-12 is TheSky's version of the usual sky map we've been showing you, limited to magnitude 2.5. The area outside the viewable circle gives the context of what's almost viewable, and the shading across the display shows the location of the Milky Way. The stars show up well according to brightness. The only fault we found with the display was that we couldn't find a way to eliminate the names of stars not actually being displayed.

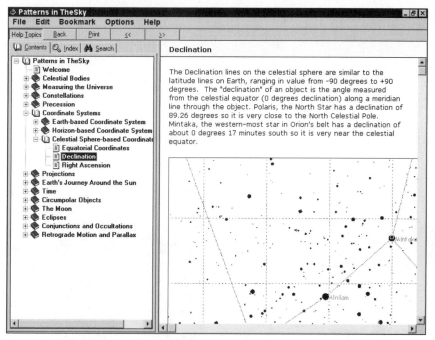

FIGURE 4-11: TheSky beginner's tutorial

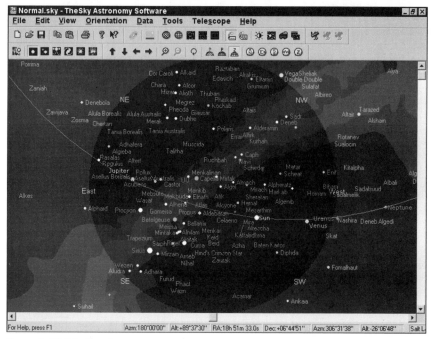

FIGURE 4-12: TheSky sky map

Even in the City, You Can See More Than the Moon and Planets

Don't assume all you can see inside a city will be the moon and planets. If you look back at Figure 4-7, you'll see there were a reasonable number of stars shown at magnitude 3.0. We turned on *all* the celestial objects in TheSky and turned off names to remove the clutter to get this sky map:

Far more than the moon and planets are visible from within even bright cities.

The objects you see in the figure, including stars, nebulas, and galaxies, should be visible even in very large cities.

An article in the April 2003 *Sky & Telescope* magazine, "111 Deep-Sky Wonders for Light-Polluted Skies" by James Mullaney (skyandtelescope.com/magazinearchive/ to purchase a downloadable copy), details what you can expect to see.

You can find freeware to control your telescope too, including Hallo Northern Sky (HNSKY). You'll also need the ASCOM software to interface HNSKY to the telescope. HNSKY controls the telescope, lets you adjust the sky map (see Figure 4-13) to limit the minimum brightness, and uses varying size dots for stars. We had some problems with telescope communications hanging at times and with program faults now and then. Nevertheless, although we found the program quite serviceable, the biggest problem we had was that the sky map was harder to correlate with the sky above us than those from the other programs or the Your Sky Web site.

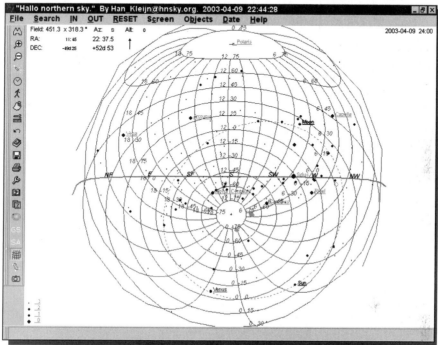

FIGURE 4-13: The Hallo Northern Sky sky map window

Building Your Telescope Tracker to Your Own Design

Astronomy is a field in which knowledge of programming, photography, and building instruments all come into play.

Build Your Own Telescope and Motorized Base

You really can build your own telescope using the instructions documented at Web sites such as the following:

- www.usno.navy.mil/8inchdob.html, tie.jpl.nasa.gov/tie/dobson/
- www.funsci.com/fun3_en/tele/tele.htm
- www.exploratorium.edu/exploring/space/activity.html

The great interest people have in building telescopes means you can find good books on the subject, including *Build Your Own Telescope, Complete Plans for Five Telescopes You Can Build With Simple Hand Tools* by Richard Berry (Scribner, 1985).

Nor do you need to abandon the idea of a motorized base. A Google search on *build telescope motor tracking* produced over 3,500 hits, including a number of sites describing how to build your own motorized base for your telescope. You can get plans for one of those designs in the book *Amateur Telescope Making* by Stephen Tonkin (Springer Verlag, 1999).

You'll need to be relatively adept with hand tools to complete either of these projects, but there's no question that when you're done you'll know your equipment inside and out. It will be somewhat harder to adapt the motor controls to respond to the common LX200 control protocol, but even that's well defined at the Meade site: `www.meade.com/support/CommandSet.html`.

Photography

Beautiful as what you see with your telescope can be, it's transient. Slew the telescope away and it's gone.

Unless, of course, you couple a camera to your telescope. The mechanical setup is easy with the ETX-90EC, because Meade makes an adapter to go between a port at the back of the telescope and a standard camera threaded ring. You can find the part (#64 T-Adapter) at `www.meade.com/catalog/etx/etx_accy.html`. If you want a camera designed for telescope photography, they also offer their Pictor CCD camera at `www.meade.com/catalog/meade_pictor/index.htm`.

Image processing might be a different story. We haven't yet tried photography with our telescope, but we did come across the Image Reduction and Analysis Facility (IRAF) site `iraf.noao.edu/`. IRAF is very heavy duty image processing software specifically intended for astronomical data. It runs on a PC only under the Linux, FreeBSD, and Solaris operating systems — Windows users need not apply. The operating system doesn't concern us so much as the need for the software at all; nevertheless, the camera adapter is so inexpensive that it's worth trying it out and seeing what you get.

Automatic Alignment

This one will be hard.

If you're a very industrious, skilled programmer, and you have significant time on your hands, you could try writing software to automatically align your telescope. You would need to use a CCD camera for the sensor, and collect enough pattern recognition data so that you could compare a computed sky map with what's in the camera image. Once you isolate the target star, you'd then issue commands to the telescope to slew it until the star is precisely centered.

If money were no object, you could write a check to solve the problem instead, , because you can buy telescopes (such as Meade's GPS models) with built-in GPS receivers, compasses, and inclinometers (levels). Stand them up, turn them on, and they align themselves. Unfortunately, they also cost thousands of dollars. If you chose to buy the complete camera setup, such as the Meade Pictor 208XT (www.meade.com/catalog/pictor/208xt.html), you'd be investing less than $1,000. (We found it for under $500 using Epinions, www.epinions.com/Meade_Pictor_208XT_CCD_Camera__Camera_07551xt) Given that, all you need to do is write the software.

Summary

Looking up at the sky has fascinated people for as long as there have been people, whether out of curiosity, appreciation for the beauty of what's there, or other reasons. Too many people give up on taking a closer look at the night sky because of the difficulty of getting started with telescopes and astronomy. Tying your PC, a motorized base, and the controller electronics to your telescope removes most of the initial complexity and gives you the opportunity to investigate the heavens with push-button simplicity, so you can focus on what you see rather than on the mechanics of the instruments.

Monitor Your Workout

I feel about exercise the same way that I feel about a few other things: that there is nothing wrong with it if it is done in private by consenting adults.

~Anna Quindlen, *Living Out Loud*

One of the widely recommended forms of exercise is a cardiovascular workout, meaning exercise in which you work hard enough to elevate your heart rate and breathing rate into a target band for a given period of time.

You're going to read about exercise in this chapter and how to use your computer to track your exercise program. The following should be completely obvious, but we want you to read and understand this disclaimer:

The content of this chapter is for informational purposes. You should not interpret anything in this chapter as medical advice or as guidance for how you should treat any medical condition. You should consult your physician before you start any fitness program.

We're not your doctors and don't intend in this chapter to tell you what's best for your individual body.

It's All About Information

The American College of Sports Medicine recommends you exercise with your heart rate within a zone they define between 60 to 90 percent of your maximum heart rate (www.acsm.org/pdf/Calculate.pdf) and suggests you exercise three to five times per week. Only very fit people will be in the middle to upper end of the zone, and recommended target guidelines vary. Figure 5-1 plots a reduced guideline, limited to 85 percent of maximum heart rate. Walking, jogging, swimming, and bicycling are all good exercises at your target heart rate.

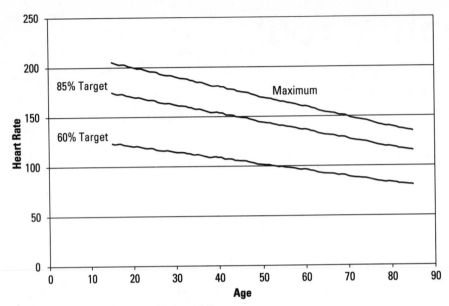

FIGURE 5-1: Cardiovascular workout guidelines

The consensus is that you compute your maximum heart rate — the maximum number of times your heart can beat in one minute — as 220 minus your age, although that rule of thumb doesn't necessarily extend to fit athletes. (So, if you're 40, your maximum heart rate computes as 220 - 40 = 180.) Consensus is also that a well-designed cardiovascular exercise includes warm up, the main exercise, and cool down.

> **Warm up.** Five to ten minutes of low intensity activity during which you gradually increase your heart rate and increase the blood flow to your muscles and heart. We've seen suggestions that your warm up be at 30 to 50 percent of your maximum heart rate. (So, if you're 40, your warm up would be in the range of 54–90 beats per minute.)

> **Exercise.** Most of your workout is in this phase, during which you want to keep your heart rate in the target zone.

> **Cool down.** Do another five to ten minutes of gradual slowing to return your heart rate to the same point it was at when you started your warm up.

One approach is to warm up for 5 to 10 minutes, maintain guideline intensity for 20 to 60 minutes, then gradually cool down for 5 to 10 minutes. You need information to make this plan work, primarily information about how fast your heart is beating.

Sensors, Computers, and Data

This is where your PC comes in. As with so many of the PC Toys, you'll use sensors and your computer to gather the data you'll use. Figure 5-2 is a block diagram of the system.

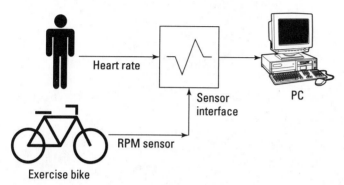

FIGURE 5-2: Workout monitor block diagram

The idea is to monitor your heart rate directly, not to estimate it from the exercise level as we've seen recommended in many places, and to monitor the exercise rate (the RPMs of the stationary exercise bike in the block diagram) as a measure of how hard you're working. We designed the project *not* to require a PC at the exercise bike, instead recording the data separately and downloading it to a PC for analysis. We used the same equipment that we used to monitor a fish tank (Chapter 8) and a weather station (Chapter 11), building the system around a small microcomputer called a *data logger*. Coupled with the right set of sensors, the data logger forms a complete data acquisition system you use to gather data you'll later transmit to a PC.

Building and Using Your Workout Monitor from Kits

Although we've seen plans to build heart rate sensors from infrared emitting and sensing diodes, the data logger we chose provides a complete heart rate sensor as one of its options. More challenging was constructing a means to monitor the rotation rate for the exercise bicycle. We ended up attaching a magnetic field sensor probe (see Figure 5-3) to the body of the bike and attaching a magnet to one of the pedal cranks as shown in Figure 5-4.

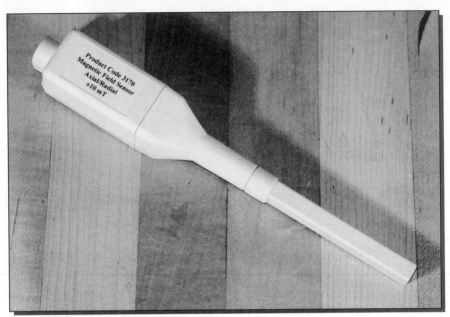

FIGURE 5-3: Magnetic field sensor

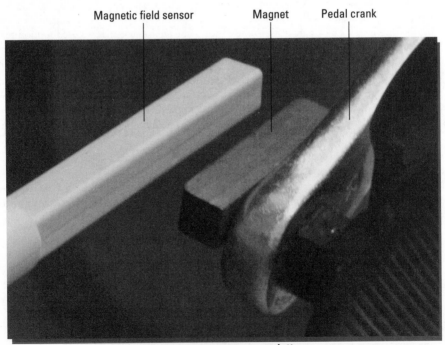

FIGURE 5-4: Magnetic field sensor set up to measure revolutions

Every time the magnet rotates near the magnetic field sensor (set up for axial field measurement, parallel to the sensor body), the measured field strength goes up. The response time for the sensor is easily fast enough to catch the field pulse as long as measurements are recorded often enough.

Parts List

The requirements for the PC you'll use to monitor your workout are minimal. Even a processor slower than 300 MHz running Windows will do, because all you're doing is data reduction. The rest of the parts we used are shown in Table 5-1.

Table 5-1 Workout Monitor Parts List	
Part	*Manufacturer and Model Number*
Data Logger	Data Harvest EasySense Advanced ($349) `www.dataharvest.com/Products/easysense/logger_features.htm`
Heart Rate Sensor	Data Harvest 3135PK ($119) `www.dataharvest.com/Products/easysense/sensors/heart.htm`
Magnetic Field Sensor	Data Harvest 3125PK ($89) `www.dataharvest.com/Products/easysense/sensors/magnetic_field.htm`

Figure 5-5 shows the data logger. Sensor probes connect to the front; the PC and power cables connect to the rear. Internal rechargeable batteries support operation for hours when the logger is disconnected from a power source. The meter button provides quick access to real-time readings, which are displayed on the LCD panel in the upper-left corner, while the other buttons operate the menu system to access more complicated functions.

Figure 5-6 shows the heart rate sensor. The clip is made to go over your finger or on an ear lobe. Either position lets the light emitted from the sensor pass through blood flow and be captured by the measurement diode. The electronics in the white sensor body interpret the sensed intensity waveform and convert the readings to heart beats per minute. You may want to loop the cord over your ear if you've clipped the sensor to an ear lobe to keep the clip from falling off.

If you're only going to use the Data Harvest data logger for this one project, you might want to consider the Polar 720i heart rate monitor (`www.polar-usa.com/polar-s-series.html`) as an alternative. It offers wireless speed and cadence pickups for bicycles plus 22 hours of data storage at five-second intervals and downloads to a PC via IR interface.

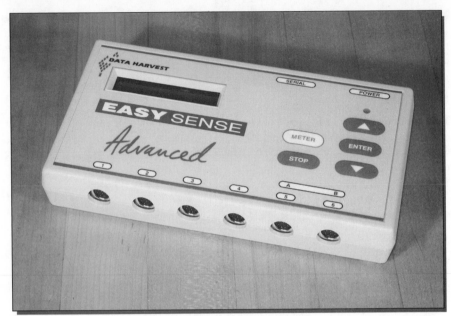

FIGURE 5-5: Data Harvest Easy Sense Advanced data logger

FIGURE 5-6: Heart rate sensor

Processing the Data

The magnetic field sensor doesn't directly convert the physical data to RPMs for you, so you're going to have to plan both how to collect the raw data and how to convert it to RPMs.

Even collecting the data is more complex than you might initially think. If you simply start the Easy Log routine on the data logger, it captures data at a relatively fast rate for a while, then slows the sample rate. Aside from the computational problems that changing the sample rate can cause, you might lose data. Figure 5-7, a plot of the magnetic axial field strength versus time in tenths of seconds, shows the problem you face. The pulses are only two-tenths of a second wide (less if you're pedaling even faster), so if the data logger is only sampling a few times per second, you're going to miss pulses.

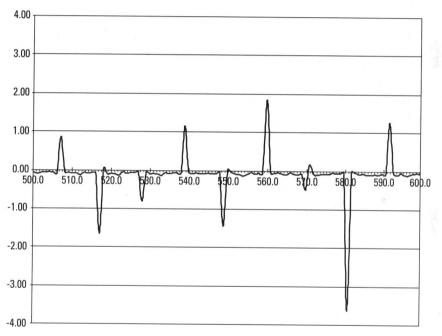

FIGURE 5-7: Detail of raw magnetic axial field data

The Easy Sense Advanced has two modes that let you control the sampling rate, Remote and Fast Log. Setting the Remote mode for a half-hour workout resulted in a sample rate of two per second, though, so we used the Fast Log with samples at a fixed tenth of a second interval. The resulting raw data set, collected over 400 seconds, is shown in Figure 5-8. The heart rate is the plot mostly in the top half of the graph and uses the scale on the right, while magnetic axial field is in both halves and uses the scale on the left.

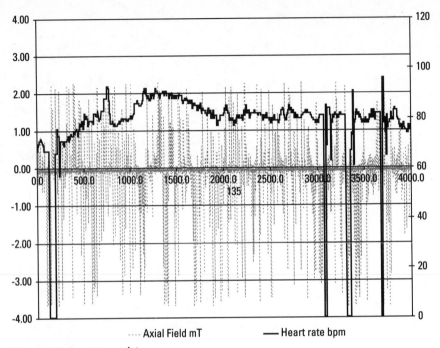

FIGURE 5-8: Raw sensor data

The data in Figure 5-8 has multiple problems that you'll need to solve while processing the data. Most obvious is that the pulse rate sometimes goes to zero. The test subject didn't suffer medical emergencies at those points, the sensor data simply dropped out. You could ignore the drop outs, substitute the last known reading until new data is available, or linearly interpolate over the data points framing the zero data. For simplicity, we ignored the drop outs.

More difficult is that the magnetic field pulses go both positive and negative, and the amplitude of the pulses varies a lot. You can solve that problem by using the absolute value of the field measurement (since you don't care whether the field is positive or negative, just that it's present), and by thresholding the measured values to determine whether a pulse is present. We added a test to eliminate pulse indications in two consecutive measurements, since the pedals will never turn that fast and we were seeing data with extra pulses due to measured data being over threshold for more than one sample. We used a threshold value of 0.2 milliTesla (mT; we gauged the threshold by looking at a plot of the data), producing data for which a section of the overall plot is shown in Figure 5-9. You can see the pulses occur at regular intervals, suggesting the thresholding operation worked properly.

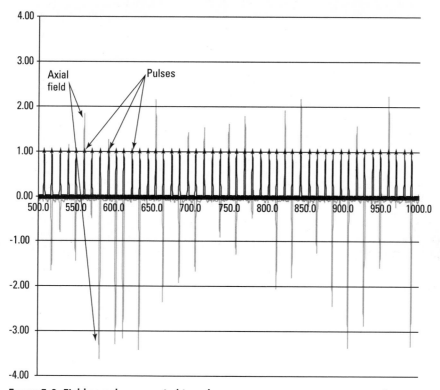

FIGURE 5-9: Field samples converted to pulses

After processing magnetic field strength measurements to pulses in time, you now need to use the pulses to estimate RPM. One way to do the computation is to count the number of pulses over one second, recognizing each pulse as a revolution of the pedal crank; then multiply by 60. You could equally count pulses over two seconds and multiply by 30, over four seconds and multiply by 15, etc. We tried all three of those methods, and found the results didn't differ much.

Figure 5-10 plots heart rate (for comparison against the RPM computation, since the two are correlated), computed RPMs, and a trendline for the RPMs averaged over 50 points. The computed RPM data isn't directly useful, since the computed values are coarsely spaced and the relative spacing of values conveys as much information as does the actual value. The trend line, however, is a reasonable approximation of the actual RPM.

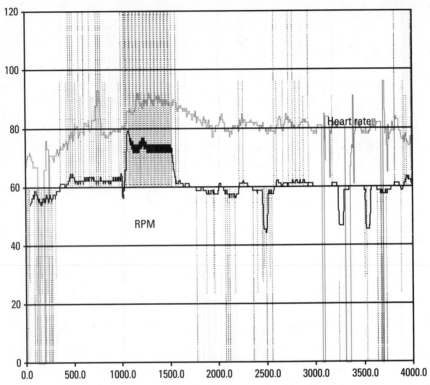

FIGURE 5-10: Heart rate and RPM (magnetic pulse count method)

Another way to compute RPMs is to calculate the time interval between pulses; then use the reciprocal of that interval to calculate the instantaneous RPM. Figure 5-11 shows the result of that calculation, along with a trend line and heart rate. The calculated RPMs are intuitively far more what you'd expect to see, even though the trend lines in Figures 5-10 and 5-11 are very similar.

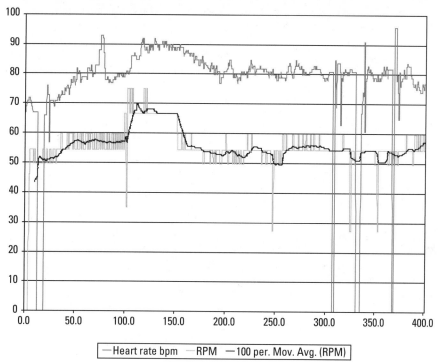

FIGURE 5-11: Heart rate combined with RPM trend line (magnetic pulse interval method)

Building Your Workout Monitor to Your Own Design

What you want to take away from these two approaches to calculating the RPMs is that there's not necessarily only one right way to do data reduction — several approaches may be valid. Which is better may depend on the characteristics of the data you have. For example, a different design of the magnetic sensing setup could use two magnets and sensors, one for each pedal, producing pulses twice as often, or could use multiple magnets on a wheel rotating past a single sensor. The more frequent pulses would increase the required sample rate, but in exchange would increase the number of samples per second, which would in turn improve the accuracy of the counts-based estimate. With enough counts per second, the calculated data would be a good approximation of the actual RPMs without the need for a trend line.

Moreover, the examples we showed above were limited to 4,000 samples because we used the data logger to collect remotely, without connection to a PC, at 0.10 second intervals. That's less than seven minutes. If you connect a PC to the data logger, however, the PC can record data in real time for an indefinite time. You use the *Graph* application that's part of the Sensing Science Laboratory software to do the data collection. Figure 5-12 shows both the controls you use to start the process and the key dialog window for setting up the collection.

Use a continuous timespan
recording to collect data indefinitely

Pick a recording duration to set
the sampling interval (the duration
is ignored for continuous recording)

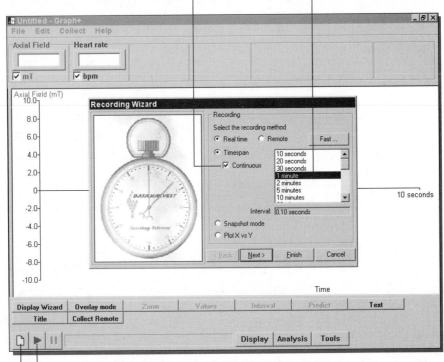

Click on Go after the wizard completes to start recording data

Click on New to start the recording wizard, preparing to collect data in real time

FIGURE 5-12: **Recording from the data logger directly into a PC**

You'll need a serial connection from the data logger to your PC. You could string cables, or search for an affordable wireless serial connection. Alternatively, you could use the Belkin Powerline USB Adapter to extend a USB connection from your PC to where you're exercising; then use a USB to serial converter to connect into the data logger. If all else fails, you could set up a laptop right next to the data logger.

Summary

For many people, better information is the key to better exercise. The monitoring capabilities of your PC, augmented by a data logger and the right sensors, might be just what you need.

Security

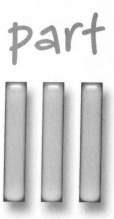

Home Surveillance with Internet Remote Access

You don't put kids under surveillance: it might frighten you.

~Garrison Keillor, "Easter," *Leaving Home*

F riends of ours built a retirement home some years ago and became concerned about theft and vandalism while they waited in another city to sell their old house and move in. Being the sort to use technology to solve problems, they installed a Black Box VueMate Hub (`catalog.blackbox.com`), to which they connected closed circuit television cameras. A long-distance call from their PC to the hub gave them access to the cameras, letting them monitor the site whenever they chose.

The unfortunate part of this story is that the VueMate Hub goes for close to $700, plus the cost of cameras. The long-distance phone bills to actually *use* the system seem like chump change in comparison, and despite spending all that money, they could only access the cameras from a PC with the necessary software loaded.

Never Be Out of Reach

As with seemingly everything else, the Internet has revolutionized what you can build for remote surveillance and security. Low-cost video cameras, driven by the market for desktop video conferencing and webcams, have improved to where they generate reasonably high-quality video and provide embedded video compression. Broadband Internet access offers both speed advantages and a permanent connection to the net, making it suitable for remote monitoring. The global reach of the Internet means that you can monitor your home from Abu Dhabi, if you happen to be there.

One of the things that tends to raise the initial cost of the Black Box unit is its ability to multiplex four separate cameras. This is an important feature, because it's impossible to monitor your entire home from just one camera unless that camera is quite a way above the house. You can also increase the coverage you get from each camera with a motion sensor and tracking camera base. You'll see how to set up these features in this project, along with how to integrate your surveillance system with the Internet and access it from any computer with a Web browser.

Sensors and Alerts

Figure 6-1 shows the organization of the overall surveillance system. We used video cameras because they are inexpensive and widely available, and because video cameras are easier to interface to a PC than a still camera. Most video cameras can take still images, too. The system looks simple, consisting of only the camera(s), PC, and broadband modem, but is difficult to implement because of the mismatch between the data rate from the video camera and the uplink rate through the broadband connection. You could see as much as 4 MBps (32 Mbps) from each camera, yet a typical uplink rate is only 128 Kbps. That's roughly a 30:1 differential, which means you're not going to be pumping broadcast quality video out to the Internet.

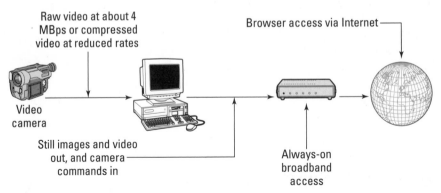

Raw video at about 4 MBps or compressed video at reduced rates

Browser access via Internet

Video camera

Still images and video out, and camera commands in

Always-on broadband access

FIGURE 6-1: Surveillance system block diagram

You have many options for using the available Internet bandwidth. For example, if you're working with still photos, you can:

- Transmit on command
- Transmit at set intervals
- Transmit at set intervals whenever there's motion

The still photos can be large or small, and can be compressed with lossless or lossy compression — such as JPEG — if you really need to make them small.

Video is much like a rapid succession of still images, so choosing your resolution still matters. The video *frame rate* is similar to the interval between still photos, with *slow scan* video referring to video at only a few frames per second. If you get the frame rate high enough so that *motion compensation* can compactly encode object motion differences between successive frames, video compression technologies — such as MPEG-1, MPEG-2, or MPEG-4 — are usable.

Building and Using Your Surveillance System from Kits

Our baseline design for the surveillance system solves the bandwidth problem by using compressed still images triggered by motion in the camera field of view, and minimizes the number of cameras needed by following moving objects with the camera. A tracking camera detects movement at a distance, then keeps the moving object in the field of view as it gets closer; the result is that you need fewer cameras to cover the surveillance area.

Parts List

We expected this to be a difficult project when we started to design it, largely because when we had last looked at webcams they did nothing but capture a small video image — no zoom, no tracking base, and no triggering when there's motion. However, our Google search for *pan/tilt camera mount* turned up nearly 18,000 hits. SmartHome was the first hit (www.smarthome. com/7742.html), but at $399.99 for just the camera mount, their equipment was impractical for this project. More refined searching *(pan/tilt camera mount motion tracking)* turned up the TrackerPod robotic camera base and TrackerCam software from Eagletron which, together with a webcam like the Logitech QuickCam Pro 4000, gave us a low-cost system with strong capabilities. The parts we used are shown in Table 6-1.

Table 6-1   Home Surveillance Parts List

Part	Manufacturer and Model Number
Motion Base and Software	Eagletron TrackerPod and TrackerCam Software ($174.99) www.pantiltcam.com/TCamWeb/productdes.htm
Camera	Logitech QuickCam Pro 4000 ($70 and up; see www.shopper.com) www.logitech.com/index.cfm?page=products/ details&CONTENTID=5042

Figure 6-2 is an overview of how the TrackerPod and a camera combine into a surveillance system. The camera and TrackerPod both have USB connections. The camera interface carries audio and video to the computer, and zoom, resolution, and image adjustment commands to the camera. The TrackerPod interface carries position information to the camera and pan, tilt, and LED commands to the servo base. Under control of the TrackerCam software, you can point the camera, record video and stills, upload to Web sites, and monitor or control the camera remotely.

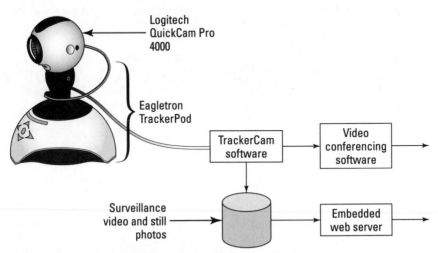

FIGURE 6-2: TrackerPod, camera, and software integration
Logitech® and QuickCam® are registered trademarks of Logitech.

The Logitech QuickCam Pro 4000 (Figure 6-3) provides surveillance images and sound, offering video resolution up to 640×480 pixels at up to 30 frames per second and still photos at resolutions up to 1280×960 pixels.

FIGURE 6-3: Logitech QuickCam Pro 4000
Logitech® and QuickCam® are registered trademarks of Logitech.

Powering the TrackerPod

The TrackerPod requires power from the USB port to drive the motors in the base. The Dell 4550 computer we used couldn't supply as much power to the USB port as our model of the TrackerPod wanted, causing the TrackerPod to constantly reset and the TrackerCam software to lose control. Eagletron has auxiliary power supplies for the early TrackerPods to work around this problem, and added current limiters to the motor base circuits in a revised version to reduce the peak draw. The TrackerCam software detects when there's a power problem, giving you this dialog box:

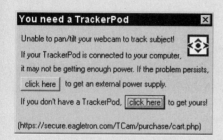

You'll need an auxiliary power supply if your computer can't supply enough power at the USB port. Click on the first button to bring up a Web page from which you can order the necessary power supply.

Dismount the camera from the base, then use a screw-in mount supplied with the TrackerPod to attach the camera to the motion base and form the assembly shown in Figure 6-3. Be sure to install the software before connecting the camera and base to the computer, because the software installation supplies the necessary USB drives.

Working with the TrackerCam Software

Once you install and start the TrackerCam software (you'll have to work through several configuration dialog boxes; the one to go online/offline can be canceled for now), and connect the camera and TrackerPod, you'll see the display on the right of Figure 6-4, labeled Initial TrackerCam Window.

Initial TrackerCam window

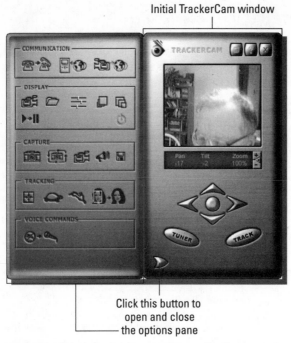

Click this button to
open and close
the options pane

FIGURE 6-4: Initial TrackerCam window and controls window

Click the button in the lower left to open the options window and use the button next to the right edge of the display pane to make the display window larger (see Figure 6-5).

FIGURE 6-5: Expanded TrackerCam window

The window that opens when you click on Tuner in the TrackerCam window (lower left of Figure 6-5) is the interface you use to set up the enormous number of settings for TrackerCam. The defaults are reasonable, for the most part, with the exception of left/right directions. If TrackerCam is set up correctly, clicking on a point in the video window should slew the camera to make that point the center of the image. If the base goes the wrong way, reverse the control direction. Do that by bringing up the tuner (not to be confused with the Configuration Wizard, which is what TrackerCam opens as the tuner when it first starts up and asks if you want the tuner), then in the Display and Camera section select Specify Field of View. On that page, make the existing value for Horizontal FOV negative and the controls will reverse direction. Click on Enter FOV Values, then test your work in the video window.

Live Internet Surveillance

The easiest way to set up surveillance with TrackerCam is to enable the embedded Web server and access live video with a Web browser. Figure 6-6 shows what TrackerCam video looks like in a browser. The video display updates at the rate shown in the lower left; you can use the tuner to adjust the update rate. Using TrackerCam across a LAN permits the full 30 frames per second (fps), while you'll have to throttle down the rate across the Internet. The requirement to run at slow frame rates across the Internet rules out video compression like MPEG-1 or MPEG-2, so TrackerCam uses JPEG compression on individual frames.

FIGURE 6-6: See what's going on from anywhere with slow scan video.

JPEG compression outputs variable image sizes depending on the image resolution, scene complexity, and compression quality setting. A typical 320×240 image shrinks to 3KB after JPEG compression (24 Kb), so you'd need 24 Kbps for 1 fps. The bandwidth requirement scales with frame rate, so you need 48 Kbps for 2 fps, 72 Kbps for 3 fps, and so on. You might get 2 fps through a 56K modem if you get a good connection; the 128 Kbps uplink common to ISDN, DSL, and some wireless systems may support 5 fps. You're using 720 Kbps for 30 fps at 320×240 resolution.

The Communication pane in Figure 6-4 lets you access the controls to turn on the embedded server for live video. Click on the rightmost icon in the pane to get the dialog box in Figure 6-7 and turn on Put Me Online and, optionally, Guests Allowed. After you make sure the IP address in the lower right is correct, the URLs at the bottom can be copied and pasted into Web browsers for remote access. Disable guests and create user accounts unless you want the camera images open to everyone or unless you've taken other access security measures.

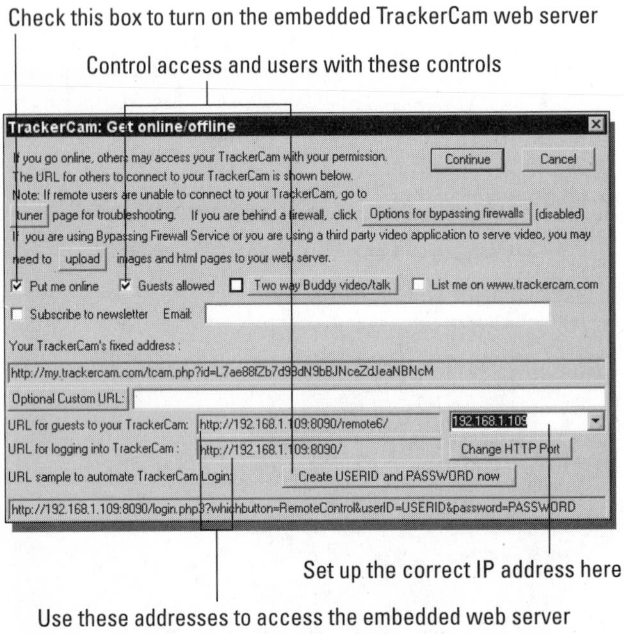

FIGURE 6-7: The Online/Offline dialog box gives you controls for remote access to TrackerCam.

Recorded Internet Surveillance

The problem with live surveillance is that if something happens when you're not looking, you miss it. TrackerCam lets you record surveillance images on disk and access those images either locally from a computer with local or shared network disk access, or across the Internet using a

Cable/DSL Router Security and TrackerCam

You already know that you're vulnerable to attack any time your computers are connected to the Internet. One of the best ways to protect your computers from attack is to use an external hardware router providing Network Address Translation (NAT), because most of those routers can be set up to allow no unsolicited access to your computers from outside your LAN. That's the approach we use (which is why our IP addresses you see in this chapter are sequences like 192.168.1.109), and the logs we get from our router make it evident we're being probed constantly. The problem with routers like the Linksys we use, though, is that it takes some work to permit outside access when you want it.

This screen shot from the browser interface to our router shows how we set it up for remote access to both TrackerCam and HomeSeer (see Chapter 3). The idea is that anytime an external network request to access one of the indicated ports or port ranges arrives at our router, it's diverted to the internal address shown. We turned on both TCP and UDP access rather than have to research whether UDP is needed in addition to TCP, but if you're even more paranoid than we are, you'll try the software with only TCP enabled and see what happens.

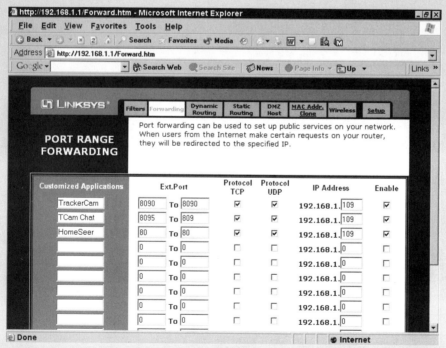

Use port forwarding on your router to direct incoming requests to a specific computer.

Continued

Continued

In practice, though, we don't leave any of those ports open on a regular basis—we open them when external access is required and close them again when the need goes away. We get from tens to hundreds of probes of our network every hour, so it's just prudent to keep the ports closed if they don't need to be used.

Web browser. Set up surveillance through the tuner (click on the Tuner button in the main TrackerPod window, Figure 6-5, then pick Surveillance—Capture Stills, found under Communications. The configuration page (see Figure 6-8) lets you choose how often you save an image, how much disk space surveillance may use, and when surveillance is active.

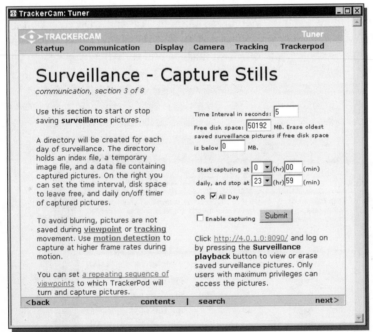

FIGURE 6-8: Use the Surveillance—Capture Stills page to enable still photo surveillance, define how often to capture an image, control disk use, and set times.

You can do more than simply position the camera and have it snap images. For example, from the tuner contents section choose Viewpoint Order in the Tracking section. Define a sequence of viewpoints (places at which the camera points) on this page (see Figure 6-9), and let surveillance visit the viewpoints in sequence. The grid you see is a plane in front of the camera, so by choosing a box you specify both pan and tilt. Define viewpoints by clicking in the box where the camera should point; if you clear all existing points you can simply click all the viewpoint positions in sequence to create the path. If you name them using the pane on the right, those names will show up in the remote browser window and can be selected to point the camera. You can define the times at which viewpoints are active, too.

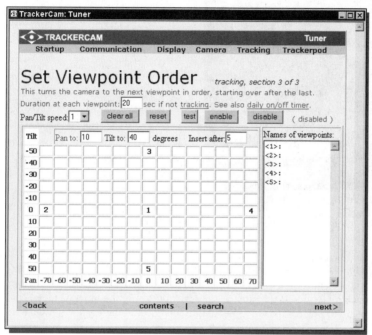

FIGURE 6-9: Set up viewpoints to have the camera scan an area under surveillance.

Motion Detection and Tracking

You can also set up your system to recognize motion and start collecting images when motion is present. The TrackerCam software has algorithms built in to detect and follow motion in the frames received from the camera. Figure 6-10 shows the motion detection algorithm in operation. The white bounding box in the figure shows the area of the image in which it has identified motion, in this case because the dog had just turned around. You can set the threshold for motion detection to be more or less sensitive, depending on the size and speed of the motion you want to see or exclude.

Once TrackerCam detects motion and establishes a bounding box, it can use that detection to trigger snapping a still image or motion clip. Basing your surveillance on motion detection helps eliminate recording useless images. TrackerCam can also slew the TrackerPod to follow the bounding box, keeping in the field of view as the object in the box moves. Test the motion tracking not only for sensitivity, but to check the speed at which the TrackerPod slews — too slow, and it can't keep up.

FIGURE 6-10: A bounding box in the camera view shows the area TrackerCam identified as containing motion.

Detailed settings for tracking and motion capture are in the Capture Motion page under Communication, shown in Figure 6-11. The top part of the right column lets you enable or disable motion tracking (which is the same as the Track button in the main window), and set the detection threshold. The rest of the right column sets the parameters for motion-based video capture.

Video Conferencing

One of the problems with desktop video conferencing is that the camera is so close that if you move to one side to do something you're out of the picture. The TrackerPod solves the basic problem by being able to track your movements, but because there are so many video conferencing applications (including CUseeMe and Microsoft NetMeeting), it's impractical for the TrackerCam software to include the equivalent of all those programs. Instead, TrackerCam implements a "pseudo camera," interposing itself between the actual camera and any application wanting access to video from a camera. This feature makes the motion tracking functions available invisibly to the other application, which simply thinks it's getting a video stream from a fixed camera.

The left-hand icon in the Communication pane in the options window starts your video conferencing application. The first time you click on the icon you'll get a dialog box used to identify the application; after that, the application simply starts. Figure 6-12 shows how this works. TrackerCam is running behind NetMeeting, while the identical image in both the NetMeeting and TrackerCam windows shows you that they're getting the same video feed.

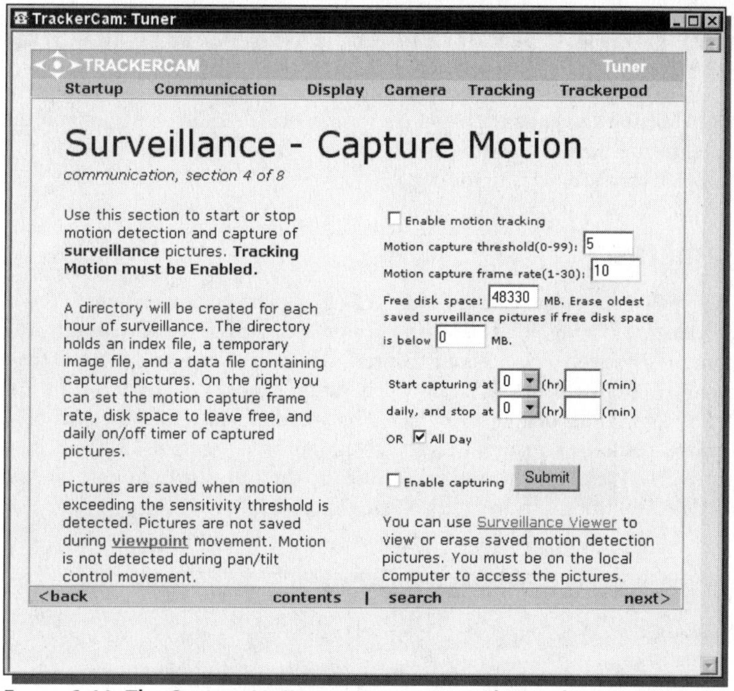

TrackerCam: Tuner

‹◆›TRACKERCAM   **Tuner**

Startup   Communication   Display   Camera   Tracking   Trackerpod

Surveillance - Capture Motion
communication, section 4 of 8

Use this section to start or stop motion detection and capture of **surveillance** pictures. **Tracking Motion must be Enabled.**

A directory will be created for each hour of surveillance. The directory holds an index file, a temporary image file, and a data file containing captured pictures. On the right you can set the motion capture frame rate, disk space to leave free, and daily on/off timer of captured pictures.

Pictures are saved when motion exceeding the sensitivity threshold is detected. Pictures are not saved during **viewpoint** movement. Motion is not detected during pan/tilt control movement.

☐ Enable motion tracking

Motion capture threshold(0-99): 5

Motion capture frame rate(1-30): 10

Free disk space: 48330 MB. Erase oldest saved surveillance pictures if free disk space is below 0 MB.

Start capturing at 0 ▼ (hr) ____ (min)

daily, and stop at 0 ▼ (hr) ____ (min)

OR ☑ All Day

☐ Enable capturing   Submit

You can use Surveillance Viewer to view or erase saved motion detection pictures. You must be on the local computer to access the pictures.

<back   contents | search   next>

FIGURE 6-11: The Capture Motion settings page in the TrackerCam Tuner

FIGURE 6-12: Configure NetMeeting to use the TrackerCam Capture camera and you'll have motion tracking from within NetMeeting.

Building a Surveillance System to Your Own Design

There's really no end to what you can do with a home surveillance system. You can start with the basic system we describe and enhance it to meet your specific requirements, or you can start with entirely different equipment and software. The driving factors are what you want to accomplish and how much you're willing to spend.

Multiple Cameras

You will need more than one camera if your objective is to watch your entire house. You can easily tie multiple cameras to your PC if they're webcams with USB interfaces, but if you're using standard composite video you'll need a PC interface able to accept and digitize the analog video signal. One possibility is the Webcam Corporation Model WCSP100-4, a PCI board accepting four NTSC or PAL analog video signals. The board includes software to monitor the cameras and give you a combined quadrant display of all four (see Figure 6-13). You can watch the video remotely with a Web browser, and you can set up the software to initiate video recording when it detects motion and to send you an e-mail alert.

FIGURE 6-13: Simultaneous quadrant display from four cameras

Long Cables and Wireless Cameras

For the same reason that it's hard to put full-motion video onto the Internet—it's hard to transmit lots of bits a long distance—the camera's data rate makes it difficult for you to set up your cameras a long way from your PC. You don't always have a choice, though, so you may need to design remote cameras into your surveillance system. The following sections discuss some of your options.

Long Cables

Many webcams use a USB interface into the PC, which would normally limit you to keeping the computer in the same room as the PC. Eagletron, the maker of the TrackerPod we used in the baseline design, makes an adapter that will extend USB cables as far as 200 feet. At $160 for the 150-foot version, those adapters (`secure.eagletron.com/TCam/purchase/cart.php?Item=H2002E150`) are expensive, so you'll want to be careful where you use them.

Wireless

One possibility is a wireless pan/tilt camera, but these are expensive too. The X10 Vanguard is representative ($799.99 list; $499.99 special offer in early 2003; see `www.x10.com/products/vanguard_sg1.htm`). Equivalent cameras we researched were even more expensive.

You also have the option of a stationary wireless camera, such as the X10 Xcam2 ($79.99 at `www.x10.com/products/x10_vk45a.htm`). It's an order of magnitude cheaper, but you'll need more cameras to get full area coverage.

If you already have cameras that produce standard composite video, Radio Shack makes wireless audio/video senders (catalog number 15-2572 at `www.radioshack.com/`) for under $100. These units transmit the composite video plus stereo to the paired receiver; if your requirements are within their range, which is affected by walls, metal, people, and other interference, they're small and simple.

Integrated Home Automation

You can combine video surveillance with home automation (see the coffee pot controller in Chapter 3 for an introduction to X10 equipment). The X10 Floodcam is an example (`www.x10.com/products/x10_vt38a.htm`); it combines a wireless camera, floodlights, and a motion sensor, and transmits the motion indication to your X10 system for further response. The camera can be turned on and off from the X10 system, too.

On a simpler level, the power supply for the stationary X10 Xcam2 will respond to your X10 controls, turning the camera on and off.

Archiving to Removable Storage

Security installations in which permanent storage of what's recorded is necessary often record the video to videotape. You could do that, but it's difficult to do if you're using the motion tracking features of the TrackerPod. Instead, if you have a CD-RW or DVD writer, you could dump the captured files to optical disk. You could use one of the many available programs to make your optical drive work like a read-write drive, then either write a program to dump directories to disk or use something like the Unison file synchronizer (`www.cis.upenn.edu/ ~bcpierce/unison/`). If you need control over the times at which the application runs, consider using a Windows scheduled task.

Summary

The essence of surveillance is making images of interesting events available remotely. As you dig into building a surveillance system, you'll grapple not only with the camera issues of resolution, image quality, and field of view, but also system control and communications bandwidth. You'll need to strike a balance among those characteristics if you want to keep costs within reason.

Monitor Your Refrigerator and Freezer

chapter

7

in this chapter

☑ Temperature switches

☑ Temperature sensors

☑ Sensor interfacing

☑ Handling power failures

Even when I was little, I was big.

~William (Refrigerator) Perry, Chicago Bears defensive tackle

It's seductively easy to take some of our most important technologies for granted. Refrigerators and freezers have been around for so long and are so dependable that we forget how different life would be without them. Power grids are also quite reliable in developed countries, and the combination of dependable power and reliable appliances lets us forget how convenient and important storing fresh food and inventories of frozen food really is.

The Dinner You Save May Be Your Own

We learned that lesson some years ago when we went on vacation, leaving the house and dogs in the care of a good friend. The circuit breaker powering a refrigerator/freezer in the garage tripped, and by the time anyone noticed, everything inside was spoiled. Our friend was mortified, but since we don't periodically check for this kind of trouble, we decided it wasn't reasonable to expect any one else to, either. People have better things to do.

Your PC, however, is an ideal candidate for the job. It never sleeps, you can protect it from power failures using an uninterruptible power supply (UPS) long enough to warn you, and it never gets bored or forgets to pay attention. You need a way for your PC to know what's going on inside the refrigerator and freezer, and once you have that in place, e-mail can warn you of any problems.

Figure 7-1 is a block diagram of the overall system. We designed the monitor using the same X10 technology and the HomeSeer software we used in Chapter 3 to control a coffee pot. You saw there how to generate e-mail in HomeSeer to warn you that the batteries had failed in your motion sensors; here, you'll extend that idea to e-mail you a warning when there's a problem that could affect food in the refrigerator or freezer.

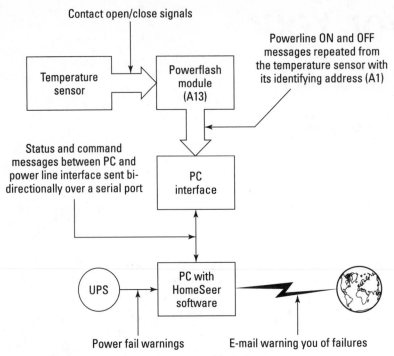

FIGURE 7-1: Refrigerator/freezer monitoring block diagram

The lower part of the block diagram is similar to the coffee pot controller in Chapter 3 — your PC watches for messages on the power lines through the attached X10 PC interface and responds accordingly.

Sensors and Alerts, Redux

The US Department of Agriculture Web site (www.fsis.usda.gov/OA/pubs/pofeature.htm) gives the following guidelines for food storage, which we've incorporated into our design:

> Always keep meat, poultry, fish, and eggs refrigerated at or below 40°F and frozen food at or below 0°F. This may be difficult when the power is out. Keep the refrigerator and freezer doors closed as much as possible to maintain the cold temperature. The refrigerator will keep food safely cold for about four hours if it is unopened. A full freezer will hold the temperature for approximately 48 hours (24 hours if it is half full) if the door remains closed.

The design requires two new elements beyond the basic X10 and HomeSeer components:

- A way to transmit status from the temperature sensors to your computer.

- A way to discover whether the temperature inside the box is above or below these threshold temperatures. There's no need to know the actual temperature, just whether the temperature is too high.

We started with the transmission problem because there are fewer products available for this task than for temperature sensing. We decided to use X10 remote signaling because it's far more convenient than placing a computer next to each refrigerator and freezer — we didn't want to have to run cables across rooms, and there's no straightforward, inexpensive way to remote temperature sensors across a wireless link. X10 has its own problems in this application, though — the system isn't intended to transmit ranges of values (other than dimmer settings), only the on/off status. People have adapted the signaling for values (using different house and unit codes for specific ranges), but the resulting method is clumsy and difficult or impossible to set up for more than one or two devices.

The fact that we don't need actual values, only threshold status, eliminates the drawbacks of using the X10 interface. The module you need is called both the Burglar Alarm Interface and the PowerFlash module (we'll call it PowerFlash from here on out). The PowerFlash module has three modes; Mode 3 is what we want. In Mode 3, when a contact opens or closes, the module sends out an on or off message, respectively, to the house and unit code address of the PowerFlash. Your X10 PC interface sees that message, just as it did the on/off messages from the motion sensors in Chapter 3, giving HomeSeer the information it needs.

The PowerFlash electrical interface is simple — you connect a switch across the contacts. Any thermometer that drives a switch to open/close at the temperature you want will connect directly and complete the sensor suite.

Building and Using Your Refrigerator and Freezer Monitor from Kits

Our search for temperature sensors compatible with the PowerFlash was initially one of the more difficult parts searches we did for this book. We needed to be able to put the temperature probe in the refrigerator or freezer as well as close a contact. We initially found only one useful temperature sensor (shown in Figure 7-2), a preset sensor switching at 39 degrees Fahrenheit we discovered on the SmartHome site (www.smarthome.com/7152.html). After ordering and receiving the part, we realized from the packaging label that it was made by Winland Electronics, leading us to a wealth of options in the temperature and humidity sensor section of their Web site (see www.winland.com/demo.php3?id=7).

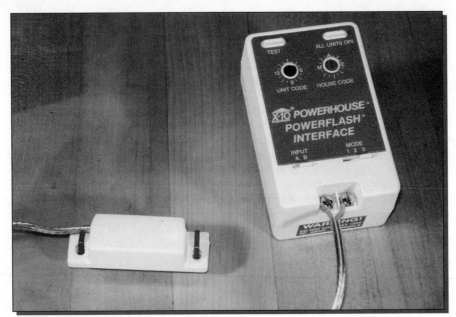

FIGURE 7-2: Preset temperature sensor
Courtesy of X10 Wireless Technology, Inc.

Figure 7-2 shows the Winland sensor on the left, and the X10 PowerFlash on the right. The wires from the sensor connect directly to the terminals on the PowerFlash module; make the wires as long as required (within reason) so you can position the sensor in the refrigerator. The mode switch on the right towards the bottom of the PowerFlash is set to Mode 3, while the input switch on the left is set to Mode B (so the PowerFlash expects a contact closure).

Parts List

As with the coffee pot controller, the PC requirements for monitoring your refrigerator and freezer are minimal. Even a processor slower than 300 MHz running Windows will do, since you don't need voice recognition for this application. Make sure you have an available serial port to connect the CM11A PC interface to the computer, or use the SmartHome PowerLinc USB PC interface ($34.99; see www.smarthome.com/1132u.html).

The parts we used (several of which duplicate items in Chapter 3) are shown in Table 7-1. The Winland Electronics fixed temperature sensor is available from SmartHome; the TempAlert variable sensors are available from several sources (search the Internet for *DTA-1* or *TA-2HLD*).

Table 7-1   Refrigerator/Freezer Monitor Parts List

Part	Manufacturer and Model Number
Temperature Threshold Monitor	All the following are made by Winland Electronics: TA-40 Mechanical Fixed Temp Alert ($9.76 from SmartHome) www.winland.com/details.php3?id=9 DTA-1 Digital Temp Alert with #1024 Low Temperature Sensor /www.winland.com/details.php3?id=30 TA-2HLD Digital Temp-Alert with #1107 Low Temperature Sensor www.winland.com/details.php3?id=42
Power Converter	Radio Shack Catalog No. 273-1631 ($14.99) www.radioshack.com/product.asp?catalog%5Fname= CTLG&category%5Fname=CTLG%5F009%5F001%5F001% 5F002&product%5Fid=273%2D1631
PowerFlash Module	X10 Model PF284 ($29.99) www.x10.com/security/x10_pf284.htm
PC Interface	X10 Model CM11A (The CM11A is difficult to find other than packaged with several modules in the X10 ActiveHome kit, $49.99) www.x10.com/automation/x10_ck11a.htm
Control Software	HomeSeer Technologies, HomeSeer ($99.95 for unlock keys; download the 61MB application from the Web site or order a CD for $5) www.homeseer.com

The Winland TA-2HLD is significantly less expensive than the DTA-1, so unless you find a DTA-1 on sale, you'll probably want the TA-2HLD. The DTA-1 operates only with an external remote sensor probe, while the TA-2HLD can operate with either a built-in temperature sensor or an external probe. Both are rated for only 32–130 degrees and aren't rated for high humidity, so you shouldn't put the unit inside a refrigerator or freezer to make use of the internal sensor.

Both units require an external power source. Although they'll operate on a variety of power converters, we picked one readily available from Radio Shack that converted wall power to 12 VAC. The converter has a switch you use to select the output voltage, so be sure to set it correctly before plugging things in. The Winland TempAlerts also expect raw wires for the power source, not a connector, so cut the connector off and strip the wires back a half inch or so. It's best if you then tin the wires (get them hot with a soldering iron and apply a little rosin core 60/40 solder) to prevent them from unraveling.

All connections to the DTA-1 are on the bottom of the unit (see Figure 7-3). The power connection is on the left, the switch contacts you'll connect to the PowerFlash are in the middle, and the sensor connection is on the right. The coil of wire on the right comes with the sensor, which you can see at the end of the wire. Because the connections are external and designed for durability, the DTA-1 is suitable for a variety of placement or mounting configurations.

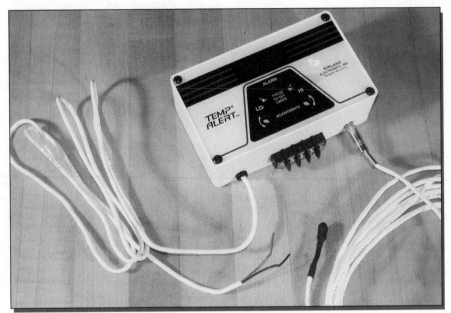

FIGURE 7-3: Winland DTA-1 TempAlert with low temperature sensor

The TA-2HLD (see Figure 7-4) is somewhat more compact, but is built for wall mounting. All the connections for the device are internal, along with a number of jumper blocks you set to determine the specific configuration you're using. You would typically mount the unit on a hollow wall or a 3-gang electrical box, so it's going to be a little more complicated to run the sensor wires out of the wall and over to the refrigerator.

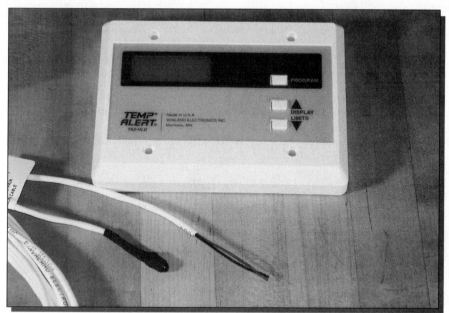

FIGURE 7-4: Winland TA-2HLD TempAlert with low temperature sensor

Hooking Up the Sensor and PowerFlash

You can set up the X10 PowerFlash in several different ways, so it's important to choose the correct switch settings. You can select three modes of operation with the switch on the front:

- When the switch contacts close, Mode 1 turns on all lamps and wall switches with the same house code, and turns on any modules with the same house and unit code. Lamp and wall switch modules at the same house code and different unit codes stay on when the contacts finally open, but any modules with the same house and unit code turn off.

- Mode 2 is almost the same as Mode 1, except lights connected to lamp or wall switch modules will flash on and off.

- Mode 3 is designed for signaling, not controlling a wide range of devices. All modules with the same house and unit code as the PowerFlash turn on when the contacts close, and turn off again when the contacts open.

The PowerFlash can either supply power across the contacts, or can expect the contacts to supply their own power. If you set the input switch on the PowerFlash to A the unit expects the contact circuit to supply 6-18 volts AC, DC, or audio; if you set it to B it expects simple contacts and supplies the necessary voltage itself. The sensors listed in this chapter provide simple contacts, so set the switch to the B position.

Figure 7-5 shows the terminal strip on the DTA-1 you'll use to connect the sensor to the PowerFlash. Connect one of the two wires to the common terminal, and the other to the normally open one. When the DTA-1 senses an alarm condition (either over or under temperature), it will close the normally open contacts, setting off the PowerFlash.

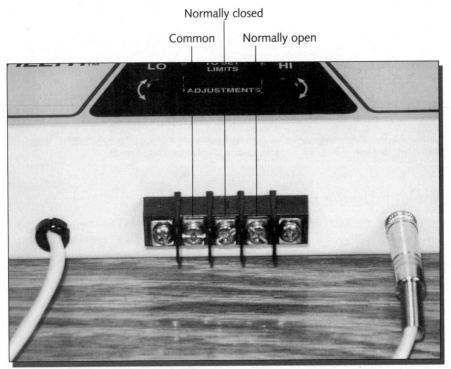

FIGURE 7-5: DTA-1 contact terminal strip

Figure 7-6 shows the corresponding hookup points for the TA-2HLD. Power, contacts, and sensor connections all run to the terminal strip on the left, with power at the top, high and low limit contacts in the middle, and sensor connections at the bottom. Set jumpers for the power source you're using; the default J1 position is right for the 12 VAC power block in the parts list. If you use 12 VDC, move the jumper to position J9. The factory default uses the internal temperature sensor, not a remote one, so you have to move the jumpers at positions J3 and J5 to the top pair of each group of three pins from the default bottom pair.

Sensor

High limit

Power

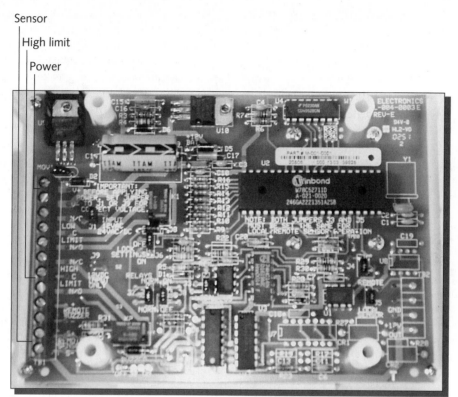

FIGURE 7-6: TA-2HLD terminal strip

The TA-2HLD gives you an interesting option to configure the relay contacts that will activate the PowerFlash. You can set up the relay to be either normally energized or normally inactive. If you set the jumpers so that the relay is normally energized, the relay will trigger if the unit loses power in addition to when the high limit is exceeded. To configure the high limit relay to be normally energized, move jumper J8 up to the normally on pair of pins (J7 controls the relay for the lower limit). Normally energizing the relay reverses the sense of the normally open/ normally closed connections on the terminal strip, so you'll connect the PowerFlash to the common and normally closed terminals. If the power goes out to the TA-2HLD (put it on the same circuit as the refrigerator and freezer), or the monitored temperature gets too high, the relay will switch and the contact will close, firing off the PowerFlash.

Two on the Cheap

Because you're setting up the PowerFlash to go active and raise the alarm when contacts close, you don't need a separate PowerFlash for every sensor. Instead, wire all the sensors in parallel across the PowerFlash inputs. Normally all the sensor contacts will be open; if *any* sensor contact closes, the PowerFlash turns on and wakes up HomeSeer.

You can use this idea to monitor a refrigerator and freezer next to each other. Wire a TA-40 Mechanical Fixed Temp Alert switch in the refrigerator (to warn any time it gets to 40 degrees or above) in parallel with the contacts on either a DTA-1 or TA-2HLD monitoring the freezer. You'll get an e-mail from HomeSeer if either appliance goes toes up.

Setting Up HomeSeer

With all the electronics in place, the rest is software. Refer to the "E-mail Alerts" section in Chapter 3 for how to configure HomeSeer to send e-mail; once you've done that, you need only configure the PowerFlash and create the lone event shown in Figure 7-7. HomeSeer doesn't have a specific definition for the PowerFlash, but you can use the Status Only device type. Be sure to create the event to fire when the PowerFlash status changes to on, not simply when it is on, so you only get one e-mail from a failure, not thousands of them. Define the event to send an e-mail to a mailbox you can monitor with a wireless PDA, and you're done.

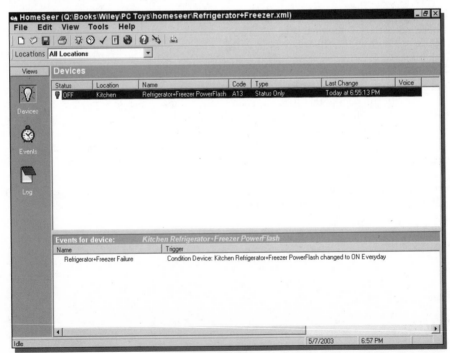

FIGURE 7-7: HomeSeer event to monitor temperature

Building Your Refrigerator and Freezer Monitor to Your Own Design

This refrigerator and freezer monitor design is only the beginning of what you can do once you have the ability to determine whether temperatures have crossed a high or low limit threshold. The following sections contain some ideas for extending the design.

Get Help When Power Fails

One of the weaknesses of the monitor as described in the last section is that, if your entire house loses power, you won't be alerted. You can give your PC a few minutes with a UPS, but then it needs a way to send out that dying gasp e-mail. Many of the larger systems will allow you to connect a status port to your PC so that you can monitor the UPS, and some will send you e-mail alerts when the unit encounters a problem.

Alternatively, you can add UPS monitoring your UPS to your HomeSeer configuration. HomeSeer can run Visual Basic scripts, and defines a number of functions you can use to let the scripts interact with HomeSeer — see the HomeSeer help file. Using a script and the information at www.apcupsd.com/manual/upsbible.html, here's a script to monitor an APC UPS connected to COM2:

HomeSeer Script to Monitor an APC UPS

```
sub main()
  dim result

  result = hs.OpenComPort(2,
                          "2400,N,8,1",
                          0,"comm_apc.txt","apc_event")
  if result <> "" then
    hs.WriteLog "Error",
                "Error opening COM port for UPS: "&result
  end if
end sub

sub apc_event(data)
  if data = 1001 then
    hs.TriggerEvent "event_name"
  end if
  end sub
```

The script, which you configure HomeSeer to run on startup, works like this:

1. HomeSeer runs the `main()` function when it initializes the script, and as a result hooks the `apc_event()` subroutine to be called any time there's a character at the serial port or status change at the port.

2. Whenever `apc_event()` is called, the UPS has passed a character to the PC or there's been a status change on the port. The parameter to `apc_event()`, `data`, is a status code for the port. The `apc_event()` subroutine checks the status to see whether the UPS has sent a break condition to the port, which would indicate that it has lost line power, and if so triggers an event.

3. The triggered event sends you an e-mail.

The script language uses the Microsoft MSComm control internally to manage the serial port. More documentation on the control is available from Microsoft at `msdn.microsoft.com/library/default.asp?url=/library/en-us/comm98/html/vbobjcomm.asp`. The set of error codes that can be passed to the callback subroutine — `apc_event()` — are defined in Table 7-2; of these, the value 1001 is useful because it indicates when the UPS has sent a break to indicate loss of line power.

Table 7-2   Communications Callback Serial Port Script Status Codes

Code Name	Value	Definition
ComEventBreak	1001	Break received — which means that the line used to send data to the PC has been held high for longer than one character time.
ComEventFrame	1004	Framing error — the pulses expected on the transmit data line sending to the PC did not correspond to the requirements of the RS-232C standard.
ComEventOverrun	1006	Port overrun — characters were received from the UPS faster than they were consumed by the script.
ComEventRxOver	1008	Receive buffer overflow — the array defined to store received characters is full.
ComEventRxParity	1009	Parity error — the received data character has been corrupted.
ComEventTxFull	1010	Transmit buffer full — there is no more room to store a character to be transmitted.
ComEventDCB	1011	Something went wrong internally in the communications software.

Protect Your Air Conditioner's Compressor

The people who maintain our air conditioner tell us that running the compressor when it's below 50 degrees outside will damage the compressor. The outside temperatures can drop significantly where we live, from daytime temperatures in the high 80s or 90s to 50 at night and often 25 degrees in 15 minutes when a front comes through. The daytime temperatures are high enough to warrant running the air conditioner to cool the house down at night, but without a safeguard running it is risky in early or late summer when the nighttime temperatures could drop below 50.

Change your refrigerator/freezer monitor design to move the temperature sensor outside, and program the lower limit to 50 degrees, and your PC can detect when the outside temperature drops too low. All you need to complete the project is a thermostat your PC can control to turn off the air conditioning system. The SmartHome page at www.smarthome.com/x10thermostat.html lists several thermostats; included on that page is the Bi-Directional X10 HVAC Controller (www.smarthome.com/3049b.html) which directly responds to X10 commands and is already compatible with HomeSeer.

Summary

Your PC is the perfect sentry, needing only the right sensors to let it detect conditions you care about. As you saw in this chapter, finding an adequate threshold sensor wasn't as difficult as it seemed at first. Don't give up too soon when looking for the sensors you need — the problem may be that you're looking the wrong way.

Monitor Your Fish Tank

chapter

8

in this chapter

☑ Be both careful and curious

☑ Tracking values or limits

☑ Data loggers

☑ Computations

If water is too clear, it will not contain fish; people who are too cautious will never gain wisdom.

~Chinese proverb.

The first part of the proverb points out that you can overdo working with a fish tank—fish want the right environment, but they also very much dislike rapid change. It's easy to do too much too quickly, and your fish will suffer if you do. Even so, the second part of the proverb applies too—you'll keep fish successfully only after investigating what works and what doesn't.

This chapter is as much about chemistry as it is about fish, because what your fish want from you is an environment identical to what they lived in before they were caught. This project helps you monitor the critical chemistries in your tank, which involves more than just plugging things in and loading some software. You're going to need to remember and work with some simple chemistry.

The Clock Is Ticking

We're not going to pretend that we're experts in the care and feeding of fish. We've maintained fresh and salt water tanks for several decades, but they are not the professionally built and maintained ones you see in commercial displays. Nevertheless, over those years we've developed a set of guidelines that help us keep our fish alive:

- **Don't overfeed.** Seemingly every fish care book names overfeeding as the number one sin people make. Don't do it.

- **Do almost nothing.** We need to emphasize what we've already said. Fish *really* don't like change, so whatever you do, do it slowly. You float the bags containing new fish to slowly accustom them to the new temperature; any other changes you make need to be just as slow or slower. Doing almost nothing includes limiting how often you change the water, stir up the gravel, or clean the insides of the tank, because any time you do these things you change the fish's environment.

- **Have fewer fish.** We've found that it's much easier to keep a tank functioning and stable if there's a lot of water and not very many fish. In a 75-gallon salt water tank, we tend to limit the population to slightly less than one full-grown inch per gallon, while conventional wisdom is closer to one and one half full-grown inches per gallon.

- **Use lots of pumps.** If anything, we suggest you err on the side of too much pumping and filtration instead of not enough. In a 75-gallon salt water tank, we use two large powerhead pumps with biological undergravel filters plus an external pump and mechanical filter. We put water wands on the outputs of the powerheads to create upward-pointing streams and increase aeration.

- **Bigger is better.** If something goes wrong, a bigger tank has more water to buffer the consequences and give you the chance to fix the problem. Small tanks have less margin for error.

- **Keep hardy fish.** Some fish are tougher than others. Until you've shown yourself that you can keep the more delicate sort, stick to the tough ones. In salt water, for example, we've found tomato clowns, anemone clowns, wrasses, and damsels to be survivors.

The idea behind this chapter is to help you track your tank closely enough that its condition never gets out of hand, ensuring you can intervene gently yet still correct what problems you have. The longer you wait after problems start, the more you'll have to do and the more you'll stress the fish. For fresh water tanks, at a minimum you'll want to track pH and temperature; for salt water tanks, you'll also track salinity. There are other tests you'll do that we're not covering here, including ones to measure ammonia, nitrite, and nitrate concentrations.

Sensors and Alerts, Part Three

Figure 8-1 shows the block diagram for the fish tank monitor. The design includes sensors for key parameters, including temperature, pH, and salinity (which we plan to measure using a conductivity sensor). The challenge in the design is (aside from finding the sensors themselves) to interface these three sensors to a PC.

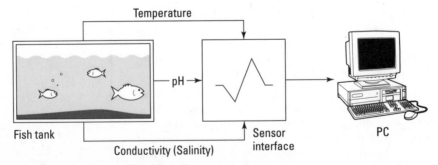

FIGURE 8-1: Fish tank monitor block diagram

As we did in Chapter 7, we assume you won't want to locate a PC immediately next to the monitored system, and won't want to run cables across your house from the tank to the PC. We're still looking for affordable wireless equipment that will extend an RS-232 serial port, and don't have the option of simply monitoring thresholds as in Chapter 7, so for this design we decided the sensors and interface would have to run autonomously, recording data that periodically gets downloaded to the PC and analyzed. A sensor interface that operates that way is called a *data logger*. Searching Google for *"data logger"* (in quotes) and *windows* lists lots of them, including several you can set up with the sensor suite in Figure 8-1.

The overall system, then, has a real-time component and an analysis component. The real-time component reads sensor values at regular intervals and records them in memory. When you're ready to run an analysis, you move the data logger to the PC, read out the values and analyze them, then hook the data logger back up to the sensors.

The idea behind using a conductivity sensor to measure salinity is that increasing salt levels makes water more conductive. Ocean sea water salinity (total dissolved salts per parts of water) averages about 35 parts per 1,000, varying between 34 and 36. Aquarium salinity is also expressed as the specific gravity of water, typically ranging from 1.020 to 1.023. Check the requirements for the fish you'll keep, because some want the salinity as low as 1.018, while others want it as high as 1.027. The relationship between specific gravity and salinity is temperature dependent; Table 8-1 from www.algone.com/salinity.htm lets you convert from one to the other.

Table 8-1   Specific Gravity to Salinity Conversion

Temperature	Specific Gravity							
°F (°C)	1.020	1.021	1.022	1.023	1.024	1.025	1.026	1.027
74.0 (23.3)	28.0	29.3	30.6	31.9	33.3	34.6	35.9	37.2
75.0 (23.9)	28.2	29.5	30.8	32.1	33.5	34.8	36.1	37.4
76.0 (24.4)	28.4	29.7	31.0	32.3	33.7	35.0	36.3	37.6
77.0 (25.0)	28.6	29.9	31.2	32.5	33.9	35.2	36.5	37.8
78.0 (25.6)	28.8	30.1	31.4	32.7	34.1	35.4	36.7	38.0
79.0 (26.1)	29.0	30.3	31.6	32.9	34.3	35.6	36.9	38.2
80.0 (26.7)	29.2	30.5	31.8	33.2	34.5	35.8	37.1	38.5
81.0 (27.2)	29.4	30.7	32.0	33.4	34.7	36.0	37.4	38.7
82.0 (27.8)	29.6	30.9	32.3	33.6	34.9	36.3	37.6	38.9
83.0 (28.3)	29.8	31.2	32.5	33.8	35.2	36.5	37.8	39.2
84.0 (28.9)	30.1	31.4	32.7	34.1	35.4	36.7	38.1	39.4
85.0 (29.4)	30.3	31.6	33.0	34.3	35.6	36.9	38.3	39.6
86.0 (30.0)	30.5	31.8	33.2	34.5	35.8	37.2	38.5	39.8
87.0 (30.6)	30.8	32.1	33.4	34.8	36.1	37.4	38.8	40.1

The key question is how to convert conductivity measurements (in units of microsiemens per centimeter) into salinity. The standard reference for the calculation is UNESCO Report No. 37, 1981, which defines the Practical Salinity Scale (PSS). You can find code to do the PSS calculations on several Web sites, including the Visual Basic version at `ioc.unesco.org/ oceanteacher/resourcekit/M3/Classroom/Tutorials/Processing/CTDData Process.htm`. Fortunately, you don't have to do the work to compile and test the code — `www.fivecreeks.org/monitor/sal.html` contains a converter using the UNESCO equations. You'll need both temperature and conductivity, which you can get from the monitor.

If you want to do the calculations yourself, but want a simplified conversion, go to the U.S. Environmental Protection Agency Web site (`www.epa.gov/volunteer/spring97/ mettec14.html`), which recommends using this single equation:

```
Salinity (ppt) = 20
                + 0.69608 (C-K)
                + 0.0013094 (C-K)²
                - 0.000011918 (C-K)³
                + 0.00000017392 (C-K)⁴
                - 0.0000000031112 (C-K)⁵
```

C is the measured conductivity in millisiemens (not microsiemens!) per centimeter at 25 degrees Celsius, and K is the constant 32.188.

It's worth checking the credibility of any Internet reference you find. For example, while researching this chapter, we found a page that said you can convert from conductivity in microsiemens per centimeter (no temperature defined) to sodium chloride (salt) concentration in parts per thousand simply by dividing by 2,000. This didn't sound right, and calculations later in the chapter show that it's not.

Building and Using Your Fish Tank Monitor from Kits

Given the design plan and science background in the previous section, all that remains is the engineering to build the monitor. The key selection parameters we used were:

- Cost
- Capability to simultaneously measure temperature, pH, and conductivity
- Ability to collect all three data streams independent of a PC for a relatively long time
- The ability to download the data to a PC for later analysis

From the selection we found on the Internet (try searching Google using *"data logger" pH conductivity temperature windows*), we chose the Data Harvest EasySense Advanced data logger.

Parts List

The requirements on the PC you'll use to monitor your fish tank are minimal. Even a processor slower than 300 MHz running Windows will do, because all you're doing is data reduction. The rest of the parts we used are shown in Table 8-2.

Table 8-2   Fish Tank Monitor Parts List

Part	Manufacturer and Model Number
Data Logger	Data Harvest EasySense Advanced ($349) www.dataharvest.com/Products/easysense/logger_features.htm
Conductivity Sensor (salt water tanks only)	Data Harvest 3135PK ($119) www.dataharvest.com/Products/easysense/sensors/conductivity.htm
pH Sensor	Data Harvest 3125PK ($89)
Temperature Sensor	Data Harvest 3100 ($39) www.dataharvest.com/Products/easysense/sensors/general_temperature.htm

In addition, you'll probably want to calibrate the sensors periodically, for which you'll need potassium chloride (KCl), pH 4.00 buffer, and pH 7.00 buffer from the local chemistry supply store. (If you can't find one locally, try searching Google for *"chemistry supply"*.)

The EasySense Advanced data logger (Figure 8-2) is virtually foolproof, because it's designed for use in schools, which are equipment torture chambers in all respects. The unit contains batteries, a processor, display, memory, and sensor ports. Plug your sensors into the ports on the front; then use the keys on the top to configure settings or start logging. The back panel (not visible in the photo) contains the serial port for interface to your PC, plus the power connector.

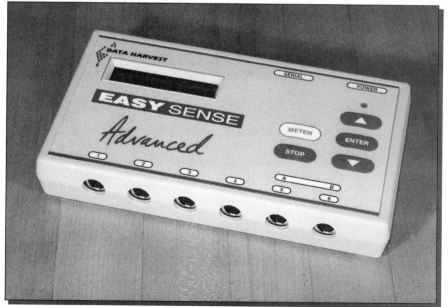

FIGURE 8-2: Data Harvest Easy Sense Advanced data logger

The simplest operation is using the logger as a real-time meter, initiated by pressing the Meter button. The display shows current readings for all sensors, although you'll have to scroll up and down if you have more than two.

The Easy Log function starts logging at a fairly rapid rate, 40 samples per second on all connected sensors, but slows the sample rate after a while and blanks the display. Depending on the sensors connected, data collection can continue, as long as the device has power, for as long as a month before you'll run out of memory. The remote logging function lets you specify the length of time you want to log data, modifying the sample rate as required.

Sensors

We've specified three sensors in the parts list: a temperature probe (Figure 8-3), conductivity probe (Figure 8-4), and pH probe (Figure 8-5). There's nothing to using the temperature probe — you simply put the tip in the water (more is OK, but don't put the wires in the water).

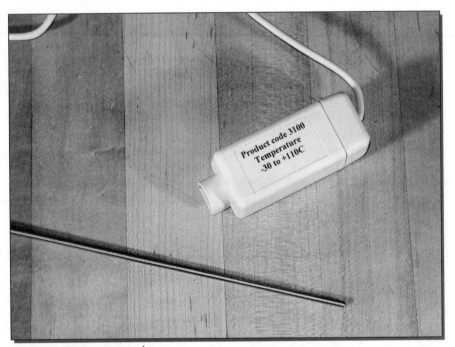

FIGURE 8-3: Temperature probe

The conductivity probe has an electrode (visible in Figure 8-4) in the middle of the outer tube. Prepare the probe by soaking it in distilled water for at least 30 minutes, then making sure the end cell is clean. If you want to calibrate the probe, put it in an accurate 0.1 M KCl solution, stirring to make sure any trapped bubbles dissipate. Calibrate the reading using the temperature/conductivity chart packaged with the sensors. Rinse all probes carefully with distilled water before putting them away.

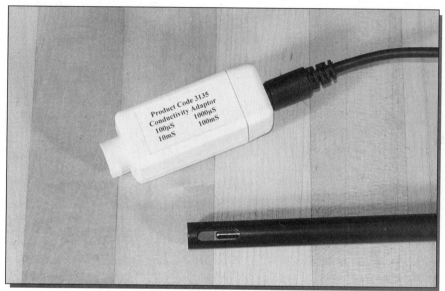

FIGURE 8-4: Conductivity probe

The pH probe (see Figure 8-5) is more complicated, in that it has a small glass ball at the end inside the plastic fingers and a secondary electrode at the end between the ball and a finger. The ball can't be allowed to dry out, so it comes with a canister that you place over the probe's tip when storing the probe. The secondary electrode can require replacement. You must make sure you have no bubbles in or on the ball in order to get accurate readings.

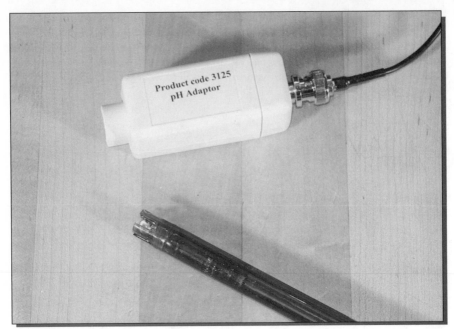

FIGURE 8-5: pH probe

The pH probe comes with a calibration table loaded into the interface (which the data logger uses if you choose the default calibration). You can calibrate the probe yourself, but you'll need accurate pH 4.00 and 7.00 buffer solutions.

Measurements

We monitored our 75-gallon salt water tank and came up with very stable readings. That's not surprising, because that much water simply doesn't change characteristics quickly. Read through the following steps to track our salinity measurements and calculations.

Measuring Conductivity and Calculating Salinity

1. Put (at least) the temperature and conductivity probes into the tank. If you also put in the pH probe, keep it as far from the conductivity probe as possible to prevent interference between the two.

2. Start the logger (or switch on the metering function), and record your sample data. We measured 50,800 microsiemens conductivity at 23.5 degrees C.

3. Convert the measurements using the page at www.fivecreeks.org/monitor/sal.html. Our measurements converted to a salinity of 34.50 parts per thousand. For comparison, note that the equation at www.epa.gov/volunteer/spring97/mettec14.html results in a computed salinity of 33.35 parts per thousand. Part of the

error is due to the measurement not being at the 25 degrees C temperature assumed by the equation. (Recall also the Web page that told us to simply divide the conductivity by 2,000, which gives a result of 25.4—not even close.)

4. Use Table 8-1 to convert salinity to specific gravity. Our measurements resulted in specific gravity between 1.024 and 1.025, which (depending on the fish you have) could be a little higher than ideal.

Building Your Fish Tank Monitor to Your Own Design

There's a lot you can do once you can measure and record the temperature and other water characteristics of your fish tank. For instance, you can:

- Monitor the temperature of your swimming pool and use the pH readings to make sure you add acid as necessary.

- Monitor the temperature of your spa remotely (you might want a direct connection from the logger to the PC for this) so you know when it's up to temperature and ready for you.

- Monitor the temperature of your wine cellar to make sure you're keeping the bottles at the optimum point.

Summary

Data loggers expand the range of sensor types you can interface to your PC and give you the ability to record data from locations distant from the computer. The three sensors in this chapter are only the beginning—Chapter 5 used the data logger to monitor your workout, Chapter 11 will use it as a weather station, and the Data Harvest Web site offers even more sensors you can use to interface your PC with the environment.

Out and About

part

IV

Do Your Own Automotive Diagnostics

. . . I appeal to any, who have been but moderately conversant in the history of mankind, and looked abroad beyond the smoke of their own chimneys. Where is that practical truth, that is universally received without doubt or question. . .

~John Locke, *An Essay Concerning Human Understanding*

The computers jammed (and later engineered) into cars in the late 20th century did nothing for the shade-tree mechanic. Previously, mechanics could make do with a shop manual and some oddly shaped tools. Computer-controlled engines, transmissions, and instruments, different in each manufacturer's cars and lacking any universal characteristics, quickly threatened to make automotive repair so arcane that none but factory-trained and sponsored mechanics had a prayer.

Computers Be Damned, the Gearhead Is Back!

Government-imposed smog regulations were a key reason why computers began to appear in cars. Early onboard computer implementations sapped so much power and ran so poorly, however, that many people wrote off smog equipment and worked to convince anyone who would listen that electronics in cars should be eliminated.

Eliminating electronics in cars hasn't happened. The latest BMW 7 series includes a simplified computer trackball and a user interface that your grandparents won't get out of park. That's an extreme example, but even conventional-appearing cars are filled with computers and processors. You don't set the spark plug timing, set the fuel mixture, adjust for high altitude, or shift the automatic transmission (despite those manual shift positions). Computers do.

Cars now universally use computer-controlled fuel injection, and the combination of faster, more reliable computers and decades of testing and improvement have resulted in cars that are more powerful, run smoother, and require less maintenance than their older versions. The computers and controls are so good that some states permit emissions testing based on simply checking the readouts of the onboard computers, not actually sampling the car exhaust.

Surprisingly, governments intervened to solve many of the early problems amateur mechanics had with automotive computers, requiring manufacturers to implement a standard interface to the onboard systems. The state of California required systems compliant with On-Board Diagnostics I (OBD I) on all 1991 and newer vehicles. The United States Environmental Protection Agency required systems compliant with On-Board Diagnostics II (OBD II) on all 1996 and newer vehicles. These requirements apply to all cars sold in the United States, regardless of where the vehicle was made. The standardization created by these requirements created a market for inexpensive, universal OBD II data access and logging equipment, giving home mechanics access to the information previously locked inside their cars' computers.

Standardization Is Your Friend

OBD II requires that all cars sold in the United States use one of three hardware interfaces to send and receive data through the OBD II port. The Society of Automotive Engineers (SAE) is responsible for the standards used by Ford and General Motors, while the International Standards Organization (ISO) is responsible for the standard used by Chrysler and most foreign car companies. Above the electrical level, the generic *diagnostic trouble codes* (DTCs) are the same for every vehicle; individual manufacturers add their own vehicle-specific codes as required.

All OBD II systems work in the same way, following the block diagram in Figure 9-1. Your car still has a conventional internal combustion engine, but it's been augmented with sensors and actuators. The sensors, including ones that monitor timing, fuel, oxygen, and other parameters, report to the *Engine Control Unit* (ECU), a small microcontroller in the car. Software in the ECU monitors the sensor readings, uses the actuators to time the spark for each cylinder and adjust the engine operation, and to watch for problems. When problems occur, the ECU logs a failure snapshot and may turn on the Check Engine light (called the *Malfunction Indicator Light*, or MIL, in the OBD II standard).

Standard Connectors and Locations

Aside from requiring a minimum level of monitoring functionality to be in every car, OBD II benefits you by standardizing the mechanical, electrical, and messaging-level interface between the data capture and analysis function and the ECU. Car manufacturers are free to implement the OBD II specification any way they want, using sensors and actuators tailored for the engine and car, but they must implement the standardized interface. You plug a scan tool into the standard connector (see Figure 9-2), which by law has limits on where it can be placed.

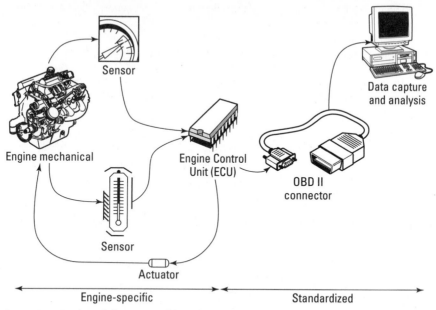

FIGURE 9-1: On-board diagnostics block diagram

FIGURE 9-2: A standard OBD II interface connector

The Society of Automotive Engineers (SAE) Recommended Practices J1962 concerning the connector location says, in part:

- *The vehicle connector shall be located in the passenger compartment in the area bounded by the driver's end of the instrument panel to 300mm beyond the vehicle centerline, attached to the instrument panel, and accessible from the driver's seat. The preferred location is between the steering column and the vehicle centerline. The vehicle connector shall be mounted to facilitate mating and unmating.*

- *Access to the vehicle connector shall not require a tool for the removal of an instrument panel cover, connector cover, or any barriers. The vehicle connector should be fastened and located as to permit a one-handed/blind insertion of the mating test equipment connector.*

- *The vehicle connector should be out of the occupant's (front and rear seat) normal line of sight but easily visible to a "crouched" technician.*

Figure 9-3 shows the suggested interpretation of this guidance, defining the allowed and pre-ferred areas for the connector.

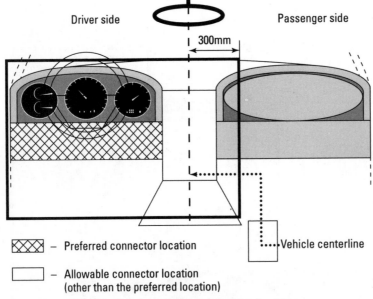

FIGURE 9-3: **Allowed and preferred OBD II connector locations**

You'd think directions this explicit would make the connectors straightforward to find, but if so you're apparently not qualified to work for car manufacturers. Connectors can be so hard to find that the state of Texas maintains a great reference document on a Web site (www. txdps.state.tx.us/vi/Misc/connectors.pdf), titled *Hard to Find OBD II*

Connectors. The document is organized by manufacturer and model, and in most cases includes annotated photographs showing the connector location. Figure 9-4 shows why our roadster was listed in the file — the connector is hidden behind the fuse box cover, and unless you remove that cover, you'll never find it.

CarChip installed in OBD II connector

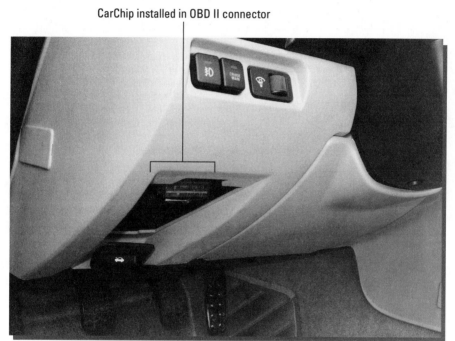

FIGURE 9-4: OBD II connector location behind fuse box cover

Standard Codes

OBD II standardizes the error codes reported by the ECU for much of what can go wrong in your engine. For example, the code P0505 will always mean *Idle Control System Malfunction.* Figure 9-5 shows the structure used to create codes, which consist of a letter and four numbers. Codes are defined both for common (generic) codes, which are defined by the SAE, and for vehicle-specific codes, which are defined by the *original equipment (car) manufacturer* (called the OEM in Figure 9-5).

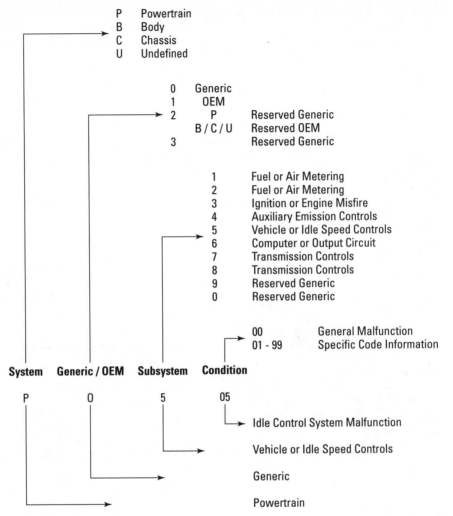

FIGURE 9-5: Standard OBD II code structure

The Colorado State University OBD II Research Center keeps a list of the generic codes at www.obdiicsu.com/Docs/DTC/DTCData.html. You can look up codes, including vehicle-specific ones, at either the Actron (www.actron.com/code_lookup/index.php) or Gendan (www.gendan.co.uk/diagnostic/dtcs.php) Web sites. On the Gendan site, for example, the OEM code P1101 results in *MAF Out Of Range (Mazda)* for the Miata, while it's not found on the Actron site. (MAF stands for *Manifold Absolute Pressure*.) There's also an index of generic and OEM OBD II trouble codes at autorepair.about.com/library/ts/obd-ii/bl-obd-main.htm.

Simple Automotive Diagnosis from Kits

The major difference between a thing that might go wrong and a thing that cannot possibly go wrong is that when a thing that cannot possibly go wrong goes wrong it usually turns out to be impossible to get at and repair.

~Douglas Adams

Information about the inner state of your engine and powertrain is useful, whether you're a total gearhead or a victim on four wheels. OBD II gave your car the ability to tell you a lot of useful information; what you need is a way to get at it. You have two choices—you can passively log the data as the car runs, then upload to your PC, or you can connect a PC to the car. The first approach is less immediate, but far more convenient if you want to record the data while you drive. The second approach would be good if you're actively tuning or servicing the car in a shop.

We chose to use a data logger, because it works both for diagnosing, if you are your own mechanic, and for giving data to your repair shop (or double-checking what they tell you). Figure 9-6 shows the system-level block diagram for this project; the key to the system is the Davis Instruments CarChip, which clips into your car's OBD II socket for days or even weeks until you're ready to download its contents, then transfers all the recorded data to your PC.

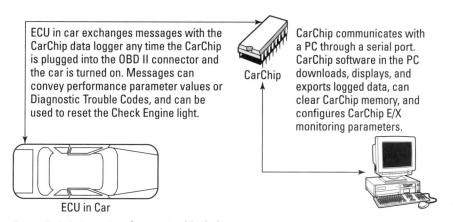

ECU in car exchanges messages with the CarChip data logger any time the CarChip is plugged into the OBD II connector and the car is turned on. Messages can convey performance parameter values or Diagnostic Trouble Codes, and can be used to reset the Check Engine light.

CarChip

CarChip communicates with a PC through a serial port. CarChip software in the PC downloads, displays, and exports logged data, can clear CarChip memory, and configures CarChip E/X monitoring parameters.

ECU in Car

FIGURE 9-6: Automotive diagnostics block diagram

Parts List

The PC requirements for using the CarChip are minimal—any PC capable of running Windows 95 or later and having both 5MB free disk space and a free serial port will do. Information on the CarChip is in Table 9-1.

Table 9-1 Automotive Diagnostics Parts List

Part	Manufacturer and Model Number
Data Logger	Davis Instruments CarChip ($139) `www.carchip.com/drive/products/drive_product.asp?pnum=8210`
	CarChip E/X ($179) `www.carchip.com/drive/products/drive_product.asp?pnum=8220`

The CarChip is available in two versions. The standard version logs the time, date, and distance for each trip, plus the vehicle speed every 5 seconds. If the ECU detects a malfunction, the CarChip notes the DTC and status of other engine parameters when the code occurred. The CarChip E/X does everything the standard version does, and also stores up to 300 hours of data for up to 4 engine parameters (from a selection of 23), recording values every 5–60 seconds.

Setting Up Your CarChip

Easy as they are, we don't recommend precisely following Davis' instructions for setting up your CarChip, because they omit some important configuration steps, including clearing the CarChip, setting the clock, and choosing the added CarChip E/X parameters you want to record.

To Set Up CarChip

1. Find an available serial port on your PC and plug in the CarChip data cable. Plug the auxiliary power supply into a wall socket and into the connector on the data cable.

2. Install the CarChip software.

3. Plug the CarChip into the data cable. The connector is a small slot on the side of the CarChip; the cable goes in with the release button facing away from the OBD II connector on the CarChip.

4. Start the CarChip software. It should recognize the CarChip's presence and give you a dialog box with which you can give a name to the CarChip.

5. Make sure your computer clock is set accurately, then use the CarChip, Set Clock and CarChip, Clear CarChip Memory commands to initialize the CarChip.

6. If you have a CarChip E/X, use the CarChip, Choose Other Parameters command to select the four parameters other than vehicle speed that you want to track, and set the sampling interval for all the parameters.

7. Disconnect the CarChip, find the OBD II connector in your car, and plug in the CarChip.

Figure 9-7 shows the CarChip installed in an OBD II socket. You simply push it in gently until it stops — no force is required.

FIGURE 9-7: Installed CarChip E/X

CarChip is a trademark of Davis Instruments Corp.

Solve That Missing Serial Port Problem

The PC industry is working hard to get rid of the serial and parallel ports we've used for years, replacing them with USB and other newer technologies, because the older ports are relatively hard to use. A lot of support calls result from problems with serial and parallel ports, so the industry expects to both save money and help users avoid problems by eliminating these ports.

The problem is, of course, that far too many devices currently use serial and parallel ports for this plan to work in the near future. Not only do external modems and many of the popular Palm and Blackberry handheld assistants use serial ports, so do telescopes, X10 interfaces, and the Winland and Dataharvest data loggers we use in several chapters. With most recent computers offering only one externally available serial port, you're going to run out of ports in a hurry.

Continued

Continued

You have two alternatives. One is to add a PCI card to your computer that provides more serial ports; a search on `www.shopper.com` for *pci serial port* results in several options, the lowest price of which was a $26, two-port card made by StarTech. Your second alternative is to use a USB–serial port adapter, such as the Belkin model F5U103, which we found for $42 and up. Both will work; you pay somewhat more for the USB version in exchange for the convenience of not having to open the computer and install a card.

Configuring Your CarChip E/X

You can configure the CarChip E/X to record four parameters besides vehicle speed. The parameters you can select from include:

- Air Flow Rate
- Battery Voltage
- Coolant Temperature
- Engine Load
- Engine Speed
- Fuel Pressure
- Fuel System Status
- Intake Air Temperature
- Intake Manifold Pressure
- Long Term Fuel Trim (B1–B2)
- O2 Sensor Voltage (B1–B2, S1–S4)
- Short Term Fuel Trim (B1–B2)
- Throttle Position
- Timing Advance

Vehicle speed is always selected. Not all cars implement all parameters, so you'll want to test yours before making trips. For instance, our roadster (with an inline four-cylinder engine) has only one bank of cylinders, so it reads out only short- and long-term fuel trim for B1, and O2 sensor voltage for B1/S1–S4. Our four-wheel drive vehicle has eight cylinders in a V8 configuration, so it implements both banks and all four sensors in each bank.

What parameters you record depends on what you're trying to do. If you're troubleshooting a problem cranking the engine in cold weather, you might want to record the battery voltage, fuel pressure, timing advance, and engine speed. If you're looking at low gas mileage, you might want the fuel trim values. If you're hoping to double-check a mechanic's recommendation to change an O2 sensor, you might look directly at the voltages on the sensor.

Be sure to download any values from the CarChip and clear its memory before you set a new parameter configuration.

Using the CarChip Software

Your typical cycle using CarChip goes like this:

CarChip Diagnostic Cycle

1. Clear the CarChip and (for the CarChip E/X) set the parameters you want to monitor and the sample intervals.
2. Install the CarChip in the car's OBD II connector.
3. Drive.
4. Park and remove the CarChip from the car.
5. Connect the CarChip to your PC and start the CarChip software.
6. Open the data file for the car you're working on (or make a new one), and download the data from the CarChip.
7. Save the data file, and after the save is complete, clear the CarChip memory.
8. Plot and analyze the data you collected.

Don't let the software automatically clear the CarChip memory when you download, and don't clear the memory until after you've saved the download into a CarChip file on your disk. If you clear the memory before you've saved the data and then have a computer problem (or a software crash), you've lost the data and will have to rerun the test.

Where and how long you drive depends on what you're doing; generally, you want the car to exhibit the behavior you're trying to troubleshoot. If you have a GPS receiver and mapping software on your laptop, it's useful to synchronize clocks for all the computers you're using, and for the CarChip, then record the path you drove. Later, when you're analyzing the data, you can correlate interesting parts of the CarChip data with road conditions using the time stamps.

Once you've collected the data, you need to analyze it, and you'll want to look at both absolute and relative values in that analysis. For example, large offsets in fuel trim probably indicate a problem, but so do offsets between banks that are significantly different. The tabular data displayed in the CarChip software (see Figure 9-8) is good for looking at absolute values, but tedious for making comparisons.

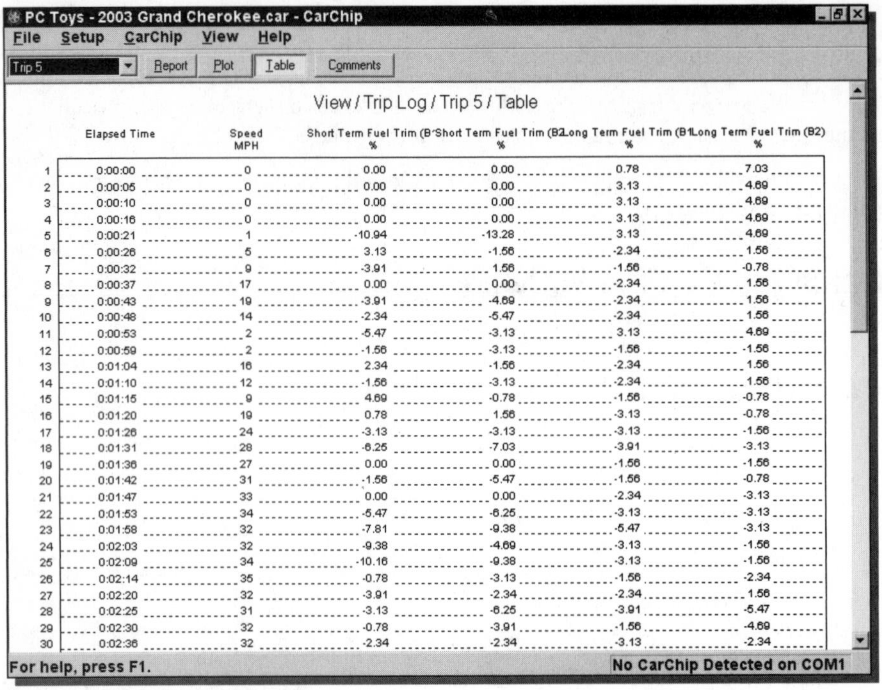

PC Toys - 2003 Grand Cherokee.car - CarChip

File   Setup   CarChip   View   Help

Trip 5 ▼   Report   Plot   Table   Comments

View / Trip Log / Trip 5 / Table

#	Elapsed Time	Speed MPH	Short Term Fuel Trim (B1) %	Short Term Fuel Trim (B2) %	Long Term Fuel Trim (B1) %	Long Term Fuel Trim (B2) %
1	0:00:00	0	0.00	0.00	0.78	7.03
2	0:00:05	0	0.00	0.00	3.13	-4.69
3	0:00:10	0	0.00	0.00	3.13	-4.69
4	0:00:16	0	0.00	0.00	3.13	-4.69
5	0:00:21	1	-10.94	-13.28	3.13	-4.69
6	0:00:26	5	3.13	-1.56	-2.34	1.56
7	0:00:32	9	-3.91	1.56	-1.56	-0.78
8	0:00:37	17	0.00	0.00	-2.34	1.56
9	0:00:43	19	-3.91	-4.69	-2.34	1.56
10	0:00:48	14	-2.34	-5.47	-2.34	1.56
11	0:00:53	2	-5.47	-3.13	3.13	-4.69
12	0:00:59	2	-1.56	-3.13	-1.56	-1.56
13	0:01:04	16	2.34	-1.56	-2.34	1.56
14	0:01:10	12	-1.56	-3.13	-2.34	1.56
15	0:01:15	9	4.69	-0.78	-1.56	-0.78
16	0:01:20	19	0.78	1.56	-3.13	-0.78
17	0:01:26	24	-3.13	-3.13	-3.13	-1.56
18	0:01:31	28	-6.25	-7.03	-3.91	-3.13
19	0:01:36	27	0.00	0.00	-1.56	-1.56
20	0:01:42	31	-1.56	-5.47	-1.56	-0.78
21	0:01:47	33	0.00	0.00	-2.34	-3.13
22	0:01:53	34	-5.47	-6.25	-3.13	-3.13
23	0:01:58	32	-7.81	-9.38	-5.47	-3.13
24	0:02:03	32	-9.38	-4.69	-3.13	-1.56
25	0:02:09	34	-10.16	-9.38	-3.13	-1.56
26	0:02:14	35	-0.78	-3.13	-1.56	-2.34
27	0:02:20	32	-3.91	-2.34	-2.34	1.56
28	0:02:25	31	-3.13	-6.25	-3.91	-5.47
29	0:02:30	32	-0.78	-3.91	-1.56	-4.69
30	0:02:36	32	-2.34	-2.34	-3.13	-2.34

For help, press F1.   No CarChip Detected on COM1

FIGURE 9-8: Tabular CarChip data

CarChip is a trademark of Davis Instruments Corp.

The plots available in the CarChip software (see Figure 9-9) don't really help for comparison analysis either, because you get only a plot of one parameter at a time.

A better solution is to export the data from CarChip to a spreadsheet such as Microsoft Excel. You can right-click on the CarChip data table and copy the data to the clipboard as text, then paste it into an empty spreadsheet. Create an XY plot using the elapsed time as the X axis and you get something like Figure 9-10. The plot lets you see that although there's some offset between the two banks, the short-term and long-term fuel trim for both banks follow each other closely and are within a few percent of each other.

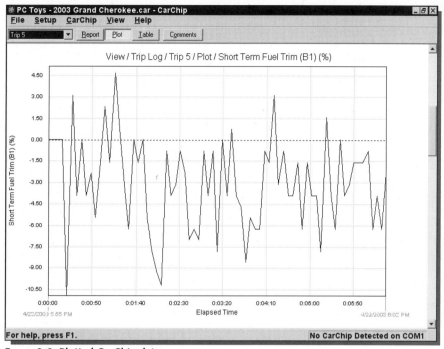

FIGURE 9-9: Plotted CarChip data

CarChip is a trademark of Davis Instruments Corp.

Plotting an analysis of overheating while driving up a canyon would be harder — you'd need to export the position/altitude data you collect with your GPS and laptop with time stamps, then correlate that data in Excel with coolant temperature data collected with the CarChip. Once you have your data correlated, you can plot the combined data to see whether elevation or steepness of ascent are related to engine temperature.

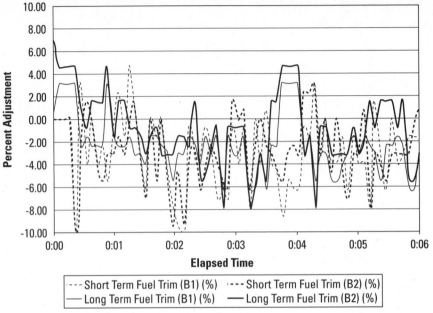

FIGURE 9-10: CarChip data plotted in Microsoft Excel

The Internet Is No Substitute for a Good Mechanic

We're unabashed fans of the Internet, because there's seemingly no limit to the information you can find there. One of the services the Internet brings you is Carfax, at www.carfax.com, where (among other things) you can check a vehicle's history and specifically whether accidents have been reported by the DMV, police, or other sources. The site is a great idea, but like all other information sources, what's reported is dependent on fallible sources not under the control of Carfax.

For example, the Carfax accident record was completely clean for a car we submitted for a report, including a clean police accident record. Carfax can't report what they don't know, however, and contrary to the clean status of the Carfax report, about $20,000 spent at the local collision center suggests otherwise. Both police reports and insurance claims were filed, but no one has an obligation to file with Carfax, leading to situations like this one.

You won't find out whether a car has been wrecked through its OBD II system either, but if the onboard computer thinks the car has residual engine damage, you and your mechanic (you do have used cars inspected before you buy them, don't you?) will know.

Trouble

When the ECU detects a problem in the engine or powertrain, it logs a DTC. There are two categories of DTC, Type A and Type B. Both are emissions-related, but Type A is more severe. The ECU turns on the Check Engine light after a single failed driving cycle, and stores a freeze-frame record of data concerning the failure.

You can perform a complete driving cycle in under 15 minutes by following these steps:

Perform an OBD II Driving Cycle

1. **Cold Start.** The engine coolant must be colder than 50 degrees C (122 degrees F) and within 6 degrees C (11degrees F) of the ambient air temperature when you start the engine. If you must wait for the engine to cool, make sure the ignition switch is off.

2. **Idle.** Run the engine for two and a half minutes. You should have the air conditioner and rear defroster on; the more electrical load the better.

3. **Accelerate.** Turn off the air conditioner and all the other loads, then accelerate at half throttle until you reach 55 mph (preferably on a freeway).

4. **Hold Speed.** Keep your speed steady at 55 mph for three minutes.

5. **Decelerate.** Let off the accelerator pedal and coast until you slow to 20 mph. Don't shift, brake, or depress the clutch.

6. **Accelerate.** Accelerate again, this time at three-quarters throttle until you're going 55–60 mph.

7. **Hold Speed.** Keep your speed steady at 55 mph again, this time for five minutes.

8. **Decelerate.** Coast to a stop.

The ECU only logs a Type B failure after two consecutive failed driving cycles, storing the freeze-frame data after the second cycle. Figure 9-11 shows a typical freeze-frame report from the CarChip software. The report gives you the fuel-trim and fuel-system status whether you're monitoring those parameters or not.

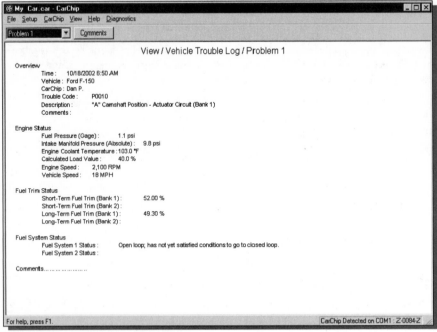

FIGURE 9-11: CarChip freeze-frame report

CarChip is a trademark of Davis Instruments Corp.

Intimate Conversations with Your Car

OBD II and your CarChip can tell you a lot about your car, but they're not diagnostics you can apply indiscriminately. Problems can have subtle causes and may be discussed in the vehicle service manual, where you're likely to find both possible causes and tests you can perform to isolate the trouble. For example, suppose the manifold pressure sensor reports a bad value. The problem could be a leak in the manifold, the sensor, or the wiring to the sensor. Similar problems apply to the other sensors, and can propagate to other systems and sensors. For example, suppose the manifold air flow sensor is fouled and giving incorrect readings. Those bad readings will cause the fuel trim to be wrong, and if sufficiently off, could lead to the O2 sensors reporting a fuel mixture failure. Only deeper investigation and backup testing will let you know for sure.

OBD II is a solid, reliable source of information, but you shouldn't trust it blindly—sometimes it's right, and sometimes it gets fooled. The following three case studies illustrate the point.

- In the case study at www.obdiicsu.com/Studies/2002CaseStudies/ O2Codes/O2Codes.html, technicians encountered differing results from the OBD II codes and a direct O2 sensor test. Believing the direct test, they returned the car to the field. In retrospect, after much more experience with OBD II systems, they concluded the sensor probably was bad, but was not detected as faulty in the short-duration bench test they performed.

- The case study at www.asashop.org/autoinc/july2002/techtotech.cfm also reports a trouble code for an O2 sensor, but goes through the analysis the technician did to discover both a weak fuel pump and a hole in an intake housing.

- Finally, www.asashop.org/autoinc/aug2002/techtotech.cfm provides reports on three different vehicles. One had a bad O2 sensor, one had a failed thermostat causing the engine to run too cold, while the third seemed as though it had a bad manifold air flow sensor, but actually had a failed ECU.

Summary

Onboard computers have evolved from obscure, irritating, power-sucking boxes corrupting the pure operation of your car, into reliable components that not only improve performance but also give you good insight into the operation and problems in your engine and powertrain. A simple data-logging attachment brings the data from your car to your PC, where you can see everything your car has to say.

Build Your Own In-Car Navigation System

In the mountains the shortest route is from peak to peak, but for that you must have long legs.

~Friedrich Nietzsche, *Thus Spake Zarathustra*

Ah, the joys of business travel.

Your partner was assigned a new, plum client to visit and handed a ticket to Tuscon, Arizona. The client, according to the boss, is just outside of town, in Sierra Vista. Your partner never returned and was never found. The client still wants to see someone, though, so the boss hands you a duplicate set of tickets and wants you on the plane this afternoon. You trundle off.

Asking for Directions May Not Be a Guy Thing, but Electronics Are

Not, however, directly to the airport — you stop at your desk, fire up DeLorme's Street Atlas USA 2003, and plot a route from the Tucson airport to Sierra Vista. Looking at the result (see Figure 10-1), you conclude your boss is either homicidal or a moron, because Sierra Vista is slightly more remote than the middle of nowhere.

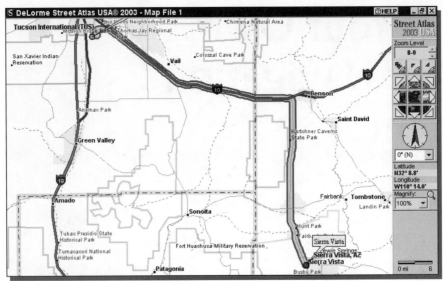

FIGURE 10-1: The business trip from hell

How GPS Works

Getting to where you're going in unfamiliar territory can be challenging even with a map, and is harder still in the dark. Knowing where you are is the first requirement for navigation, and since the early 1990s the best way to know where you are is by using the Global Positioning System (GPS) constellation of satellites, a collection of at least 24 satellites orbiting 26,560 km above the Earth. Ignoring blockage from mountains, buildings, and such, three satellites are guaranteed to be visible from most places on Earth, enough to closely approximate your latitude and longitude. Four or more satellites are usually visible, enough to determine your position in three dimensions using the approach shown in two dimensions in Figure 10-2.

Your GPS receiver computes the distance from you to each of the visible satellites by measuring the time it takes for a radio signal to travel from each of the satellites to you. It combines that interval, the speed of light, and an accurate knowledge of the satellite's position to compute the distance from you to the satellite. The distance from you to each satellite defines a circle on which you must be in Figure 10-2. (You're on the surface of a sphere in real life.) Your position is on each of those circles simultaneously, at the common intersection of all the circles (spheres).

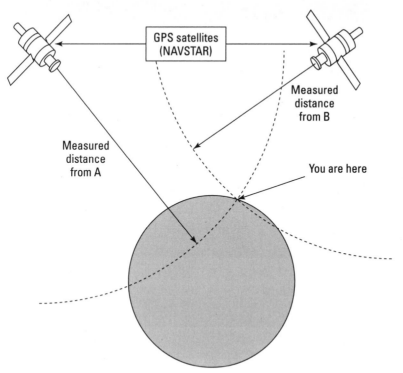

FIGURE 10-2: GPS geolocation using combined distance measurements
From PC Upgrade and Repair Bible, Third Edition, by Barry Press and Marcia Press. Copyright © 1999 by Wiley Publishing, Inc. All rights reserved. Reproduced here by permission of the publisher.

Simple and precise as those computations may sound, GPS is not perfectly accurate. Even though the US Department of Defense stopped deliberately introducing controlled position errors — what's called Selective Availability, or SA — into the signal in the year 2000, circumstances can still significantly degrade the system's ability to pinpoint your location. For example, consider the views from far over your head in Figures 10-3 and 10-4. The satellites are optimally positioned in Figure 10-3, so the point at which the distance arcs intersect is accurately defined. Using standard civilian GPS equipment (that is, the Standard Positioning Service, SPS, without differential GPS or other accuracy-increasing augmentations), optimally aligned satellites can give you accuracy on the order of 10 to 15 meters.

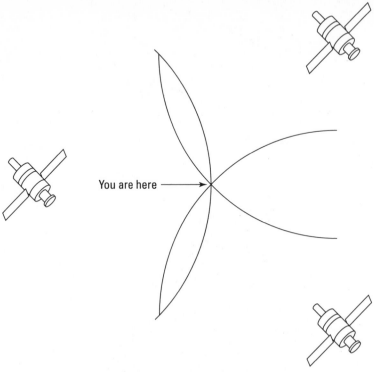

You are here

FIGURE 10-3: Optimum satellite positioning

The satellites are poorly aligned in Figure 10-4, because the two satellites on the right are too close together. As a result, your vertical position in the figure is not as well defined, leading to increased position error in the estimate your receiver gives you.

Many GPS receivers report a set of values collectively addressing a *Dilution of Precision* (DOP) measure, which indicates the degree to which satellite position and other factors are introducing errors into the system's estimate of your position. The higher the DOP, the more error is present — DOP is a multiplier on the errors, so if the DOP value is 2, the error is twice the inherent error in the raw inputs.

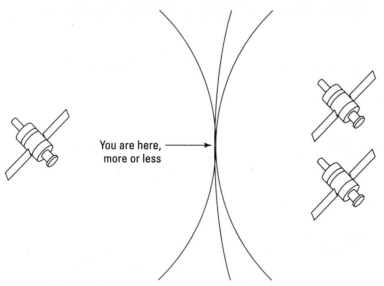

You are here,
more or less

FIGURE 10-4: Degraded satellite positioning

DOP has several components. The most significant component for automobile navigation is the *Horizontal Dilution of Precision* (HDOP), which directly characterizes the error in the latitude and longitude estimates. HDOP varies as satellites move, drops as your receiver acquires data from more satellites (because the added satellites improve the relative geometry of the visible constellation), and increases as satellites go out of view and the number of satellites decreases. We've seen HDOP values as low as 0.8 (more later on how that happened), around 6 without augmentation systems running, and as high as 22 when few satellites were visible. There's more discussion of DOP at `gpsinformation.net/main/dopnontech.htm`, and a more mathematically intensive discussion at `users.erols.com/dlwilson/gps.htm`. (The home page at `gpsinformation.net` contains many, many useful links and is worth a visit.)

One of the ways you can improve the GPS estimate of your position is to average position measurements reported over a long interval. The VisualGPS program (`www.visualgps.net/VisualGPS`) reads data from your GPS receiver, decodes it, and plots the result (see Figure 10-5). You'll have to install the optional serial drivers supplied with the USB GPS receiver we've recommended to use VisualGPS.

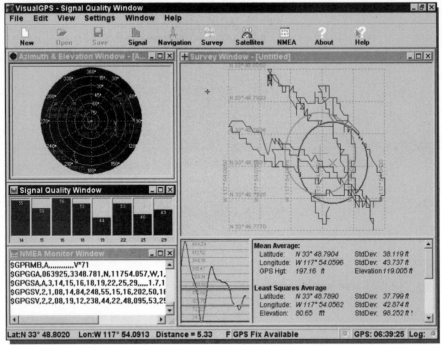

FIGURE 10-5: VisualGPS display

The upper-left pane in Figure 10-5 shows a plot of which satellites are visible from your position (the center of the plot), much as the sky maps do in Chapter 4. The trails extending away from the satellites indicate their path across the sky, helping you see which ones will soon be out of view.

The larger pane on the right plots the positions reported by the GPS receiver, along with a pair of estimates of the ellipse bounding the space containing your actual position. A related plot of your elevation is in the bottom-left corner of the pane, with corresponding upper and lower elevation bounds.

The middle pane on the left shows the relative signal strength from the satellites, with eight signals visible in the figure.

The Standard GPS Receiver Interface

The lower-left pane in Figure 10-5 shows the raw data from the receiver. Most GPS receivers, and nearly all GPS-related software for the PC, support the NMEA 0183 interface standard defined by the National Marine Electronics Association (NMEA). NMEA 0183-compliant *talkers*, such as a GPS receiver that sends data to your laptop, format their data into lines, or *sentences*. The lines shown in the NMEA Monitor Window pane in Figure 10-5 are each a sentence conveying a unit of information, such as the current time, position, and other data. In those lines, the $ character is required at the start of every line, while the GP characters in the next two positions indicate the information comes from a GPS receiver. The following three characters define the format for the rest of the sentence. Some of the standard GPS sentences include:

- GGA — Global Positioning System Fix Data

- GLL — Geographic position, latitude and longitude

- GSA — GPS DOP and active satellites

- GSV — Satellites in view

- RMB — Recommended minimum navigation information

- RMC — Recommended minimum specific GPS/Transit data

- ZTG — Universal Time Coordinated, and time to destination waypoint

A list of GPS sentences and which receivers output what sentences is at www.gps information.org/dale/nmea.htm.

NMEA 0183 receivers may also transmit manufacturer-proprietary sentences, all of which have P as the first character after the $ character, followed by a three-character manufacturer ID. You can find a list of manufacturer ID codes at pcptpp030.psychologie. uni-regensburg.de/trafficresearch/NMEA0183/manufact.txt.

Reducing the Position Error

Minimizing the error in the GPS estimate of your position is important for automobile navigation — for example, it matters a lot whether you're on an interstate highway or the frontage road paralleling it, but the difference could be only a few tens of meters. Uncorrected standard GPS signals can contain errors that mask the difference, making timely navigation difficult.

Correcting the limits on GPS accuracy has historically been important for low-visibility maritime approaches to harbors, especially when the selective availability errors were still being introduced, and led to the creation of *Differential GPS* (DGPS). Mobile receivers could be corrected by DGPS using a signal from an accurately surveyed receiver close to the mobile one. The DGPS receiver would determine and broadcast the correction necessary to adjust the current GPS signal to the known accurate location. Mobile receivers reasonably close to the DGPS receiver (so that the same corrections applied) would decode the correction signal and apply the same corrections, leading to accuracies measured in centimeters.

Unfortunately, DGPS worked only if you were close enough to the DGPS receiver, which themselves were located primarily along coastlines. The US Federal Aviation Administration is interested in a GPS system useful for aircraft navigation, however, and is deploying the *Wide Area Augmentation System* (WAAS) to use a similar approach of having mobile receivers apply corrections based on an auxiliary signal. The key differences between DGPS and WAAS are that WAAS applies across all of North America (there are no ground reference stations in

South America to derive the necessary corrections), and is based on a distinct signal received from two Inmarsat geosynchronous satellites. WAAS lets receivers correct for GPS satellite orbit and clock drift and for signal delays caused by the atmosphere and ionosphere. The combination of GPS and WAAS gives very good accuracy — the DeLorme Earthmate USB GPS receiver we've used in this project is capable of ±3 meter estimates with WAAS available. The times we've seen HDOP as low as 0.8 were when we had at least six satellites visible, plus the WAAS signal.

The specific Inmarsat satellites used for WAAS are the AOR-W and POR birds, shown in the coverage maps at `217.204.152.210/support_maps.cfm`. You must have a clear line of sight to the satellite to receive the WAAS signal, making its use difficult in deep natural or urban canyons. The satellites aren't very far above the horizon for users in North America (you can follow the line from any local satellite TV dish to approximate the elevation angle). The AOR-W satellite is above Brazil, east of Florida, while the POR satellite is slightly west of Hawaii.

Just a Simple Matter of Software, Now That the Satellites Are Up

Being able to know where you are anywhere on Earth opened up seemingly limitless possibilities, including simple compasses that monitor the direction and speed in which you're traveling, navigators that give you bearing and range along a preset series of waypoints, and trackers that show your position on a moving map. As the necessary electronics became smaller, all these functions migrated into handheld, battery-powered units.

You can use a navigator to drive from one place to another, but you have to figure out the route — the navigator gives you only the general direction in which you have to go. Moving maps help you navigate by plotting the GPS position estimates on a map, and by keeping your current position centered on the display. Figure 10-6 shows a moving map in operation, and shows one of the problems you'll have to live with — the maps aren't perfect, and those problems combined with GPS position errors can leave you thinking that you're driving through someone's back yard.

The reality is that not only does your reported GPS position contain errors, the maps do too. New streets may be missing, and any street may be in the wrong place. Roads can be renamed and renumbered, and the data in the maps you get may not be the latest. Of course, all this is true — even more so — of paper maps, but you don't get the GPS trace on a paper map to highlight its failings. Remember that even the US Geological Survey 1:24,000 series has a positional accuracy tolerance of only ±8 meters.

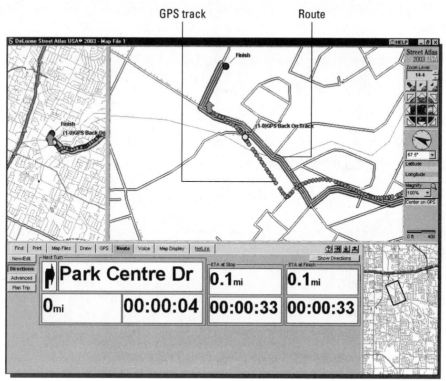

FIGURE 10-6: Divergence between GPS track and map

Making Maps More Accurate

The data on the maps you display on a PC need not come from precise, highly accurate sources. People have been making digital maps for far longer than GPS has been around, using aerial photos and surveyed markers to plot street and boundary locations. Errors in registering those photos and surveys to each other and to the correct coordinates lead to errors in maps derived from the data.

People used the standard precision data with selective availability-induced errors ever since the advent of GPS, and although a variety of approaches worked to minimize the added error, it wasn't possible to take all the error out. Don't be fooled by software that fakes the trace of where you've been, snapping it to the road the program thinks you're on. Every map has errors, and every GPS has errors. If your moving map is always on the road, it's lying.

Continued

Continued

However, having to tolerate sometimes significant mapping errors is about to change. The increased navigational accuracy possible today using GPS and WAAS, and the increased resolution available from aerial and spaceborne cameras, mean that photoimagery can now be used to correct mapping errors. DeLorme's effort to collect the necessary imagery and update its maps is described on the TopoBird Web site, `www.topobird.com`.

Routing and Directions

A computer has the capacity to find routes, but to do that it needs sophisticated maps that define not only the highways and roads, but also road classifications (so that the computer knows possible travel speeds), one-way streets, road names and numbers, ramps onto and off of limited access highways, and more. The combination of highly accurate GPS location data with computer-generated routes, in turn, lets the computer look forward from where you are to know what you should do next.

You can see in Figures 10-1 and 10-6, however, that the maps are too detailed and the controls too complex to use while you're actively driving. You'd need a navigator to use them for you. Text to speech technology, available in the Microsoft Text to Speech Software Development Kit (`www.microsoft.com/downloads/details.aspx?FamilyId=5E86EC97-40A7-453F-B0EE-6583171B4530&displaylang=en`), gives software developers the ability to give you information verbally; a corresponding speech recognition technology lets programs recognize commands you give verbally. Together, sophisticated maps, GPS, routing, computer directions, and speech technologies — all neatly packaged with your laptop computer — give you an automated navigator to assist with your trips to unfamiliar areas.

Building and Using Your Navigator from Kits

The only specialized hardware you'll need for your navigator is the GPS receiver — your laptop (which should have speakers, a microphone, and a USB port) does the rest.

Parts List

The most important characteristic the Windows laptop PC you'll use for your navigator needs is a big, bright display so that you can easily read it outside. Even a processor slower than 300 MHz running Windows will do — here's DeLorme's minimum requirements for Street Atlas USA 2003:

- Intel Pentium II (or equivalent), 233 MHz or higher processor (300 MHz recommended)
- 64MB RAM (128MB recommended)
- 405MB of available hard-disk space (580MB recommended for voice)

- Super VGA card running under Windows

- CD-ROM drive

- Sound card, microphone, and speakers (for voice capabilities)

The GPS receiver can be the DeLorme Earthmate we used, a DeLorme GpsTripmate, or any fully compatible NMEA receiver from GARMIN, Magellan, Brunton, Rockwell/Conexant, Lowrance/Eagle, or Trimble.

The list of the parts we used is shown in Table 10-1.

Table 10-1   Navigator Parts List

Part	Manufacturer and Model Number
GPS Receiver	DeLorme Earthmate ($129.95) www.delorme.com/earthmate
Mapping and Routing Software	DeLorme Street Atlas USA 2003 (included with GPS receiver) www.delorme.com/streetatlas2003
Power Converter	Xantrex Portawattz 300 ($49) www.xantrex.com/products/product.asp?did=146

We specified a power converter to transform the 12 VDC in your car to the 120 VAC (or 240 VAC) your laptop requires. You plug your usual laptop power brick into the converter. We've also used mobile laptop power adapters that plug directly into the 12 VDC source (ours is from Xtend Micro, now part of iGo, igo.ententeweb.com), but they're significantly more expensive than a DC-to-AC converter. A converter is a good idea if your drive time will come anywhere close to the battery lifetime. Don't forget that the GPS receiver may draw power from the laptop, shortening battery life, and that if you have to increase the brightness on the display you'll reduce battery life drastically.

Software for operation in Europe is available; search Google for *gps map windows Europe.*

Here's a list of features we've found useful in GPS and software packages, although we've not found all these features in any one package:

- Voice command and response

- Clear map visuals

- Notification of the route to follow when the road is just bearing left or right at a fork, not making a full turn

- Automatic and manual route replanning

- Accuracy of plotted position versus car position

- Driving cues in advance, such as notification that you have to make a turn in a few minutes or a few tenths of a mile

- Address and place lookup with a robust directory of cities, streets, places, and landmarks

- Knowledge of one-way streets

- Moving and rotating map position so the car location remains centered and forward is up on the map

- Automatic zoom, with a broader scale view available

- Good position update rate — at least once per second

Driving with Your Navigator

Figure 10-7 is the essence of why a navigator is valuable — you're in unfamiliar territory, possibly having lost your sense of direction, and have to choose which way to turn. Your navigator knows where you are, where you're going, and which way your route turns. Because it requires little more than your laptop, it's easy to carry with you.

FIGURE 10-7: Where you want a navigator

To set up your navigator, first install the GPS receiver in your car. You want to make sure that you put it in a place where it has an unobstructed view of the sky, ideally one with an unobstructed view of the geosynchronous satellite over the equator transmitting the WAAS signal. Figure 10-8 shows the receiver installed in our roadster.

FIGURE 10-8: Earthmate GPS installed on dashboard

The receiver rests on the dashboard at the junction between it and the windshield. A suction cup on the USB cable between the receiver and the laptop anchors the cable to the windshield, keeping the receiver from sliding off the dashboard.

We thought about suspending the receiver under the car's convertible top, but decided not to bother because we got good GPS and WAAS coverage for all vehicle headings except due north, when the WAAS signal tended to disappear. If the convertible top's material had any conductive component, that placement wouldn't have worked well. Similarly, if your windshield has a metallic screen, you may find GPS reception is poor through the windshield. You can find a list of vehicles with metallized windshields at www.e-zpassny.com/static/info/exteriortags.html.

Most laptops include hardware and software for power management, which reduce the system's power consumption to extend battery life. Turning off the LCD display is one of the first things you can expect power management to do, because (under battery management test software) the display is between 30 and 40 percent of the total system power drain. Your system will continue to monitor the GPS and announce turns with the display turned off, but if it spins down the disk or puts the laptop into suspended mode, everything stops. We countered that behavior by turning on what our laptop calls *presentation mode*, meaning all power management is temporarily turned off. Battery life suffers because of that, which is why we recommend an automotive power converter for anything but short trips.

Once you get rolling, the rotating map view centered on the GPS location ensures the map display matches what you'll see out the windshield. Figures 10-9 and 10-10 show the correspondence. We took the photograph and map display screen shot during a road trip in western Utah. You can see our position as the arrow in the bottom center of the map in Figure 10-10, showing the road extending roughly straight until it reaches the hills visible in the photograph in Figure 10-9, at which time it bends left to a pass through the hills.

FIGURE 10-9: The view out the windshield

Figure 10-10 also shows the alternate map views Street Atlas USA 2003 provides. The view on the left is particularly useful, giving a wider area view of your route and position.

Don't be surprised or confused when the directions the computer gives you seem inappropriate. We've had the navigator tell us to turn onto a street when we had no choice but to follow a bend in the road, making the directed turn pointless. The navigator gives these false directions in response to street name changes or other information in the underlying map database.

The navigator attempts to tell you how to fix the problem when you make a wrong turn, too. The left map pane in Figure 10-11 shows a missed turn; the navigator still highlights the original route it plotted (the top horizontal route), the new route it's suggesting (the bottom V-shaped route), and the path we took (between the two routes). The navigator continued to give us suggested turns until we rejoined the planned route, even though we weren't where it recommended. There's also a *back on track* function in the software that lets you command the computer to plot a new route based on your current location.

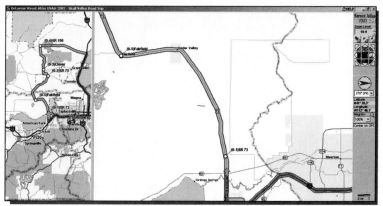

FIGURE 10-10: Map view screen shot corresponding to Figure 10-9

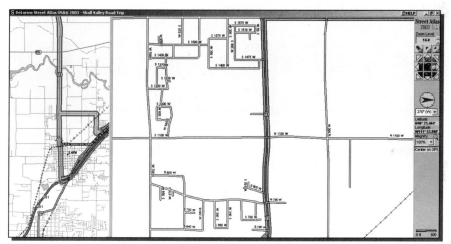

FIGURE 10-11: Routing after a missed turn

You'll discover that traveling with the navigator has advantages, but you need to check its routes. For example, Figure 10-12 shows a part of our road trip where the navigator diverted us off the numbered highways on to a road called Lincoln Highway. That road was difficult to spot flying by at highway speeds — we'd have missed it without the GPS and map and continued to the vertex at the left edge of the larger map — and Lincoln Highway when we reached it didn't have the look of a road that went anywhere useful (Figure 10-13). In practice, however, the road never got any worse than what you see in Figure 10-13, and the computer's recommendation shaved several miles off the route.

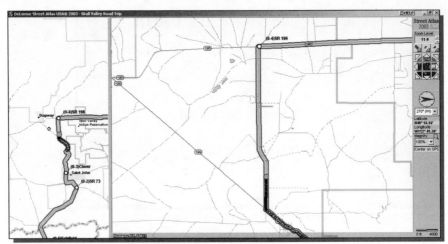

FIGURE 10-12: Lincoln Highway on the map route

FIGURE 10-13: Lincoln Highway in reality

Driving with the GPS and navigator can lead you into trouble if you're not careful when you plan your trip. Enough cell phones, computers, and satellite visibility to kill a horse won't help if your cell phone has no signal when you have a breakdown — you could be stuck until some-one shows up.

Building Your Navigator to Your Own Design

Running Street Atlas USA 2003 with your GPS on your laptop is just the beginning of what you can do. For example:

- If you build a Windows processor board and LCD display into your car, you could include both an MP3 library and player (Chapter 2), and a GPS navigator. You'll need to "ruggedize" the installation somewhat so that it can handle heat dissipation, shock, and vibration, and clean up noisy power. Sourceforge has lots of software you can use (www.sourceforge.net) that works with an NMEA 0183 compatible GPS, or you can use the commercial products in this chapter. You can also find a lot of useful information on GPS and NMEA 0183 atvancouver-webpages.com/peter.

- Different grades and elevations present varying loads on your car's engine. If you find the engine is misbehaving on specific road segments, you can correlate CarChip data (Chapter 9) by time with a map trace recorded from the GPS data.

- People are building "hot spots," sites that make wireless IEEE 802.11b Internet connections available in restaurants, airports, and many other popular locations. Hot spots aren't always well marked, but you can identify them and record their location using the Netstumbler program (www.netstumbler.com).

Summary

The integration of GPS position identification anywhere on the Earth, digital map data, and route computations on a laptop computer creates a navigator able to give you route directions from wherever you are to your destination. We've loaded the entire Street Atlas USA 2003 database into our laptop and made the Earthmate GPS a permanent addition to our laptop carrying case.

On the road again . . .

Build a Weather Station

Climate Control: or How to Predict the Weather Using a Pig Spleen

~Ken Gregory, at www.cheapmeat.net/ClimateControl.html

We spent more time searching the Web for this chapter than for any other project in the book. During our research, we came upon the Web page with the title above at www.cheapmeat.net/ClimateControl.html, and aside from being funny, it's not a bad highlight for what we found. The project in this chapter not only collects data from a weather station you'll build, it gives you tools to use that data in making your own weather forecast. Most of what you'll find searching the Web, though, is either (a) tools to gather weather forecasts from established Web sites, (b) tools to gather data from your own weather station and do nothing else but prepare graphs, or (c) oddball rules of thumb for how to predict the weather. Pig spleens, indeed.

The Accurate Weather Report Is Outside Your Window

We used to live in Los Angeles, where being next to the Pacific Ocean made weather forecasters uncannily accurate. Their forecasts almost never varied from day to day, however, so their record had little to do with mad weather skills. Where we live now, though, actually has seasons: rain, snow, wind, and tornados. Weather forecasters earn their keep, even though they're usually wrong. It's seemingly the only profession in which you can be wrong all the time and still collect a regular paycheck.

In all fairness, forecasting the weather is hard and gets phenomenally harder as you project further into the future. A good discussion of forecasting and chaos theory can be found at `www.met.rdg.ac.uk/~ross/Documents/SchoolTalkA.html`. The article there classifies forecasts based on how far ahead they look, naming these categories and stating that they become less certain as you go to longer forecast intervals:

- **Now-cast** — up to six hours in the future
- **Short-term forecast** — up to three days in the future
- **Medium-term forecast** — up to ten days in the future
- **Seasonal forecast** — up to three months in the future

If you happen to have a recent-vintage supercomputer lying around unused, and perhaps several advanced degrees in weather forecasting, you're all set to start your own long-range weather forecast service (or have already). The rest of us can access the same results using any of the services on the Internet including

```
www.weather.com

www.intellicast.com

nws.noaa.gov

www.wunderground.com

wwwa.accuweather.com

www.earthwatch.com
```

International forecasts are available through `www.ask.com` by searching on *International Weather Forecast*. The problem with all these services, both U.S. and international, is that by necessity they cover relatively large areas (such as single ZIP codes or larger) and thus may not accurately forecast for your location.

Instant Data, Served Anywhere

Figure 11-1 and Table 11-1 together illustrate that Internet forecasts and local weather for the same place can differ. The figure shows a sample of current data from `www.weather.com` for our location as retrieved by Weather Watcher (`download.com.com/3000-2381-10049378.html`). Table 11-1 shows the actual data as recorded with a weather station built according to this chapter.

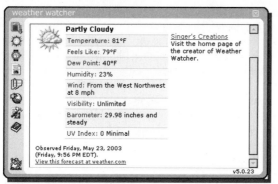

FIGURE 11-1: Weather Watcher current conditions display

Table 11-1   Actual Weather Data Corresponding to Figure 11-1

Temperature (°F)	Relative Humidity	Barometric Pressure (in Hg)
72.5	24.1	30.03

The relative humidity and barometric pressure were close, but the temperature was not. Given that you can't get really accurate current conditions, it's not very likely you'll get an accurate forecast from the Internet either. That degree of inaccuracy might not matter if all you're doing is lying in the sun on a summer day, but if you're worried whether or not you can safely plant seedlings after the last spring frost, it matters a lot. The problem isn't incompetence on the part of the weather data providers; it's that weather patterns form very complex systems in which small factors can produce significant variations. For example:

- In Napa Valley, different vineyards — on different sides of the valley, or even down the road from one another — are subject to different temperatures, rainfall, and sunlight. The result is that grapes of the same varietal from one vineyard make wine significantly different from another vineyard in the same valley.

- From *Palms Won't Grow Here and Other Myths*, by David A. Francko (Timber Press, 2003), "The National Weather Service (NWS) has been collecting official climatic data for Cincinnati since the 1860s. For most of this period, the official weather station was in the city proper, at Lunken Airfield, in a low-lying area near the Ohio River that has become strongly influenced by urbanization. In the 1970s the official reporting station was relocated to the new Greater Cincinnati-Northern Kentucky International Airport, located across the Ohio River in a rural area of northern Kentucky perhaps 10 mi (16 km) west of Lunken Airfield. Not only is Hebron, Kentucky, away from the heat island of downtown Cincinnati (although an airport itself is a heat island), the airport is sited on an exposed plateau rather than a sheltered lowland. It should not be surprising, then, that numerous temperature records have been set for Cincinnati recently."

■ The Cloudforest Web site (www.cloudforest.com/weather/weather_res. html) offers guidelines on microclimates, but itself notes that "... the temperature in your yard might still be quite different from what the official weather station down the street might be reading. We took a look at the December 1998 readings for all the stations around Santa Cruz, and the results varied significantly from location to location."

In the face of such local variability, your only resort for an accurate near-term forecast is likely to be one you do yourself. In this chapter, you'll see how to gather the data you need and develop a forecast for your site.

Building and Using Your Weather Station from Kits

Figure 11-2 shows a block diagram of the weather station project. You'll use weather simulation software to generate your forecast, combining more general data from Internet sites with local data you collect. Those combined data sets give the simulation software insight more relevant to your location than is available to the less specialized forecasts and give you better short-term forecast capability.

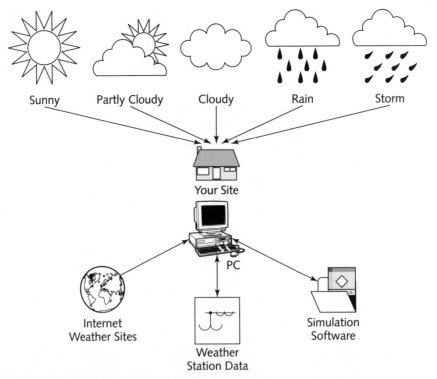

FIGURE 11-2: Weather station project block diagram

Parts List

Although long-term weather forecasts rely on massive, expensive supercomputers, the much shorter time frames and smaller region you'll analyze with simulation software in this project place far lesser demands on your PC, so much so that the requirements for the PC you'll use for your weather station really are minimal. Once again, even a processor slower than 300 MHz running Windows will do. The rest of the parts we used are shown in Table 11-2.

Table 11-2   Weather Station Parts List

Part	Manufacturer and Model Number
Data Logger	Data Harvest EasySense Advanced ($349) www.dataharvest.com/Products/easysense/logger_features.htm
Temperature Sensor	Data Harvest 3100 ($39) www.dataharvest.com/Products/easysense/sensors/general_temperature.htm
Barometric Pressure Sensor	Data Harvest 3140 ($69) www.dataharvest.com/Products/easysense/sensors/barometric.htm
Relative Humidity Sensor	Data Harvest 3145 ($74) www.dataharvest.com/Products/easysense/sensors/humidity.htm
Weather Simulation Software	WXSIM by Thomas J. Ehrensperger ($59.95) members.aol.com/eburger/WXSIM.html Download and order at www.weathergraphics.com/WXSIM/index.htm

The first step is to set up your weather station and begin collecting data. You can get complete weather stations with PC interfaces (the one available from Day Weather at www.dayweather.com/Shopping%20Cart/ws2010PC.htm is representative); we chose to use (with different sensors) the same data logger hardware we used in Chapters 5 and 8 to reduce the cost of the collection of projects. Figure 11-3 shows the data logger. Sensor probes connect to the front; the PC and power cables connect to the rear. Internal rechargeable batteries support operation for hours while disconnected from a power source. The meter button provides quick access to real-time readings, displayed on the LCD panel in the upper-left corner, while the other buttons operate the menu system to access more complicated functions.

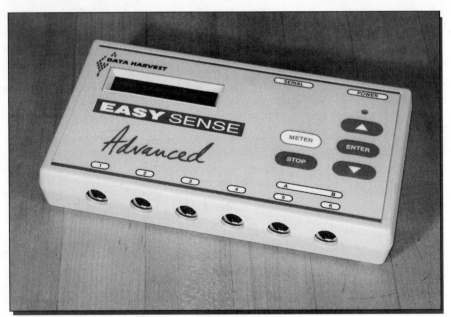

FIGURE 11-3: Data Harvest Easy Sense Advanced data logger

We chose to use the data logger remotely, collecting data independently of the PC, but if you have the ability to connect a serial cable from your PC to the data logger you can collect in real time, too. Because the data logger can capture data for well over a month without attention, and because a relatively slow sample rate is usable for this project, there's no liability to using it remotely. You'll want to make sure the logger itself is protected from water, wind, dust, salt, fog, and curious animals, although the sensors must remain exposed. Figures 11-4 through 11-6, respectively, show the temperature, relative humidity, and barometric pressure sensors.

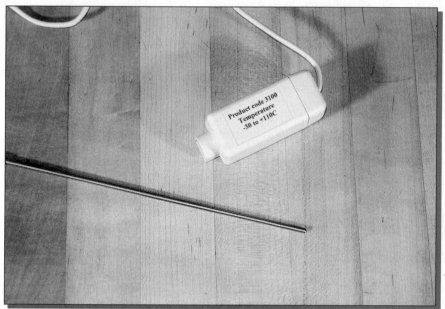

FIGURE **11-4**: Temperature sensor

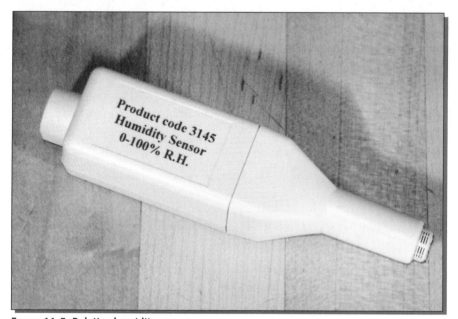

FIGURE **11-5**: Relative humidity sensor

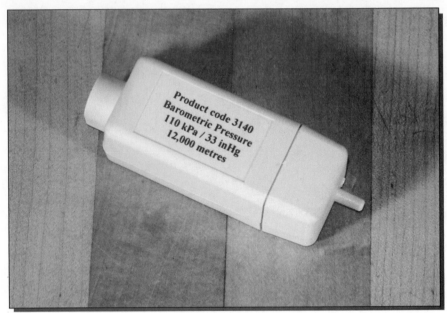

FIGURE 11-6: Barometric pressure sensor

Don't forget to calibrate your sensors. Our barometric pressure sensor, for example, recorded 84.8 kPa (kilopascals) out of the box at a time when the actual pressure was 101.7 kPa. That's a significant difference, one that would invalidate any computations you did with the offset data.

Use the remote logging function on the data logger, setting it for as many days as you want to collect before downloading data to your PC. Figure 11-7 shows a sample plot made with Microsoft Excel; to make the plot, we downloaded data with the Data Harvest Graph application, copied the data table to the clipboard and pasted into Excel, then created an XY plot using time as the X variable.

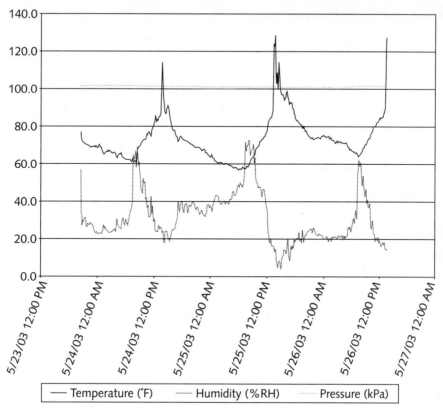

FIGURE 11-7: Sample data plot

The data comes from the logger in degrees Centigrade and kiloPascals. Cconvert from degrees Centigrade to Fahrenheit with the usual formula:

```
F = 1.8C + 32
```

Convert pressure in kiloPascals to inches of mercury with the formula:

```
in Hg = 0.2953 kPa
```

where in Hg is the pressure in inches of mercury and kPa is the pressure in kiloPascals.

Once your data is in Excel, it's also convenient to scan for the daily minimum and maximum values (using the MIN and MAX functions), which you'll need for input to the weather simulation software.

Weather Simulation

The Weather Simulator (WXSIM) software uses a local atmospheric model, with provision for you to make interactive data entries and model changes. Figure 11-8 shows how you enter information for your location using the Location ➔ Other dialog box (these values will be pre-set from a data file created just for you and accessible via the Location ➔ On File dialog box if you've purchased the software; otherwise, you have to estimate the parameters yourself). Most of the titles in the dialog box (and in the rest of the program — you'll see them in blue when you run the program) bring up help text dialog boxes when you click on them.

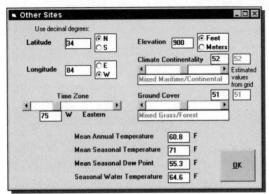

FIGURE 11-8: WXSIM location data entry screen

You can get latitude and longitude from Terraserver (www.terraserver.com, see Chapter 4) and estimate your elevation with TopoZone (www.topozone.com/findplace.asp). Alternatively, you can get latitude, longitude, and elevation from a GPS receiver (see Chapter 10). Enter data in the following sequence so that WXSIM can help you with default values for the later steps:

Enter Location Data into WXSIM

1. Enter your latitude, longitude, and elevation.

2. Set the Climate Continentality and Ground Cover sliders to match the estimated values. Use values offset from the defaults if your specific location is different than the program estimate.

3. Set the Time Zone. The numeric value is 15 times the number of hours offset from Greenwich.

4. Set the four temperatures at the bottom of the screen. WXSIM will have set reasonable defaults by the time you get to this step, but you should invest the time to research values as accurate as possible for your site in order to improve the accuracy of your forecasts. Only the first value is for annual data; the other three are for the season in which you're making the forecast.

We searched www.ask.com using the query *what is the average annual temperature in <our city>* to find sources for the required temperatures. NOAA maintains a data archive at lwf.ncdc.noaa.gov/oa/climate/research/cag3/cag3.html. Another good site, if you're listed, is that for the Teaching Architecture and Energy project at Washington University, where we found comprehensive data for several North American cities (dell2002.cap.utk.edu/ecodesign/escurriculum/CLIMATEDATA/NORMALS/climateindex.html). Other data sources for locations outside the listed cities (dell2002.cap.utk.edu/ecodesign/escurriculum/CLIMATEDATA/Climate Sources.html) are also listed.

Once you've entered the basic site data, click OK and return to the main forecast data entry screen, shown in Figure 11-9. You need to fill out this complicated-looking form before starting the simulation, but if you take it box by box it's not too bad.

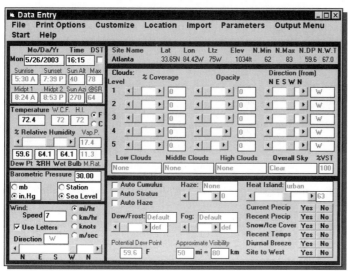

FIGURE 11-9: WXSIM location data entry screen

Start in the upper-left corner, and enter the date and time for your simulation run. The program sets as a default the time on your PC when the program starts up, assuming you want to predict the short-term future. The sunrise, sunset, and other values are computed by WXSIM, and can't be changed directly.

Enter the current temperature from your data logger (or, the temperature corresponding to the date and time you already entered in case you're not forecasting from now forward) in the next box down. Add the current relative humidity from the data logger; WXSIM will adjust the vapor pressure, dew point, and wet bulb temperature. (Alternatively, if you're not using a relative humidity sensor, you can enter measured wet bulb temperature and WXSIM will compute the relative humidity.)

The third box from the top lets you enter the current barometric pressure. If you're using a reading from your data logger, set the entry parameters to show this is a station measurement (if you use sea level values from the Internet reference them to be at sea level with the control next to the value). You can convert kPas to inches of mercury (in Hg) using the 0.2953 factor given earlier in the chapter, or (because millibars are equivalent to hectoPascals), can convert kiloPascals to millibars by multiplying by ten (that is, `millibars = kPa x 10`).

The fourth and final box in the left column records wind direction and velocity. We've not included an anemometer and wind vane in the parts list, but you can make a wind vane following the directions at `www.fi.edu/weather/todo/vane.html`, and an anemometer using the ideas at `sln.fi.edu/tfi/units/energy/dixie.html`. If you'd rather pick the wind off the Internet, recall it's available on most forecast sites (and from Weather Watcher, see Figure 11-1).

The cloud data in the middle pane of the right column (you already set up the top pane when you entered your location) is difficult to enter from observations, because you really have no way to accurately estimate the height of the cloud features you see. Worse, if there are low-level clouds, you may not be able to see the upper levels at all. Instead, your best bet for entering all but low-level clouds is to import data from the Internet. The process is (unfortunately) not deeply automated—you have to create the necessary data file by fishing around on the Internet, then import the file into WXSIM. Directions are in Section IX of the WXSIM users manual included with the software.

Finally, enter any relevant data you have into the lower box in the right column. You should have recent temperatures from your data logger, and you could use a simple rain gauge for recent precipitation (observation works for current precipitation!). The program will estimate clouds and haze if you check the three functions on the left.

At this point, you're done with the basic data entry. Use the Start → Test for Midpoints command to set up some simulation variables; then click Start → Start Calibration Run to run the simulation. You may see some interim confirmation dialog boxes; simply click OK to accept defaults. When you're done, you'll receive output like that in Figure 11-10, showing key weather parameters as the forecast progresses in time, and plotting them in the bottom of the window.

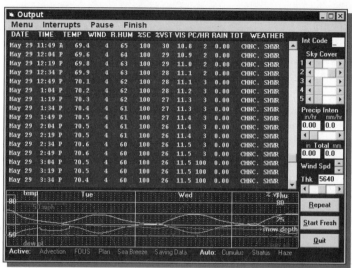

FIGURE 11-10: WXSIM simulation run

Building and Using a Weather Station to Your Own Design

If you're a programmer, consider writing software to automatically create the import data files WXSIM needs to exploit data from the Internet. Beyond that, WXSIM has more controls and features defined in the manual than could be explained in some depth in a small book. Once you make your initial run, you can change parameters (click on Repeat in Figure 11-10 to return to the data entry window and change the set up), and program in interrupts to stop the simulation in mid-run to change parameters on the spot. You can import new data on the fly too.

The Citizen Weather Observers Program (CWOP, www.fiu.edu/orgs/w4ehw/ CWOP-Main.html) is system by which people can upload real-time observations to NOAA. The software CWOP provides works with a specific set of weather stations, but because the system uses a standard protocol (Automatic Packet Reporting System; web.usna.navy. mil/~bruninga/aprs.html) you can write your own software to interface a weather station of your own design to the NOAA servers, or work with the CWOP staff to design and implement a generic interface suitable for supporting home-built weather stations.

The Web page at www.calsci.com/Weather.html suggests that BrainMaker, a neural network implementation, has been used to forecast the weather with good results. If you were to obtain a version of that forecasting system, you could develop your own weather forecasting software. The NOAA archival data (lwf.ncdc.noaa.gov/oa/climate/research/cag3/cag3.html) should provide the raw data you need to train and evaluate your implementation.

The anemometer design suggested earlier in the chapter is easy to build, but not terribly durable. Aside from making one from machined components, you could build a more durable anemometer with no moving parts using the information at www.e-insite.net/ednmag/archives/1996/092696/20di4.htm.

Finally, the National Weather Service is fielding prototype digital forecasts (go to the NWS page at www.wrh.noaa.gov/wrhq/nwspage.html, select a city, then pick Prototype Digital Forecasts from the column on the left). You could write software to interface the digital data into the formats used by WXSIM.

Summary

Forecasting the weather has many applications but is hard due to both the complexity of weather systems and the significant impact of local effects. Combining measurements you make yourself with Internet data lets you run weather simulations to create more accurate near-term forecasts for your specific site.

Pure Fun

part

V

Create and Control Your Own Robots

Let's start with the three fundamental Rules of Robotics. . . . We have: one, a robot may not injure a human being, or, through inaction, allow a human being to come to harm. Two, a robot must obey the orders given it by human beings except where such orders would conflict with the First Law. And three, a robot must protect its own existence as long as such protection does not conflict with the First or Second Laws.

~Isaac Asimov, *I, Robot*

People seem to have one of two views of robots, exemplified by either the death-dealing sentient competitors to man found in *Terminator* or *The Matrix*, or the docile, subservient androids from *Star Wars*. Asimov had the middle view implicit in his Three Laws, holding that robots could be both highly advanced and kept in check.

Feet, Hands, Eyes, and Brains

So far, though, what the science of robotics can build is hardly the threat envisioned in movies and novels, because the science of artificial intelligence can't yet even approximate broadly sentient behavior. People can build mechanisms that perform tasks with surprisingly sophisticated capabilities, but not ones that can actually think for themselves.

Although we can't yet build sentient robots, and maybe never will, we can build mechanisms of great value. Every robot, from the simplest early experiments to sophisticated assembly-line robots or the Mars Rover, has four basic components: the physical structure, sensors, actuators, and computing elements that direct the actuators based on sensor inputs. All four sets of components work together to observe the real world, make decisions, and take actions.

Lack of sentience notwithstanding, what robots — ones you can build — can do is seemingly unlimited. For that reason, this chapter is unlike the rest. It's an introduction to building robots using a commercially available kit, the LEGO Robot Invention System, not a project for one specific robot design.

Figure 12-1 shows a block diagram for robots you build with the Robot Invention System. Your robot operates independently, receiving programs you generate on your PC and running them on the RCX microcontroller. Touch and light sensors tell your robot about the environment, while motors let it take actions in response.

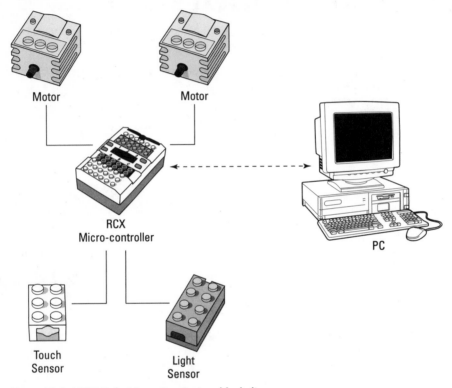

FIGURE **12-1:** LEGO Robot Invention System block diagram

Building and Using Your Robots from Kits

Nearly any Windows PC will work for the Robot Invention System — few PCs are likely to still be running that can't meet the minimum specifications shown in Table 12-1.

Table 12-1	LEGO Robot Invention System Minimum PC Requirements
Characteristic	*Requirement*
OS	Win 98/Me, Windows XP
CPU	Pentium II, 233 MHz, or compatible

Characteristic	Requirement
RAM	32MB (Win 9x), 128MB (Windows XP)
Disk	115MB
Mouse	Yes (any Windows compatible)
Sound	Yes (any Windows compatible)
CD	8x
Video	800 x 600, 4MB RAM, 16-bit color
USB	1.1 or later
Modem	Optional
Internet Browser	Netscape Navigator or Microsoft Internet Explorer

Parts List

Almost everything you need to start building robots comes in the Robot Invention System. Table 12-2 lists the parts you'll need.

Table 12-2   Robot Construction Parts List

Part	Manufacturer and Model Number
Robot Kit	LEGO Robot Invention System 2.0 ($199.95) mindstorms.lego.com
Powered USB Hub	Belkin ($49.99) catalog.belkin.com, Part No: F5U224

LEGO recommends a powered USB hub to ensure the infrared transceiver has enough power to support long-range PC → RCX communications. We've listed a USB 2.0 hub from Belkin that's backwards compatible with the slower USB 1.1 specification.

You'll build robots from four elements — the LEGO structural pieces, a control computer, sensors, and motors. The RCX (see Figure 12-2) is a microcomputer that controls the robot when it's running separate from your PC. The four-pin contact pads above the numbers 1 to 3 interface to sensors, while the four-pin contact pads below the letters A to C interface to bidirectional motors. Buttons on the RCX turn it on and off, select the active program (from five possibilities), start and stop the program, and enable a view mode that lets you directly examine the properties of attached sensors and motors. Six AA batteries fit inside the RCX to power the microcomputer, motors, and sensors.

Robots for Little Kids

The Robot Invention System looks like the blocks kids have played with for decades, but it's nowhere near that simple. You have to build mechanisms far more complex than required for most LEGO projects and then write computer programs to bring the robots to life. LEGO suggests ages 12 and up, but in practice a 12-year-old will need a few course corrections and explanations along the way; our 11-year-old was an able assistant.

The advanced characteristics of the Robot Invention System won't dissuade smaller kids from wanting to play — it's LEGOs, after all. There's a robot kit for them too, the LEGO Spybots. The Spybots are not programmable like the Robot Invention System is, but once kids assemble the robot there's a game that integrates a PC and the Spybot robot into a series of challenges and a multiplayer mode letting several players (each with his or her own Spybot) compete.

FIGURE 12-2: LEGO Robot Invention System RCX controller

LEGO and the brick configuration are trademarks of the LEGO Group. ©2003 The LEGO Group is used here with permission. The LEGO Group does not sponsor or endorse this book.

The Robot Invention System comes with two kinds of sensors, touch sensors (one is shown on the left in Figure 12-3) and a light sensor with light source (on the right in Figure 12-3). The RCX can tell if the touch sensor push button is pushed nor not, and can read the light level from the light sensor. Decision-making constructs in the Robot Invention System programming system let you read the sensors and act on the resulting input values. Contacts built into the enclosing LEGO blocks support interconnections between blocks, using wires tied into other thin LEGO blocks.

FIGURE 12-3: LEGO Robot Invention System touch and light sensors

LEGO and the brick configuration are trademarks of the LEGO Group. ©2003 The LEGO Group is used here with permission. The LEGO Group does not sponsor or endorse this book.

The motors (see Figure 12-4) resemble the sensors in that they're functional elements built into LEGO block enclosures, with contacts in the block posts. The motors run in both directions (so it's important to orient the wires on the blocks precisely as shown in the construction diagrams) at a speed controlled by the power level being output by the RCX. Figure 12-4 shows an interconnection cable on the right-hand motor, with connection blocks at either end.

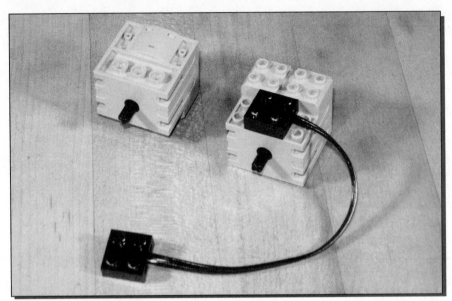

FIGURE 12-4: LEGO Robot Invention System motors

LEGO and the brick configuration are trademarks of the LEGO Group. ©2003 The LEGO Group is used here with permission. The LEGO Group does not sponsor or endorse this book.

An infrared transmission tower, a USB device you connect to your PC, transmits programs and commands from your PC to the robot. Remember to connect the tower to your PC through a powered USB hub, or it will have to run with reduced power and at shorter ranges. The Robot Invention System software includes the drivers for the tower.

We installed the Robot Invention System software on a PC running Windows XP, and although both the box and the packaged instructions say you'll need Windows 98 or Me, Windows XP works. The Mindstorms Web site addresses this issue (`mindstorms.lego.com/support/en/ris20.asp`)—there's nothing special you have to do for Windows XP other than to set up the kit in the following sequence:

1. Install the software from CD.

2. Plug in the USB tower, find the New Hardware Found window, and finish driver setup (automatic search should work).

3. Run the program.

The version of QuickTime installed on our computer was newer than that supplied on the Mindstorms CD, so we skipped the QuickTime part of the software installation. Unfortunately, our QuickTime installation lacked the Internet Extras component required to make the Mindstorms software work properly, but once we added the component by updating from the QuickTime Web site (`www.quicktime.com`), everything fell into place.

Assembling the Robot Vehicle

Once you install the software and the drivers for the tower, you're ready to build robots. The Robot Invention System includes the *Constructopedia*, a manual to show you how to build some basic robots, and training missions in the PC software to show you how to program the robots. We suggest that you work through the training course to familiarize yourself with the system. The course starts with you assembling and programming the Roverbot robot; the photographs below show you steps in building the second robot in the training sequence, the Acrobot.

Every page of directions in the *Constructopedia* has you assemble smaller subsystems, then integrate them into the robot. Figure 12-5 shows the first stage we assembled for the Acrobot, beginning to assemble what LEGO calls the *driving base*. In all their robot designs, the term *driving base* describes an assembly including at least the RCX microcontroller and the motors.

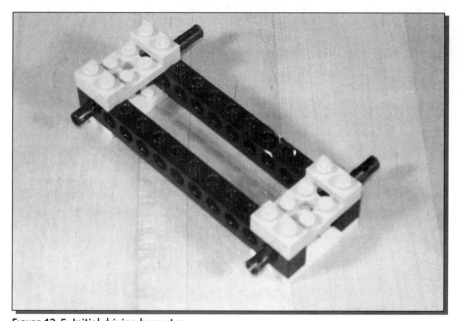

FIGURE 12-5: Initial driving base step

LEGO and the brick configuration are trademarks of the LEGO Group. ©2003 The LEGO Group is used here with permission. The LEGO Group does not sponsor or endorse this book.

Figure 12-6 builds on the starting frame in Figure 12-5, adding the motors and framework elements to lock the motors into the driving base.

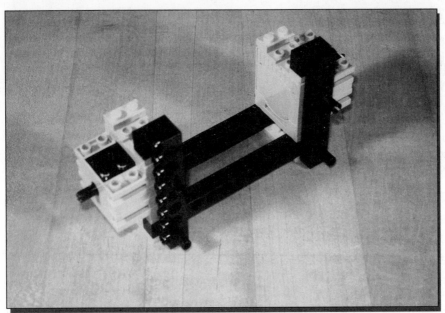

FIGURE 12-6: Intermediate driving base step
LEGO and the brick configuration are trademarks of the LEGO Group. ©2003 The LEGO Group is used here with permission. The LEGO Group does not sponsor or endorse this book.

Figure 12-7 continues framing the lower part of the driving base. The motors are now visibly at the back, with a frame structure taking shape in the front. The RCX microcontroller will fit into the bay between and in front of the motors. You'll hold the assembly together with pins rather than the usual LEGO friction fit, because the weight of the RCX combined with the reaction forces from the motors would shake the robot apart if you relied on friction.

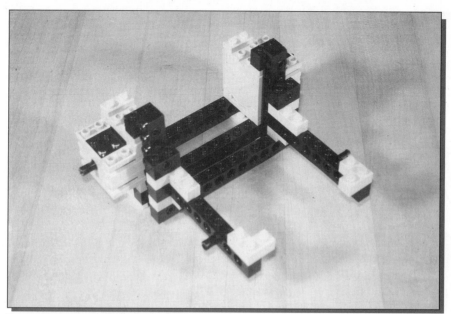

FIGURE 12-7: Intermediate driving base step—initial framework

LEGO and the brick configuration are trademarks of the LEGO Group. ©2003 The LEGO Group is used here with permission. The LEGO Group does not sponsor or endorse this book.

Figure 12-8 shows the driving base with the front of the frame complete and the RCX laid in. Be sure to orient the RCX so that the controls face upward and the infrared window points to the front of the driving base, away from the motors.

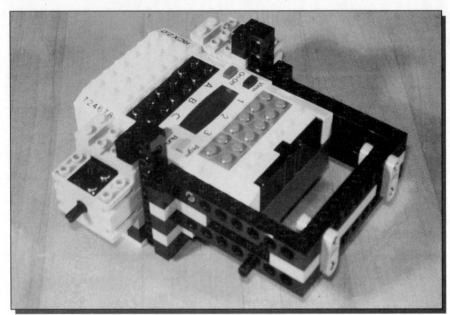

FIGURE **12-8: Intermediate driving base with RCX installed**

LEGO and the brick configuration are trademarks of the LEGO Group. ©2003 The LEGO Group is used here with permission. The LEGO Group does not sponsor or endorse this book.

Figure 12-9 shows the completed driving base, with wiring from the motors to the RCX and the kit's four big tires mounted on the motor axles and the front axles.

FIGURE 12-9: Complete driving base with wheels

LEGO and the brick configuration are trademarks of the LEGO Group. ©2003 The LEGO Group is used here with permission. The LEGO Group does not sponsor or endorse this book.

Programming the Robot

Programs you build tell the robot what you want it to do. You build those programs with your PC, then download them to the microcomputer in the RCX through the infrared tower. The Robot Invention System includes a graphical programming environment specialized for RCX software development (see Figure 12-10). Programming is through a procedural language represented as flowcharts, using an editor within the environment in which you drag and drop blocks to build flowcharts. There are primitives (indivisible blocks) for input, output, flow control, and for manipulating variables. The help file includes a block language reference, which you'll want to read to learn the details of what each block can do for you.

FIGURE 12-10: Robot Invention System programming environment

LEGO and the brick configuration are trademarks of the LEGO Group. ©2003 The LEGO Group is used here with permission. The LEGO Group does not sponsor or endorse this book.

The items along the top of the window in Figure 12-10 form the typical Windows main menu bar, although it looks different than what you'd expect in a program that strictly follows Windows layout conventions. The Download, Run, and Stop buttons are immediate commands that copy the current program to the robot, start the program running, and stop the program. The RCX has five "slots" to hold programs, independent of the maximum program size it can hold. You select the active slot by pushing the PRGM button on the RCX. The current program number shows up in the LCD window on the RCX to the right of the stick figure and is the slot into which the download operation will transfer your program.

The large, dark area in the window is where you compose your program. (You can pan and zoom the program area with the four-pointed compass tool in the bottom right of the figure.) Graphical blocks represent each element in a program. The buttons on the right of the blocks open dialog boxes you use to customize specific characteristics of the block, such as motor runtime moving the robot forward.

The column of buttons on the left of the window is your program block library. Primitive program elements are kept within the buttons as shown in Table 12-3. The Small Blocks button contains six lower-level buttons, which in turn hold the actual primitive blocks; the other five top-level buttons contain the associated primitives directly.

Table 12-3   Primitive Robot Invention System Programming Elements

Button	Available Primitives
Small Blocks	Power (On, On For, Off, Set Power, Set Direction, Reverse Direction)
	Sound (Beep, Tone, Mute Sounds, Un-Mute Sounds)
	Comm (Send IR Message, Clear IR Message, Display Value, Display Clock)
	Variable (Set, Add, Subtract, Multiply, Divide, Make Positive, Make Negative)
	Reset (Reset Light, Reset Timer, Reset Temp, Reset Rotation)
	Advanced (Set Priority, Global Reverse, Global Set Direction, Connect Power, Disconnect Power, End Program)
My Blocks	Create New My Block
Wait	Wait For, Wait Until
Repeat	Repeat For, Repeat Forever, Repeat While, Repeat Until
Yes or No	Yes or No
Sensors	Touch Sensor, Light Sensor, Timer Sensor, IR Sensor, Variable Sensor, Temp Sensor, Rotation Sensor

The Big Blocks button holds programming elements too, but they're themselves larger scale functions, specialized for specific robots (except for the Global category), and built from smaller and primitive elements. You can make your own big block equivalents, called My Blocks, by placing a My Blocks element on screen, opening it (use the button in the My Blocks upper-left corner), and dragging other elements inside.

The program area holds only one program for your robot at a time. You tie blocks to the unique program block in the upper-left corner of the program area by dragging them from the column of buttons. You can temporarily store program fragments as unattached elements in the program area, but until they're tied to the program flow, they won't do anything.

The sensor blocks tie into your program differently from the way regular program statements do. Sensors themselves are interfaces to the outside world, and the events they sense can happen asynchronously, independently of what's going on in your program. For that reason, they connect to the program block and execute an independent sequence of blocks when the condition they recognize becomes true. (If you're a programmer, you'll recognize the sensor as initiating a parallel task triggered by an external interrupt and filtered by the sensor condition.) You can use any program element block in the sequence triggered by the sensor except another sensor — all sensor blocks must tie directly to the unique program block.

We recommend that you work your way through the training missions to familiarize yourself with the programming environment. Each mission involves building and testing the corresponding robot, then challenges to develop and test small programs that illustrate specific programming concepts. Figure 12-11 shows a program that solves the first Acrobot challenge, moving the robot forward and backward indefinitely. The program starts with the unique program block, then wraps Forward and Backward blocks in a Repeat Forever block. If you collapsed the Repeat Forever block (use the button at the top left of the upper part of the Repeat Forever block), you'd hide the Forward and Backward blocks. That's useful in larger programs so that you can focus on the higher-level structure.

FIGURE 12-11: Acrobot programming challenge number one

LEGO and the brick configuration are trademarks of the LEGO Group. ©2003 The LEGO Group is used here with permission. The LEGO Group does not sponsor or endorse this book.

The Forward and Backward blocks themselves are Big Blocks held within the Acrobot button. You can expand those two blocks to see the primitive elements they contain, and can copy those primitive blocks to a My Block if you want to create a modified version. (You can't modify Big Blocks directly.)

As soon as you progress past the simplest programs, you'll need to test conditions and choose what to do accordingly. You use Yes or No blocks for that purpose, filling in the Yes and No sequences with the appropriate subsequences. You can test sensor status in a Yes or No block, which happens synchronously with program execution at the point the block fires, giving you a second way to work with sensors — you are not required to use a sensor block.

Further illustrating that Robot Invention System programs are the same as more conventional software, they're not guaranteed to work right when you first write them. The system includes a debugger to help you view the values at the sensor inputs, the commands sent to the motor outputs, and the values being stored in any variables you used in your program. You can't single-step through the program, but you can watch what's happening at a top level. Using the debugger (see Figure 12-12) requires that the robot be visible from the infrared tower.

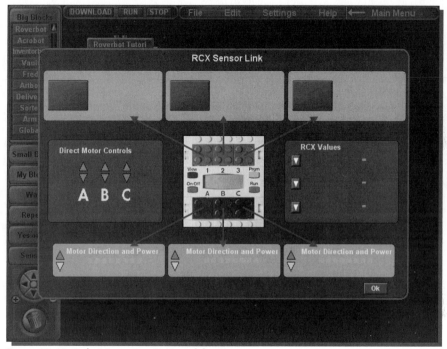

FIGURE 12-12: Robot Invention System debugger

LEGO and the brick configuration are trademarks of the LEGO Group. ©2003 The LEGO Group is used here with permission. The LEGO Group does not sponsor or endorse this book.

Building Your Robots to Your Own Design

The unlimited range of robots you can build, a result of the flexibility of the underlying LEGO blocks and the programmability of the RCX equivalent to a full textual programming language, has led to a large community of people developing with and building enhancements for the Robot Invention System.

Robot Invention System on the Web

LEGO offers an online community that lets you create your own workshop page, exchange messages with other members, and share robot designs. It's a great idea, but as long as they collect unnecessary personal information, you won't find us there. The associated privacy policy explains that they need birth-date information to identify children and to be able to comply with related legislation, but that's not justification for collecting gender, residence postal code, or the date of birth for those over 13 years of age.

Books

There are some excellent books that go into great detail about building your own robot designs, programming the Robot Invention System, and other sophisticated topics. Table 12-4 shows some of the high-level topics in several of the books we liked best; every one of these books shows you how to build robots beyond those documented with the Robot Invention System.

Table 12-4   Books on the LEGO Robot Invention System

Book	Topics
The Unofficial Guide to LEGO Mindstorms Robots by Jonathan B. Knudsen (O'Reilly, 1999)	Parts identification, building robots, programs for the robots, gears and gear ratios, transmissions, pulleys and arms, using and combining sensors, alternative programming environments, alternative robotic software architectures
	The book covers version 1.0 of the RCX. Version 2.0 is what shipped when we wrote this chapter, so you'll see things we mention (like variables in the programming environment) that weren't available in version 1.0. Some of the alternative programming environments discussed may require updates before they'll work with the USB tower.
Building Robots with LEGO Mindstorms by Mario Ferrari and Giulio Ferrari (Syngress, 2002)	LEGO sizes and units, vertical and horizontal bracing, gears, motors, sensors, mechanical design, RCX programming and environments, sound, drive trains, expansion, pneumatics, grabbing, calculations, walking, mazes, board games, racing, combat
Jin Sato's LEGO Mindstorms by Jin Sato (No Starch Press, 2002)	Assembly, motors, gears, sensors and RCX, programming languages and environments, robots to build, Computer Aided Design (CAD) software
	If you spend enough time building Mindstorms robots, you'll want the discussions of advanced topics in this book. Many of the topics listed here look like those of the other books; calibrate the difference by considering that the book covers Sato's MIBO robot, a walking/sitting/standing dog using *two* RCX controllers.

Book	Topics
Robot Invasion by Dave Johnson (McGraw-Hill/Osborne, 2002)	Racers, collision avoidance, combat, exploration, video, robot arm
	Robot Invasion extends LEGO Mindstorms in different directions than Sato's book, using parts that are far afield from the standard LEGO elements to build new designs and capabilities.

Spare and Additional Parts

You can buy additional robot kits, including these add-ons from LEGO:

- Ultimate Accessory Set, which includes a rotation sensor, a touch sensor, a lamp, extra building elements, and a remote control

- Dark Side and Droid Developer Kits, which include a simpler microcontroller with a built-in light sensor and motor, and extra building elements

- Ultimate Builder's Set, including pneumatic parts, an extra motor, and more building elements

You can also order individual parts, including a variety of motors, from the LEGO Shop at Home service (shop.lego.com/ or (800) 835-4386), or from Pitsco LEGO DACTA (www.pitsco-legodacta.com or (800) 362-4308).

LEGO Technics parts work with the Robot Invention System, so don't overlook them as a source of building elements.

Alternative Programming Systems

You can program the RCX in C, forth, Java, or raw assembly code. Perhaps the best information on the low-level operation of the RCX is by Kekoa Proudfoot (graphics.stanford.edu/~kekoa/rcx/). He details the hardware, firmware, and interpretive language that runs on the RCX, and provides links to a number of related pages with alternative programming environments.

A good way to find information on Robot Invention System alternative programming systems is a Google search on *LEGO firmdl*. One of the projects you'll find that way is leJOS, a system to let you program the RCX in Java (sourceforge.net/projects/lejos/). Released versions of leJOS in late 2002 added support for the USB tower found in the version 2.0 Robot Invention System.

Add Your Own Sensors

You can embed your own sensor designs into LEGO bricks and connect them through studs that connect to the standard LEGO wiring bricks. See Michael Gasperi's Web site for details (www.plazaearth.com/usr/gasperi/lego.htm). You'll find a variety of devices (including an analog interface, a temperature sensor, a sound sensor, an improved light sensor, a rotation sensor, a touch sensor with 360 degree coverage, a motion sensor, a motor speed/torque sensor, a pressure sensor, an angle sensor, and a galvanic skin response sensor) plus a lot of design suggestions for inventing your own sensors.

Summary

The capabilities of the LEGO Mindstorms Robot Invention System are limited only by your time and imagination. You'll have to bring both in ample supply, because designing and building your own robots isn't simple — you'll need some ability with physics, mechanical design, electrical design, computer hardware, and software development. LEGO's claim that the system is for ages 12 and up is pretty fanciful, but for the right people, it's hard to see how you get a longer-lived return on a $200 investment.

Throw a Networked Head-to-Head Video Gaming Party

These humiliations are the essence of the game.

> ~Alistair Cooke, quoted in Bob Chieger and Pat Sullivan, Eds., *Inside Golf*

Hysterical assertions that video games are turning youths into antisocial loners notwithstanding, we'll absolutely stand on this one point: every video game we've ever played that had a multiplayer option was a whole lot more fun with a room full of people second guessing and laughing at your every move. It's hard to retain a sense of pride under those conditions, but they make for an incredible amount of fun.

Let the Screaming Begin

One of the hardest things to build into video games is a realistic, intelligent opponent. It's easy to build an enemy you can never beat, but very hard to build one that is realistically difficult — one that plays as well as a human, even as well as the best humans, but no better. Multiplayer games solve that problem by providing people as opponents. People may well be better and faster than you, but they make mistakes, lose concentration, and have off days. People have characteristics you can learn, but they learn yours at the same time.

As wonderful as online, multiplayer games can be over the Internet, LAN parties with your friends within earshot are infinitely better, because the screams, taunts, and epithets from both players and spectators add a unique dimension to play. Microsoft understood this when they built voice communication into their Xbox Live Internet gaming service, but even the good implementation they built can't match the immediacy of a party.

Assuming your guests bring their own PCs, a LAN party is easy to throw. Some inexpensive network equipment and some of your time is all it takes. Well, that and good food. Here's what you'll learn to do in this chapter:

- Set up the network cabling and connections

- Make sure each person's computer can talk to the others

- Create servers to host game sessions, and directories to simplify finding and joining games

- Provide spectator camera views for bystanders to see what's happening in each game

- Track results and statistics (not that the winner needs to matter so much, but because it's one more way to compete and interact.)

Some Games Work at Parties, and Some Do Not

Games don't work at parties if players can't play them reasonably well, which means either the players must already be experienced with the games, or else the game must be simple to learn. Ideally, your guests will be at comparable skill levels, too, because it's depressing to lose constantly. Finally, parties last only so long, so you'll want to pick games in which you can complete matches or levels in a reasonable amount of time.

That said, here are our picks for great LAN party games:

Genre	Game
First Person Shooter	Unreal Tournament 2003
	Quake I, II, and III
	Halo (no matter when it's released)
	Half Life with Counterstrike Mod
Action	Diablo II with Lord of Destruction Expansion Pack
	Battlefield 1942
Role Playing	Icewind Dale
	Baldur's Gate II
Real Time Strategy (requires some experience)	Command and Conquer Generals
	Warcraft III

Guest's Computers, Your Network

Table 13-1 lists all the parts you'll need for a party, including cabling, hubs and switches, and game software. We're assuming your guests will bring their own PCs, so the only PCs you'll have to supply are the one you play on plus the one you use as a games server.

Table 13-1	Video Game LAN Party Parts List
Part	**Manufacturer and Model Number**
Category 5 Patch Cables	Patch Cable ($1.50 and up) www.cablesnmor.com/cat-5-cable.html
Ethernet Hub or Switch	Hubs ($24.95 and up) shopper.cnet.com/shopping/search/results/ 0,10214,0-1257,00.html?tag=sort&qt=ethernet+hub&cn= &ca=1257&so=1&st=0 Switches ($31.83 and up) shopper.cnet.com/shopping/search/results/0,10214,0-1257, 00.html?tag=sort&qt=ethernet+switch&cn=&ca=1257&so=1& st=0
100 Mbps Ethernet Adapters	PCI ($8.78 and up) shopper.cnet.com/shopping/search/results/ 0,10214,0-1257,00.html?tag=sort&qt=Ethernet+PCI&cn= &ca=1257&so=1&st=0 USB ($23.34 and up) shopper.cnet.com/shopping/search/results/0,10214,0-1257, 00.html?tag=sort&qt=ethernet+adapter+usb&cn=&ca=1257& so=1&st=0

Continued

Table 13-1 *(continued)*

Part	Manufacturer and Model Number
Internet Router	External ($40 and up) Belkin Wireless: `catalog.belkin.com/IWCatSectionView.process?Section_Id=201523` Wired: `catalog.belkin.com/IWCatSectionView.process?Section_Id=201487` D-Link Wireless: `www.dlink.com/products/wireless/index.asp` Wired: `www.dlink.com/products/routers/index.asp` Linksys Wireless: `www.linksys.com/products/group.asp?grid=33&scid=35` Wired: `www.linksys.com/products/group.asp?grid=34&scid=29` Netgear Wireless: `www.netgear.com/products/wireless.html` Wired: `www.netgear.com/products/routers/websafefirewall.asp` Modem: `www.netgear.com/products/prod_details.asp?prodID=33` SMC Wireless: `www.smc.com/index.cfm?sec=Products&pg=Product-List&cat=5&site=c` Wired: `www.smc.com/index.cfm?sec=Products&pg=Product-List&cat=4&site=c`

Part	Manufacturer and Model Number
Wireless Access Point	External, plug into a hub or switch ($67.27 and up)
	Belkin:
	`catalog.belkin.com/IWCatProductPage.process?Merchant_Id=&Section_Id=201523&pcount=&Product_Id=122640`
	D-Link:
	`www.dlink.com/products/wireless/dwl900ap/`
	Linksys:
	`www.linksys.com/products/product.asp?prid=157&grid=`
	Netgear:
	`www.netgear.com/products/prod_details.asp?prodID=92&view=`
	SMC:
	`www.smc.com/index.cfm?sec=Products&pg=Product-Details&prod=269&site=c`

There's no guaranteed sufficient minimum PC configuration for client or server machines — you'll have to check the requirements based on the game itself. Nevertheless, if you're playing Unreal Tournament 2003 as we describe in this chapter, you'll want to *at least* meet the requirements shown in Table 13-2 for the machine you play on. First person shooter (FPS) games usually have the most stringent hardware requirements, so you might get away with somewhat less playing other games. Don't try to cut back too far, though, because generating the graphics for any fast-paced game is demanding.

Table 13-2   Unreal Tournament 2003 Client Computer Requirements

Characteristic	Requirement
Operating System	Windows 98/ME/2000/XP
CPU	x86-compatible, 1 GHz or faster
Memory	256 MB RAM or greater
Hard Disk Space	3 GB
CD or DVD	Yes, have one
Audio	Windows compatible sound card, and perhaps headphones
Video	nVidia GeForce 2 or ATI Radeon (lesser cards will put you at a disadvantage, although even an nVidia TNT2-class card will work)
Internet Connection	33 Kbps or faster for Internet play

The most basic work you must do, and should ideally do in advance, is to set up the cabling and equipment you'll use to connect your guests' computers together. You can use cables, wireless connections, or a combination of both.

Wired

If you use wired connections, the first choice you need to make is what cabling technology to use. Nearly always, the right choice will be standard 10/100Base-T Ethernet (see Figure 13-1). You'll recognize 10/100Base-T cabling by the characteristic 8-wire RJ-45 modular connectors. Use CAT-5 wiring or better to make sure you can handle 100-megabit connections.

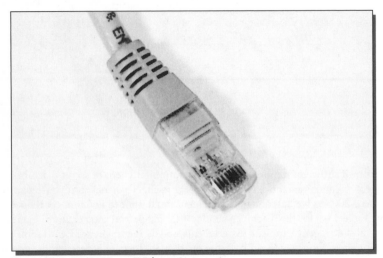

FIGURE 13-1: 10/100Base-T Ethernet connector

Unless you need cables to connect a *lot* of guests' computers to the LAN, you're probably better off buying the cables that connect the computers to the switches or hubs. Those patch cables will each cost you anywhere from $1.50 to $35 and up, depending on where you buy them. If you can plan ahead and give yourself enough time to order cables, look at the pages we listed in Table 13-1 for Cables N Mor www.cablesnmor.com/cat-5-cable.html; even a 100-foot cable there won't cost more than $28.

If you're only connecting two computers, meaning at any one time two players are head to head with each other, with no separate machines for spectators, you can use just a crossover cable to directly connect the two. Otherwise, you'll need an Ethernet switch or hub. Searching www.shopper.com for *ethernet hub* and *ethernet switch* respectively, we found five-port Ethernet hubs for as little as $24.95, and switches as low as $31.83.

The difference between a hub and a switch is that a hub can pass only one packet at a time, because all computers share the hub equally, while a switch pairs the source and destination ports for packets and can pass many packets simultaneously as long as the packets each use different pairs of ports. The ability to pass multiple packets at a time means switches can carry more traffic than hubs and will burden the receiving computers with less irrelevant traffic. That benefit won't matter if you're running only a few games at a time, but if you stack multiple switches and hubs in a tree to let *lots* of people play or watch at once, the traffic near the root (see Figure 13-2) can mount and start to bog down if you're not using a switch.

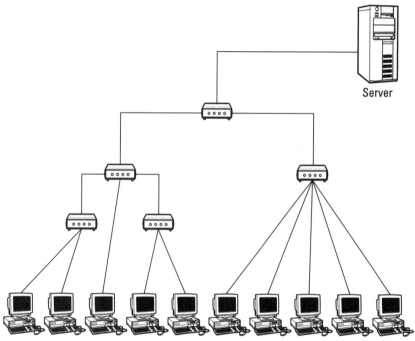

FIGURE 13-2: A tree gives you many ports for client computers.

Even if you are using switches, the traffic into and out of the server will be the sum of all the traffic in the network, so if you have a lot of clients, make sure the server is on a 100-megabit port.

Be sure you don't accidentally connect the cables to form a loop, because if you do, your network won't work. Once you've cabled the entire infrastructure and checked for the usual green link OK lights everywhere two parts are joined, it's time to wire up the computers. Unless you know that all the visiting computers have network ports, you're safest assuming that some of them won't, and therefore you'll have a few loaner network interface cards (NICs) on hand. If nobody objects to slapping a PCI card into their computer, they're a really cheap alternative. You always run a risk of problems when you open a computer or install a PCI driver, though; if you're concerned, could use the somewhat more expensive USB NICs instead. You may still have to do a driver installation, but USB drivers cause problems far less often, and you won't have to open the computer case.

Wireless

There's a saying that God watches over drunks and fools. Neither of those were in short supply in the more raucous parties we remember, and given all the other, more important problems in the world, trusting in divine providence means all those Ethernet cables strung around on the floor are disaster waiting to happen.

At some cost, you can avoid that problem by using a wireless LAN. The most commonly available wireless LAN technology, and the least expensive, follows the IEEE 802.11b (or WiFi) standard. The equipment operates in the 2.4 GHz band, which means that it's vulnerable to interference from some wireless phones and — rarely — Bluetooth computer equipment, but overall it works well. You'll want to think about the following four issues when using 802.11b wireless:

- Primary equipment configuration
- Coverage
- Security
- Latency

By *primary equipment configuration* we mean the choice of what type of wireless equipment to use. The 802.11b technology itself permits both direct computer-to-computer connections and computer-to-LAN connections (see Figure 13-3). The direct computer-to-computer, or *ad hoc* mode creates a wireless connection from every computer to every other computer, with no one computer managing the network. The computer-to-LAN, or *infrastructure* mode creates a wireless connection from each wirelessly connected computer to a central access point, with a connection to the LAN at the access point. Infrastructure mode is less expensive for your gaming network, because otherwise *every* computer needs its own wireless interface whether it's on the wired LAN or not. That's workable if you set up a purely wireless LAN, but not otherwise.

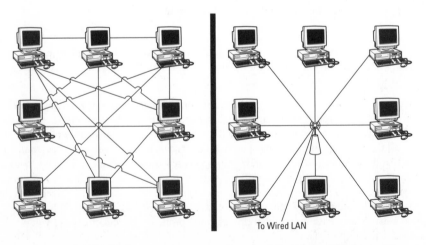

To Wired LAN

Ad Hoc Mode   Infrastructure Mode

FIGURE 13-3: The IEEE 802.11b wireless standard permits ad hoc and infrastructure networks

If you need more coverage than a single router can provide, or already have a router without wireless capability and simply want to bridge other computers into your existing LAN, you can use a *wireless access point* (WAP), which functions much like a hub with wireless connections.

Coverage describes the physical space within which computers can connect to your wireless network. Coverage isn't just a matter of distance, although it's strongly affected by distance — antenna patterns, blockage, and interference play a big role too. The wireless signals travel in a straight line, but it's likely that not all directions are equally favored by the antenna pattern. Some antennas may radiate in a circle, but not well up or down, some may radiate front to back and up/down but not side-to-side, and others will have different patterns yet.

Moreover, different materials block signals to varying extents. Metal is particularly bad, but non-metallic substances will block signals somewhat, and materials that seem non-metallic can nevertheless have metallic powders or other forms of metal in their makeup. You can be assured that only active, powered electronics will radiate interfering signals, but knowing the frequencies at which a device radiates, and how strongly, is almost impossible without instruments. Computers and monitors are potential sources of interference, but so are some wireless telephones and microwave ovens.

It's hard to predict just how an antenna will radiate by looking at it, much less how much power an access point or interface card have, what the interference sources are, and what objects are causing more or less blockage. The easiest thing to do is walk around with a laptop in different directions and at different distances, looking at the received signal strength. Doing that survey lets you map out the net effects of radiated signal strength, antenna performance, blockage, and interference.

Your wireless LAN's signal will not stop at the walls of your building, nor at your property line. The signal simply continues without boundaries until it becomes too weak to be received. It can easily overlap onto the street, into the apartment unit above or below you, and to your next-door neighbor. If you've done nothing to prohibit access from those points outside your control, your network is open and insecure. Not something you want, so here's what you need to do.

Secure Your Wireless 802.11b LAN

1. *Turn off the broadcast SSID.* The Service Set Identifier (SSID) is, effectively, a password for access to your wireless LAN. If you leave the broadcast SSID enabled anyone can join your network without knowing the password. That's nice for your guests, but you might have other visitors.

2. *Set a specific SSID that is different from the default.* The default SSID is well known for many different brands of routers: Linksys routers come set to *linksys*, Cisco routers come set to *tsunami*, Intel is *intel*, 3Com is *101*, and so on. Change the SSID, preferably to something not easily guessed. (For that matter, you might want to set one SSID for your party, and then change it afterwards.) Because you've turned off the broadcast SSID, everyone will have to set the specific SSID in their configuration.

3. *Turn on WEP.* Wired Equivalent Privacy (WEP) encrypts the transmissions over your wireless network, and adds a good (but crackable) layer of security. Set your router for 128-bit keys, then enter a passphrase into the router and generate a key. Give the key (in hex) to your guests; it's not likely you can simply have each of them enter the passphrase and end up with a working key. You tell wirelessly connected guests the specific channel number you're using if they're having problems connecting.

If you *really* want to lock down your wireless LAN, you can restrict access to specific physical hardware by their built-in unique addresses, called MAC addresses, explicitly defining the set of cards allowed to access the router. No other cards will have access. This might be overkill for a party of a few hours, but it's not a bad idea for a wireless LAN when you normally have few visitors.

The latency sending messages from one computer to another is higher over wireless links than over Ethernet cables. The difference isn't large — on our network, for example, we see ping times of 2–3 milliseconds over the wireless network and less than a millisecond over the Ethernet cables. That may not seem a lot, but some really fanatic gamers may be concerned that it's enough to give their opponent a split-second advantage. Evaluate your guests' fanaticism and proceed accordingly.

Before You Frag — Setting Up the LAN

Once you've set up connections, be they wired or wireless, you need to make sure the necessary protocols work on your LAN and make provisions for guests to use those protocols. You'll use either the IPX or TCP/IP protocols, depending on what else you do with your LAN and on what the games support.

IPX, the protocol that originated with Novell's Netware, is a great choice if you're just putting a LAN together temporarily for your party. It requires no administration beyond making sure the protocol stack is available on every computer, because it assigns addresses to computers automatically. For many years, the default Windows installation loaded IPX onto every networked computer along with the NetBEUI protocol stack, making LANs as easy to set up as could be. At one time, every multiplayer game supported IPX because it was so prevalent.

Nevertheless, IPX is becoming rare today because TCP/IP is the protocol of the Internet. There's no good reason to support both IPX and TCP/IP on a computer, and because so many LANs are connected to the Internet, TCP/IP has become the protocol of choice.

With the exception of the nonstandard behavior of Windows when it can't otherwise obtain an address, TCP/IP has no way for a single computer to automatically assign itself a network address. Instead, computers running TCP/IP either have their network addresses assigned manually or employ Dynamic Host Configuration Protocol (DHCP) to receive their address assignment. DHCP simplifies other elements of TCP/IP setup too, in that computers receiving DHCP information — the DHCP clients — can also be given their subnet mask (which lets the computer determine whether another address is on the same network segment or requires routing) and the address of a Domain Name System (DNS) server used to convert computer names to numeric TCP/IP addresses and vice versa.

TCP/IP Setup

If you're setting up a temporary LAN and not all your games support IPX, the simplest and least expensive approach is to manually assign each computer a TCP/IP address. TCP/IP addresses consist of four numbers each ranging from 0 to 255, such as 10.204.75.102.

One set of workable addresses for your temporary LAN ranges from 192.168.0.1 through 192.168.0.254; you can assign addresses from that range randomly to each computer as long as each computer's address is unique. You'll need a subnet mask too; use 255.255.255.0. You don't need to support DNS on your temporary LAN, because (if you need the actual computer names at all) you can just keep a list of which computers have which addresses and use the addresses themselves as names. Many games maintain their own internal naming for servers, such as you see in Figure 13-4, where at the top we've selected the server called PC Toys UT2003 Server; the actual name of the computer hosting the game server was Aries.

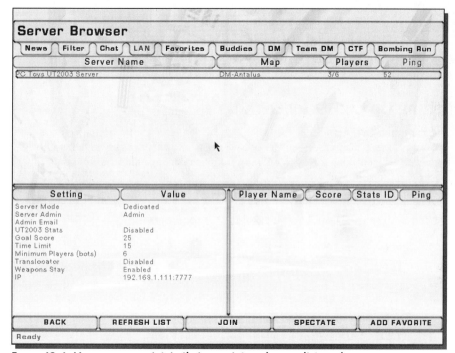

FIGURE 13-4: Many games maintain their own internal server lists and names.

If you have a LAN connected to the Internet, you may already have a DCHP server. This is likely to be true if you've connected your LAN to the Internet through a hardware router, such as those in Table 13-1, because nearly every hardware router on the market implements Network Address Translation (NAT) to support multiple PCs on your LAN using only a single TCP/IP address from your Internet Service Provider (ISP). If your hardware router is running NAT, it's providing a DHCP server unless you've changed the standard configuration. You can tell if your router is running NAT by checking the TCP/IP address on one of your computers (run ipconfig at a command line on a Windows 2000 or Windows XP box; run winipcfg on a Win9x box). If the displayed address fits one of the three private network address schemes in Table 13-3, you're running NAT. If not, you likely have live, routable Internet addresses (and all the security problems that come with them).

Table 13-3   Private TCP/IP Network Addresses

Subnet Address	Subnet Mask	First Node Address	Last Node Address	Number of Usable Addresses
10.0.0.0	255.0.0.0	10.0.0.1	10.255.255.254	16,777,214
172.16.0.0	255.240.0.0	172.16.0.1	172.31.255.254	1,048,574
192.168.0.0	255.255.255.0	192.168.0.1	192.168.255.254	65,534

If you do have routable Internet addresses, setting up your LAN for your guests is more complex than we have space to cover in this book, but probably whoever set up the LAN in the first place will know what to do.

Setting Up Clients for DHCP

If you're running NAT and therefore DHCP, setting up your guests' computers should be no more complicated than making sure they have a network interface card installed and TCP/IP loaded, and then making sure TCP/IP is set up to get network addresses automatically. The process is a little different for each Windows system (Windows 9X, Windows 2000, and Windows XP).

Setting Automatic Network Addressing: Windows 9X

1. Right click on Network Neighborhood, then left click on Properties. (Or, open the Control Panel and run System)

2. Select TCP/IP from the list of installed network components. If there are multiple lines for TCP/IP, pick the one that also names the network hardware interface you're using.

3. Click on Properties, then on the IP Address tab. If *Obtain an IP address automatically* is selected you're done and can cancel all the way out; otherwise, select that setting and then OK your way out. You may need the Windows 9X CD so the system can load some files. (We often keep a copy of the CD on disk for just this reason; later versions of Windows do that themselves.)

4. Reboot while connected to the LAN, then check the assigned TCP/IP address using `winipcfg`.

Your best approach for setting the SSID and WEP parameters for a 802.11b wireless access interface is to use the utility software provided with the interface. Using a Cisco 240 Series PCMCIA card, for example, we found we could set the SSID using dialogs standard in Windows 98, but not the WEP key.

Setting Automatic Network Addressing: Windows 2000

1. Open the Control Panel, then Network and Dial-up Connections. Right click on the correct network connection (likely Local Area Connection), then left click on Properties.

2. Select TCP/IP from the list of installed network components. If there are multiple lines for TCP/IP, pick the one that also names the network hardware interface you're using.

3. Click on Properties. You'll have a General tab; in there, check that *Obtain an IP address automatically* is selected. If so, then as with Windows 9X you're done and can cancel all the way out; otherwise, select that setting and then OK your way out. You'll probably also want to select *Obtain a DNS server automatically*.

4. You may have to reboot if the PC wasn't connected to the LAN when you booted it.

The same steps apply to both Windows XP Home and Professional.

Setting Automatic Network Addressing: Windows XP

1. Open the Control Panel, then select Network and Internet Connections. Select Network Connections, then right-click on the correct network connection (likely Local Area Connection), then left-click on Properties.

2. Select TCP/IP from the list of installed network components. If there are multiple lines for TCP/IP, pick the one that also names the network hardware interface you're using.

3. Click on Properties. Select the General tab and then make sure that *Obtain an IP address automatically* is selected. If so, then you're done and can cancel all the way out; otherwise, select that setting and then OK your way out. You'll probably also want to select *Obtain a DNS server automatically*.

4. You may have to reboot if the PC wasn't connected to the LAN when you booted it.

Most of the hardware routers we've seen let you provide addresses for 32 or more computers, so you shouldn't run out unless you're having a *really* big party. If your DHCP server permits, you'll want to assign fixed addresses to the game servers so that they can't move around at inconvenient times. Some hardware routers reserve a range of addresses (e.g., 192.168.0.1 through 192.168.0.99) for fixed server assignments, starting the automatic allocations above the reserved range. Others let you control the allocated range, which lets you create the same effect.

If your guests will be connecting to your existing LAN, you should think about what your existing security setup is and whether or not it provides the level of security you want. Suppose, for example, that you run your network behind a hardware router, protected from the Internet by the NAT layer. Under those circumstances, it would be reasonable to choose to share all the disks on all the computers, with no user names or passwords required. When your guests connect to the LAN, all those shares will be wide open to them; it's up to you whether you want copies of your checkbook, tax returns, and other personal information available to your guests. If not, a simple approach is to turn off all the shares until after the party's over.

Using a Spare PC as a DHCP Server

Microsoft built a component called *Internet Connection Sharing* (ICS) into Windows starting with Windows 98, and has maintained it in Windows 2000 and Windows XP. ICS running on a PC does much what a hardware router does—as in the figure, it runs NAT to interface a private network to a modem connected to the Internet. You'd typically run ICS on a PC with a telephone modem, but it's equally capable of tying to the Internet through a cable or DSL modem.

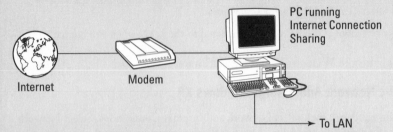

Internet Connection Sharing usually connects a LAN to the Internet through a modem.

Part of what ICS provides to the private LAN is a DHCP server. The DHCP server hands out addresses to other PCs on the LAN, and does so whether or not the Internet connection is alive. Nor does it take much horsepower in the PC running ICS to keep things going, so it's a good application for an old PC you'd rather not use for anything else.

If you set up a PC with ICS, you have a DHCP server all ready to go for your next LAN party— no hardware router required.

Setting Up Game Servers

If your plan is simply for people to play as they choose, with no one tracking wins and losses, you're done. People are hooked up to the network, and can start games and play as they like.

If your plan is more structured, with matches and perhaps a tournament, you'll want to set up dedicated game servers—machines on which no one plays—to ensure that everyone plays the same games with the same options. Game servers don't need anywhere near as much horsepower as do clients, since they're not doing the graphics computations. Unfortunately, you can easily run only one Unreal Tournament 2003 server under Windows on a single computer (it's possible to run more, but you have to be able to assign multiple TCP/IP addresses to the computer). Newsgroup posts we found on the Internet suggest that a Pentium III at 450 MHz or better, and with 256MB or more, should work well. We found those posts at www. unrealadmin.org, a good source of information on running Unreal Tournament 2003 servers.

Setting Up for Internet Access to Your Unreal Tournament 2003 Server

You'll need to do several things to make your Unreal Tournament 2003 server behind your hardware router accessible from the Internet:

- Run a dedicated Unreal Tournament server.

- Your server should have a static IP address, and the client computers may require one.

- Configure your hardware router to forward ports 7777, 7778, 7779, 7780, 7781, and 27900 to the game server, plus port 8080 for Web administration access.

- In the [UWeb.WebServer] section of the server.ini file, set the ListenPort to 8080 (to match the port above), and set ServerName to the IP assigned to the router (not the server itself) from your ISP.

Alternatively, you could just acquire another TCP/IP address from your ISP and put the Unreal Tournament 2003 server at that address and not behind the hardware router.

Unlike early multiplayer game servers, games now often include a graphical interface that lets you control the more commonly used settings. In Unreal Tournament 2003, for example, you can control the type of game (deathmatch, capture the flag, and others), the maps you'll play on, the game rules (such as whether weapons stay around for pickup versus disappear when picked up), modifications (such as low gravity), and server characteristics.

The server characteristics are on a single screen (see Figure 13-5), although you can alter other characteristics once the server starts running and you have a command line available.

The specific settings you'll want are as follows:

- **Dedicated Server.** A dedicated server is a computer on which no one is also playing the game. A player on the same computer as the server has a significant advantage, one you can eliminate by using dedicated servers.

- **LAN Game.** The game code exploits the higher bandwidth available on a LAN (versus over the Internet) to improve operations. Turn this setting on.

- **Advertise Server.** Unreal Tournament 2003 master servers on the Internet maintain lists of servers available for you to join (see Figure 13-6). If you start a server and leave the Advertise Server setting checked, your server will be among those listed by the master servers. That's probably not what you want unless you have remote guests or simply want more people playing. Moreover, you'll have to make some changes in your hardware router to make access possible from outside your LAN (see the sidebar "Setting Up for Internet Access to Your Unreal Tournament 2003 Server").

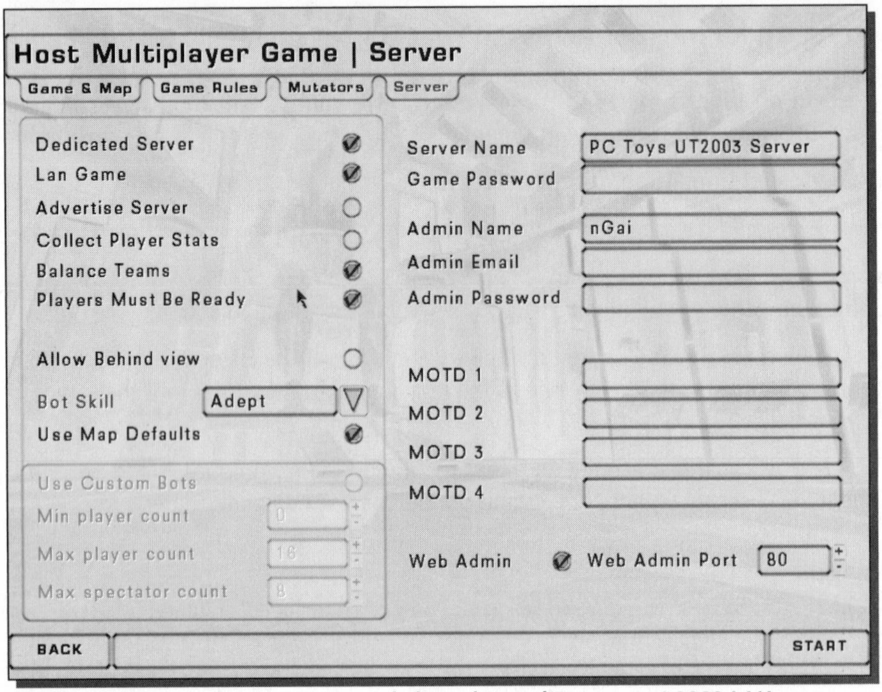

Host Multiplayer Game | Server

Game & Map | Game Rules | Mutators | Server

Dedicated Server ✓	Server Name [PC Toys UT2003 Server]
Lan Game ✓	Game Password [ ]
Advertise Server ○	
Collect Player Stats ○	Admin Name [nGai]
Balance Teams ✓	Admin Email [ ]
Players Must Be Ready ✓	Admin Password [ ]
Allow Behind view ○	MOTD 1 [ ]
Bot Skill [Adept ▽]	MOTD 2 [ ]
Use Map Defaults ✓	MOTD 3 [ ]
Use Custom Bots ○	MOTD 4 [ ]
Min player count [0]	
Max player count [16]	Web Admin ✓ Web Admin Port [80]
Max spectator count [8]	

BACK   START

FIGURE 13-5: This server setup creates a dedicated Unreal Tournament 2003 LAN server.

- **Balance Teams.** If you're playing a team game, such as team deathmatch, capture the flag, or bombing run, this setting causes the server to automatically assign players to teams to keep the number of players on each team approximately equal.

- **Players Must Be Ready.** If the game starts before everyone has joined the server and signaled they're ready to play, the early players on the server have an advantage because they can start acquiring weapons and move away from the initial positions. Enabling this setting eliminates that advantage by ensuring that the game won't start until all players say they're ready.

Collect player statistics if you want, or leave it off. If you enable Web server administration, you should consider using a password to prevent changes to the game play.

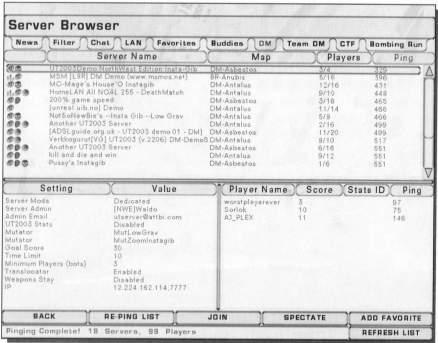

Server Browser

| News | Filter | Chat | LAN | Favorites | Buddies | DM | Team DM | CTF | Bombing Run |

Server Name	Map	Players	Ping
UT2003Demo:NorthWest Edition:Insta-Gib	DM-Asbestos	3/4	329
MSM [L8R] DM Demo (www.msmcs.net)	BR-Anubis	5/16	396
MC-Mage's House'O Instagib	DM-Antalus	12/16	431
HomeLAN All NCAL 255 - DeathMatch	DM-Antalus	9/10	448
200% game speed	DM-Asbestos	3/16	465
[unreal.uib.no] Demo	DM-Antalus	11/14	466
NotSoNewBie's --Insta Gib --Low Grav	DM-Antalus	5/8	466
Another UT2003 Server	DM-Antalus	2/16	499
[ADSLguide.org.uk - UT2003 demo 01 - DM]	DM-Asbestos	11/20	499
Verkkogurut[VG] UT2003 (v.2206) DM-DemoS	DM-Antalus	8/10	517
Another UT2003 Server	DM-Asbestos	6/16	551
kill and die and win	DM-Antalus	9/12	551
Pussy's Instagib	DM-Asbestos	1/6	551

Setting	Value		Player Name	Score	Stats ID	Ping
Server Mode	Dedicated		worstplayerever	3		97
Server Admin	[NWE]Waldo		Sorlok	10		75
Admin Email	utserver@attbi.com		AJ_PLEX	11		146
UT2003 Stats	Disabled					
Mutator	MutLowGrav					
Mutator	MutZoomInstagib					
Goal Score	30					
Time Limit	10					
Minimum Players (bots)	3					
Translocator	Enabled					
Weapons Stay	Disabled					
IP	12.224.162.114:7777					

| BACK | RE-PING LIST | JOIN | SPECTATE | ADD FAVORITE |

Pinging Complete! 19 Servers, 99 Players | REFRESH LIST |

FIGURE 13-6: A server listing on the Unreal Tournament 2003 Master Servers

Food

You can't have a party without food. Here are a couple of suggestions.

Hot Chicken Wings

Measurement	Ingredient
1 jar	Hooter's Three Mile Island Wing Sauce
6 lbs	Chicken wings (about 100)
	Bernstein's Chunky Blue Cheese Dressing (serve to dip the wings in)
	Carrots (so you can pretend you eat a balanced diet)

Continued

Continued

The day before the party, put the wings in a large plastic bag. It's okay if they're still frozen. Pour in the wing sauce and remove all the air from the bag. Let it sit overnight in the refrigerator. Preheat oven to 325 degrees. Pull the wings apart if any of them are still frozen together. Use a cookie sheet with a one-half inch lip all around (to catch the chicken fat—otherwise, use a large pan underneath it), and spray it with non-stick spray. Bake chicken at 325 degrees for 45 minutes to an hour, depending on how crunchy you like your wings. Serves 20 unless they're hungry, in which case it might only serve 10.

Chocolate Chip Cookies

Measurement	Ingredient
12 TBS	soft butter
1 cup	packed light brown sugar
1/2 cup	white sugar
2	eggs
2 tsp	vanilla
3 cups	flour
1 tsp	baking soda
1/2 tsp	salt
1 cup	walnuts
2 packages	semi-sweet chocolate chunks

Begin at least an hour and a half before you want to serve the cookies. Heat oven to 350 degrees. Mix butter, brown sugar, white sugar, vanilla, and eggs in food processor bowl until light and creamy colored. Add flour, baking soda, and salt. Blend until the dry ingredients are mixed in. Move dough to a large bowl; then add walnuts and one package of whole chocolate chunks. Run the second package of chocolate chunks through the food processor until tiny chunks remain. Stir into dough. Using a rounded soup spoon, drop dough in small balls onto ungreased cookie sheets. Bake 8–10 minutes until just golden around the edges. Let sit on cookie sheet for a few minutes then move to wire rack or waxed paper to cool. (Cookies are best when chilled overnight in the refrigerator. Chocolate chunks should solidify before serving, or they are very messy). This makes 44–50 cookies. These cookies can be frozen for months with no loss of flavor and can be shipped (freeze them first).

Summary

Throwing a great LAN party is a matter of preparation. Have your network and the food prepared, and the frenzy should start quickly and run without interruption. Louse up the network and it could quickly turn into a different kind of shouting match. (Try this! No, try that!) Louse up the food and we won't come. And don't forget the Guinness.

Set Up a Computerized Control Center for Model Trains

The press, the machine, the railway, the telegraph are premises whose thousand-year conclusion no one has yet dared to draw.

~Friedrich Nietzsche, *The Wanderer and His Shadow*

Railroads have an inexplicable fascination for children that, for many, extends well into later life. Be it memory of the size, the sounds, the feeling of power, or some other factor, the ability to recreate those childhood memories in a model railroad can be the source of countless hours of enjoyment.

In the End, John Henry Loses Every Time

Traditions notwithstanding, the history of model railroading is a march of advancing technology. From wooden models through wind-up toys and electric motors, from push toys through rheostats and computer control, technology lets model railroads do more things more realistically, opening up opportunities for the craftsman and imagination for anyone.

Until recently, complexity was unavoidable if you wanted to run layouts with multiple trains. The track layout in Figure 14-1 shows the problem. The largest loop, the one dominating the left of the layout and enclosing the two loops on the right, is large enough to contain two trains. If you simply connected a single power source to the loop track, every train on the track will respond to the voltage present—there's no direct way to make one train move while another stays put.

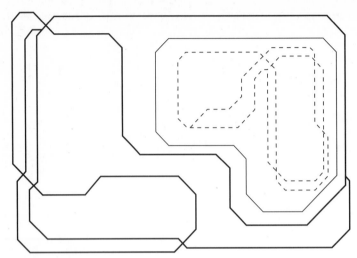

FIGURE **14-1**: Multiple-loop track layout

The indirect answer to the problem, one used by model railroaders for decades, is to divide the loop into *blocks*—each of which you power independently. Figure 14-2 shows a simple layout divided into four blocks, along with the power sources required for each block (the points at which the blocks divide the loop are arbitrary). Because the blocks are electrically isolated, the power you send to one loop has no effect on trains in the other three loops. As long as you have only one train in a block, you can control all the trains independently.

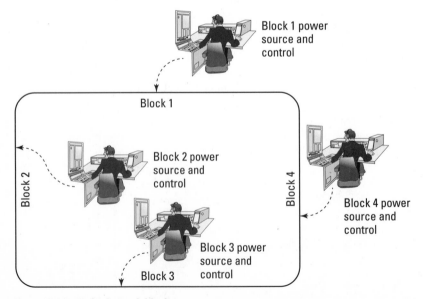

FIGURE **14-2**: Multiple track blocks

Keeping trains running realistically on a layout divided into blocks requires that you own a lot of power controllers and match the power settings at the block boundaries, remembering which control handle corresponds to which area on the layout. Try to run very many trains — particularly if they're running at different speeds — and you'll be quite busy.

Quiet the Noise and Everything Else Is Easy

Digital Command Control (DCC) fixes all that. Figure 14-3 shows how a conventional model railroad works, using a controller to adjust the voltage applied to the rails.

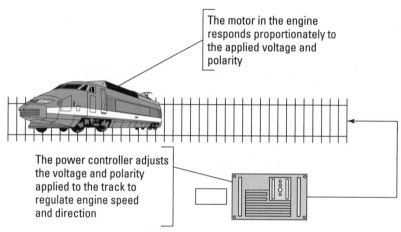

The motor in the engine responds proportionately to the applied voltage and polarity

The power controller adjusts the voltage and polarity applied to the track to regulate engine speed and direction

FIGURE 14-3: Conventional model engine control

DCC changes where the voltage control happens, moving the function to a decoder module inside the engine and using digital signaling from your PC or a handheld controller to send messages to the decoder (see Figure 14-4).

Difficult as packaging the decoder control circuits into a small enough package to fit into an HO locomotive might seem, there's much more to DCC. The motors and sliding contacts on the track generate incredible amounts of noise, enough to cause problems in your computer in addition to malfunctions in the train controls if the noise is not suppressed. The DCC electronics provide that isolation and implement a messaging system over the rails that lets your PC tell individual decoders what you want, even though all decoders simultaneously receive power and all messages from the track.

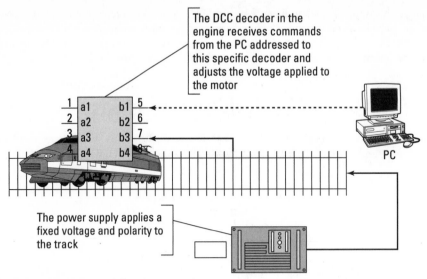

The DCC decoder in the engine receives commands from the PC addressed to this specific decoder and adjusts the voltage applied to the motor

The power supply applies a fixed voltage and polarity to the track

FIGURE 14-4: DCC model engine control

Building and Using Your Train Controls from Kits

A basic PC running a compatible version of Windows is enough to run the train control software, because the PC needs only to send and receive data from the serial port. There are no complex calculations, no large memory requirements, and no burdensome graphics processing. The software we've used in this chapter, Railroad & Co. TrainController, runs on Windows XP, Windows 2000, Windows NT, Windows 98, or Windows 95.

Parts List

We're assuming you already have a model railroad layout in this chapter, but if you're starting from scratch, your best bet is to visit your local hobby shop. You'll find plenty of model railroad starter kits—look for one with durable, reliable track if you go with a kit. You can purchase track and rolling stock separately, so you can get just the locomotive engine and cars you want and track that precisely fits the layout design you want. If you're buying a new locomotive, consider one that already has a DCC decoder installed or that is wired with a connector to make installation a plug-in affair.

Several companies—including Atlas, Digitrax, Lenz, MRC, NCE, and Zimo—build DCC electronics. We've used Digitrax equipment in this chapter because they have a good reputation on the Internet and because they offer a starter kit including everything you need to begin at a reasonable cost. DCC is an open standard from the National Model Railroad Association (NMRA; www.nmra.org), however, so you should be successful mixing equipment from several manufacturers.

A complete DCC setup consists of a command station, a booster and power supply, a throttle, and one or more decoders. The command station generates the messages sent to the engine, the booster converts the low-power signals from the command station to high-power signals on the track, the power supply provides clean, regulated power to the entire suite, and the decoders interface the engine motor to the track and messages. Table 14-1 lists the parts you'll need to supply those functions, and to interface the command station to your PC:

Table 14-1   Train Control Parts List

Part	Manufacturer and Model Number
Zephyr Starter Set	Digitrax ($199.99) www.digitrax.com/zephyr.htm
RS232 PC Interface	Digitrax MS100 ($45) www.digitrax.com/computer.htm
HO Scale Decoder(s)	Digitrax DH163D ($29.99 each, one per locomotive) www.digitrax.com/mobdec.htm#dh163D
Operating Software	Railroad & Co. TrainController ($219) Railroad & Co. TrainProgrammer ($52) www.railroadandco.com Free demonstration versions of both programs are available on the Web site

This decoder is for wiring into nonDCC engines. The Digitrax catalog (www.digitrax.com/dtprod.htm) includes decoders for a variety of engine manufacturers, including Athearn, Atlas, E-R Models, Kato, Life Like, and Lionel.

The Digitrax Zephyr Starter Set includes the DCS50 combined Command Station and Booster, the PS315 Power Supply, manuals, cables, and a decoder tester. Figure 14-5 shows the DCS50 and its key parts. The throttle controls how fast the locomotive runs, while the direction control lever controls whether the locomotive goes forward, reverses, or brakes. The keypad includes function and numeric buttons, letting you pick the operating mode of the controller and directly input addresses and other values. The track status indicator tells you if power is being applied to the track, while the LED display reads out status and address data.

The DCS50 is rated for up to 2.5 amps output to the track, which should be enough for two recent vintage locomotives (older motors may draw more current, causing more than one locomotive to overload the DCS50).

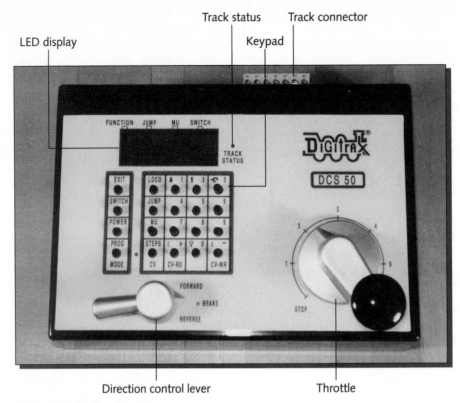

FIGURE 14-5: Digitrax DCS50

Digitrax®, Zephyr®, Jump®, and LocoNet are registered trademarks of Digitrax, Inc.

How Much Current Does Your Locomotive Draw?

You need to know how much current your locomotive engine draws, both under normal operating conditions and when stalled (powered but not turning). If you put an ammeter in series with the power to the track and run the engine at various speeds, you'll measure the normal operating current. If you stop the wheels, perhaps by holding the motor shaft after disassembling the engine, you'll measure the stall current.

This test is easiest to do with an analog power pack before you convert the engine to DCC. Double-check the power pack output voltage under stall conditions to be sure the voltage remains at 12 volts (16 volts if you're running G scale trains) or you won't have an accurate measurement.

Installing the Decoder

If you already have one or more locomotives, you'll need to install a DCC decoder. The Digitrax DH163D decoder in the parts list comes with a wiring harness you use to splice into engines not already wired for DCC.

We installed the DH163D into a Walthers model EMD F40PH locomotive. Disassemble this locomotive by removing the front and rear couplers, then removing a screw on the bottom in each of the four corners. Figure 14-6 shows the locomotive after removing the screws and gently lifting off the top cover. Don't lift the cover off very far until you identify any wires leading to lamps in the cover. The lamps in this model are secured by clips, and come free from the clips to permit the cover to be removed completely.

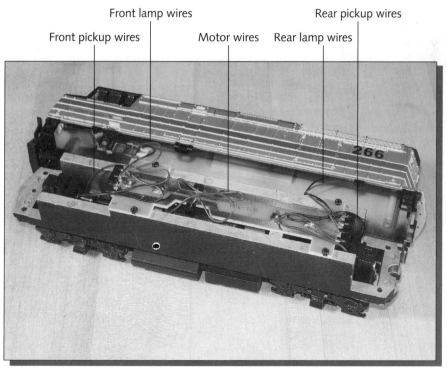

FIGURE 14-6: Disassembled locomotive

The printed circuit board you see in the middle of the metal engine frame in Figure 14-6 connects all the wiring inside the locomotive. Figure 14-7 is a schematic of the wiring. Power pickups on the front and rear wheel trucks connect directly to the motor and through diodes to the front and rear lamps. The diodes pass current in only one direction, so that only one lamp lights at a time, and are oriented so that the lamp pointing in the direction of travel is on.

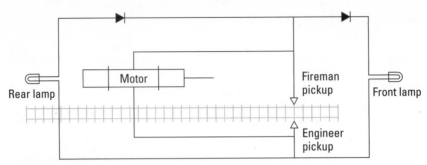

FIGURE 14-7: Locomotive schematic

It's important to understand the complete schematic inside the engine and your modifications before you start any wiring. You need to make sure the motor is isolated from the metal frame, too, or the decoder will short out and may be damaged. The Walthers engine already has the motor isolated from the frame, but that's not the case in all locomotives.

Once you understand the wiring in your locomotive, find a place for the decoder (see Figure 14-8). The decoder is a little under an inch and a quarter long and about three quarters of an inch wide, so there's lots of room in the Walthers locomotive. Other locomotive designs may require some creative placement.

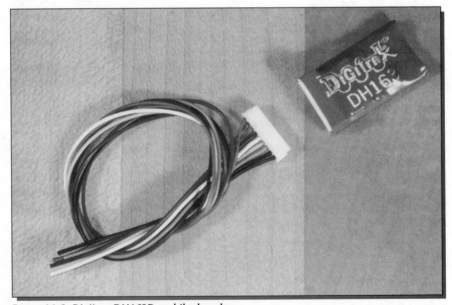

FIGURE 14-8: Digitrax DH163D mobile decoder

Digitrax®, Zephyr®, Jump®, and LocoNet are registered trademarks of Digitrax, Inc.

Table 14-2 lists the wires you'll find in the harness shipped with the decoder, in order from one side to the other. The decoder receives power and message traffic on the black and red leads. The gray and orange leads connect to the motor, while the white and yellow leads (using the blue wire for the common) drive the front and rear lamps, respectively. You can control other lights with the violet and green wires (the blue is the common for those, too), and if you need even more lighting controls, the directions from Digitrax show how to cut back the plastic cover on the decoder to reveal the F3 and F4 terminals.

Table 14-2   Digitrax DH163D Harness Color Codes

Wire Color	Function	Input	Output
Violet	F2		√
Black	Left side (Fireman's side) power pickup	√	
Gray	Motor negative		√
Yellow	F0 Reverse — rear light		√
White	F0 Forward — front light		√
Blue	Light common		√
Orange	Motor positive		√
Red	Right side (Engineer's side) power pickup	√	
Green	F1		√

It's important to identify which motor wire is the positive and which is the negative. The Walthers wiring coded the positive wire with red insulation; we verified that by setting the engine to run forward and checking polarity at the motor wires with a voltmeter.

Figure 14-9 shows the Walthers schematic after modification to insert the Digitrax decoder. The diodes are no longer used, because the decoder itself determines which lamp should be lit, and because if you left them in the circuit you'd interfere with the transponder function built into the decoder that (with the appropriate detectors) lets your PC know where the trains are on your layout.

Figure 14-10 is a close up of the printed wiring board. The two wide horizontal copper rails at the top and bottom connect to the power pickups at either end of the board and to the motor in the middle of the narrowing in the board. The shock and vibration that the locomotive is subject to led us to want to anchor the power pickup connections and the decoder connections to those circuits soundly, so we decided to detach the motor wires from the printed wiring board and use the horizontal rails as the connection points for the decoder. We cut away small gaps in the copper foil with a Dremel Moto Tool to disconnect the lamps from the diodes and used the foil to solder down the lamp control wires from the decoder.

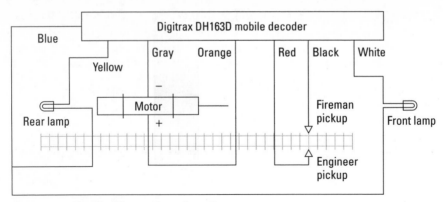

FIGURE 14-9: Modified locomotive schematic

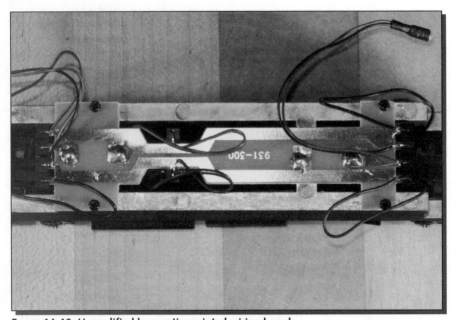

FIGURE 14-10: Unmodified locomotive printed wiring board

Finally, we spliced the wires from the motor and the common wires from the lamps to the corresponding wires from the decoder, and wrapped the connections with electrical tape to insulate them. Heat-shrink tubing would be even better, if you have it. We secured the decoder to the printed wiring board with a tiny cable tie, anchoring it as far from the motor as possible to reduce its exposure to heat. Figure 14-11 shows the completed installation.

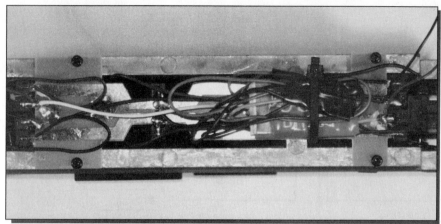

Figure **14-11: Modified locomotive printed wiring board with decoder installed**

Testing and Programming the Decoder

Once you've installed the decoder, it's time to test it. You can use a test track, wired according to the diagram in Figure 14-12. You connect the power transformer to the AC input on the DCS 50, and connect the Rail A and Rail B outputs from the DCS50 to the track. If you're using your PC in the initial testing, you connect it to either of the LocoNet ports on the DCS50 using the MS100 cable between the DCS50 and a serial port on the PC. (LocoNet is Digitrak's control bus to interconnect throttles, command stations, and boosters.) We set up our test track as the smallest oval we could make to avoid having to worry about the engine running off the end.

The DH163D decoder has short circuit protection built in to guard against a short between the motor and the locomotive frame. Place the engine on the track and turn on power. If the lights on the engine start to flash, shut down the power (or lift off the engine) immediately, because you haven't isolated the motor from the frame. Fix the problem and retest.

Every decoder has an address it uses to distinguish messages it should handle from ones destined for other decoders. The default address for all locomotive decoders is3, so if you set the DCS50 to talk to address 3, it will connect to your locomotive. Set the DCS50 to address 3 by pushing LOCO, 03, and LOCO again (see Figure 14-13).

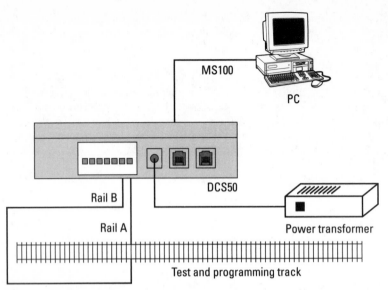

FIGURE 14-12: Test track wiring diagram

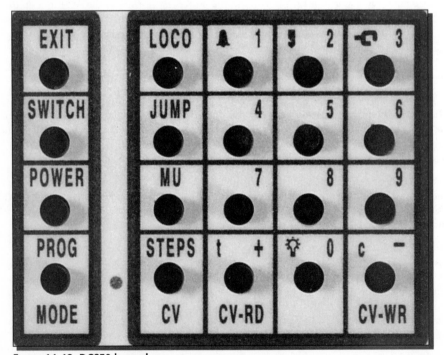

FIGURE 14-13: DCS50 keypad

Digitrax®, Zephyr®, Jump®, and LocoNet are registered trademarks of Digitrax, Inc.

Put the locomotive on the track, set the direction control level to forward, and advance the throttle at least half way. The engine should move forward. If not, try these troubleshooting steps:

1. Verify that there's power to the track. We measured over 13 VAC (not DC!) with the Track Status lamp on, and zero with it off. Another quick way to see if the track is properly connected is to apply power to the track and then use a quarter to short the rails. The Track Status lamp on the DCS50 should start to blink, and a rotating pattern should show up in the LED display. If not, the DCS50 isn't properly connected to the rails.

2. Make sure the DCS50 is addressing unit 3. You should see 3 in the LED display. Redo the LOCO / 03 / LOCO sequence if it's not.

3. Check that the decoder is really programmed to address 3. You'll need a *programming track* for this, which for now means you simply move the test track power connections from Rail A and Rail B to Prog A and Prog B on the back of the DCS50. Press PROG on the DCS50 until PAGE is displayed, then press CV (bottom left of the numeric grid); P001 should be displayed. Press CV-RD and d003 should be displayed. If the last display is something else, the decoder isn't set to address 3, and the display is the actual decoder address. Assuming you don't want to change the decoder programming, use a LOCO / *address* / LOCO button sequence to direct the DCS50 to the right address.

Be sure to reconnect the track to Rail A and Rail B before you go on.

There's starting to be a lot of literature on DCC, including more details on troubleshooting DCC problems. We suggest two titles, both of which have many good photos along with the text:

- *The Digitrax Big Book of DCC*, Digitrax, 1999. At 175 pages, if something you'd want to know is not here, either it's specific to some other manufacturer or you'll be looking in the NMRA specifications for the precise details.

- *DCC Made Easy* by Lionel Strang, Kalmbach Publishing, 2003. This is far smaller than the Digitrax book, but it covers many of the essential ideas.

Digitrax has several troubleshooting pages online, including ones for decoders (www. digitrax.com/troubleshootdec.htm) and for command stations and boosters (www.digitrax.com/troubleshootcs.htm).

Once you have the decoder running the motor, test the other functions. You can turn the front and rear lamps on and off with the 0 (zero) key on the keypad, which also has a lamp symbol to remind you of its function. The decoder installation above by default sets up the front and rear lights to follow the direction of the engine, so once you've turned on the lights, which lights are on is determined by the setting of the direction control lever. DCC is noticeably different from conventional DC operation here, in that the lamps are on at full brightness with the locomotive stopped, something that's impossible with DC control.

The DCS50, and most other DCC controllers, remembers the track status when you shut down power to the track, so you'll want to stop all the locomotives first and avoid surprises later.

Configuration Variables and Decoder Programming

DCC decoders contain microcontrollers running fixed programs to interpret and act upon received messages. You can customize the operation of the programs in those microcontrollers in a surprising number of ways by changing the values stored in what DCC calls *configuration variables* (CVs). For example, the address that the decoder responds to is kept in a CV; change the contents of the CV, and you change the address of the locomotive.

The NMRA specifies what CVs must be implemented and what they're supposed to do (www.tttrains.com/nmradcc/rp922.html) to ensure interoperability between different manufacturers' DCC equipment. Manufacturers implement different optional features in different model decoders, so you'll also want to look at their individual CV documentation. Table 14-3 lists Web links for many of the common DCC decoder manufacturers.

Table 14-3   Decoder CV Reference Pages

Manufacturer	Reference Page
Atlas	www.atlasrr.com/dcc/Atlas_Decoder_Manual.pdf
Digitrax	www.digitrax.com/decodeindex.htm (Details for the DH163D are at www.digitrax.com/dh163d.htm)
Lenz	www.lenz.com/products/decoders/currentdecoders/emfcv-v54.htm
NCE	www.ncedcc.com/catalog1.html (the manuals have the tables for each decoder)
Zimo	www.zimo.at/MX61E.PDF

You can program the CVs in your decoder directly through the DCS50 or with your PC using the MS100 cable and programming software. You're better off using a programming track connected to Prog A and Prog B on the DCS50 with either approach, because a programming track is more likely to be interoperable with different equipment and software, and because the CVs of decoders on the Rail A and Rail B main line track can't be read, just written. You can program decoders on the programming track at the same time that trains run on the main line, but you can't run trains on the programming track.

Follow these steps to program all CVs except addresses using the DCS50:

1. *Enter programming mode.* Turn on power to the track and push the PROG button until the LED display reads PAGE.

2. *Select the CV to program.* Press CV (just to the right of the PROG key). The display indicates the number of the last CV accessed by the DCS50. Key in the number of the CV you want; then press CV-RD. The display will change to show the value of the CV stored in the decoder.

3. *Enter the new value using the keypad.* You might want to make sure you understand the value read back before doing this to make sure you're entering the right value into the right CV. Press CV-WR to write the update to the decoder.

4. *Check the value written.* Repeat Step 2 and read back the value to verify the write worked properly.

Repeat Steps 2 through 4 for every CV you want to change.

The process to set the locomotive address is different:

1. *Enter programming mode.* Turn on power to the track and push the PROG button until the LED display reads PAGE.

2. *Pick the addressing mode.* Press the LOCO key repeatedly until Ad2 (for two-digit mode) or Ad4 (for four-digit mode) is displayed.

3. *Read the address.* Press the CV-RD key to read back the address for the mode you chose. Two-digit addresses are displayed with three digits (because the addresses are two hex digits ranging from 1 through 127). Four-digit addresses range from 128 through 9983. Zero is reserved for DC locomotives on your DCC track.

4. *Select the new addressing mode.* Repeat Step 2.

5. *Enter the new address.* Key in the new address, being sure to comply with the addressing ranges in Step 3.

6. *Write to the decoder.* Press the CV-WR key to write the new address value to the decoder. You can repeat Steps 2 and 3 to check the result.

7. *Exit programming mode.* Press the EXIT key to resume normal operation.

The software you need to program the decoder from your PC isn't part of the Zephyr kit or MS100 cable. We used the train programmer from Railroad & Co., but it is sold at additional cost. Free software is becoming available for model railroading, such as the Java Model Railroad Interface (JMRI, at `jmri.sourceforge.net/`), although to run that software you'll have to download the Sun Java run-time environment. The first software from the JMRI is DecoderPro, which lets you program Atlas, Digitrax, Lenz, and NCE equipment, among others.

Figure 14-14 shows the TrainProgrammer in action. We connected it to the programming track with the modified Walthers locomotive on it, then pushed the Read Decoder button (just to the right of the up arrow in the tool bar) to read all the decoder CVs. You can see that the short address is set to 3, the default, and four-digit addressing is not yet enabled. Turn on four-digit addressing, enter the four-digit address (such as 266 for this locomotive, so that the *266* label on the locomotive's body reminds you of the decoder address), and write the CVs back to the decoder. If you turn on profile mode in the software, you can write just the relevant CVs, speeding up the process.

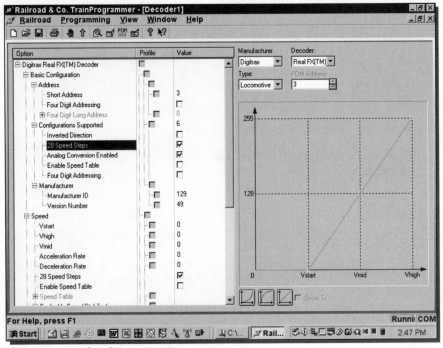

FIGURE **14-14:** Railroad & Co. TrainProgrammer

We had several timeouts while we read the CVs into our PC, but we could always restart the operation from where we'd left off, and eventually we succeeded.

Wiring Your Layout for DCC

The basics of hooking up DCC to your layout are quite straightforward. Your design is driven by the total amount of power consumed by engines and accessories on the track, leading to design decisions about booster size, wire gauge, and power districts.

- **Total power consumption.** A typical stall current for an HO locomotive is under 2 amps, while typical operating current is under 1 amp. Assuming the track voltage is 13 VAC (which leaves a little over 8 percent margin in the calculation), typical locomotives therefore draw 26 watts when stalled and 13 watts when operating.

- **Wire gauge.** Table 14-4 shows the current draw requirements based on number of locomotives, the required power bus wire gauge, and the total watts being consumed assuming no more than 10 percent of the locomotives are stalled at any one time. The table shows no recommended wire gauge for runs over 30 feet at currents over 8 amps because you probably want to re-think your design for situations like that in order to relocate auxiliary boosters near that part of the layout.

Table 14-4   HO Current, Power, and Wire Gauge Requirements

	Current Draw			Wire Gauge			
Number of Locomotives	All Stalled	All Operating	10% Stalled	30'	50'	100'	Total Watts
1	2.0	1.0	1.1	18.0	14.0	12.0	14.3
2	4.0	2.0	2.2	18.0	14.0	12.0	28.6
3	6.0	3.0	3.3	18.0	14.0	12.0	42.9
4	8.0	4.0	4.4	18.0	14.0	12.0	57.2
5	10.0	5.0	5.5	16.0	12.0	12.0	71.5
6	12.0	6.0	6.6	16.0	12.0	12.0	85.8
7	14.0	7.0	7.7	16.0	12.0	12.0	100.1
8	16.0	8.0	8.8	14.0			114.4
9	18.0	9.0	9.9	14.0			128.7
10	20.0	10.0	11.0	14.0			143.0

- **Power districts.** The Digitrax DCS50 is only rated for 30 watts, which by Table 14-4 is sufficient for no more than two locomotives (and no accessories). Boosters are devices that supply power and command packets to isolated sections of track called *power districts.* You cut gaps between sections, then wire the booster to the newly created section and to the LocoNet bus (using the other RJ12, six-wire port on the DCS50, for example). You'll find lots of tips for wiring boosters on the Wiring for DCC site (www.wiringfordcc.com/booster.htm, and more generally www.wiring fordcc.com/wirefordcc_toc.htm).

Figure 14-15 shows an oval split into two power districts. You'd use one booster for each district, the one in the DCS50 and a separate one, to drive the layout. A heavy ground wire between the two boosters helps prevent ground loops, which can cause erratic operation. It doesn't matter whether you call the inner rail A and the outer B, or vice versa, but you do need to be consistent to avoid conflicts when trains cross the gaps.

Being consistent across power districts gets harder when you put switches in your layout that allow trains to reverse direction, such as in Figure 14-16. The problem is that, depending on which way the switches are turned, rails on the middle segment might be connected to Rail A or Rail B, or if you do things wrong, might be connected to both, shorting out the booster.

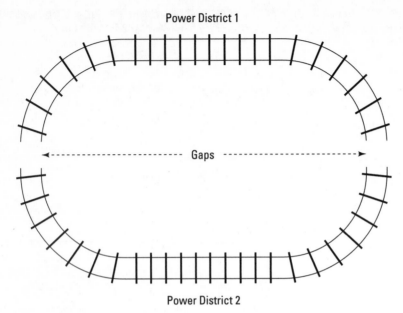

FIGURE **14-15: Power districts**

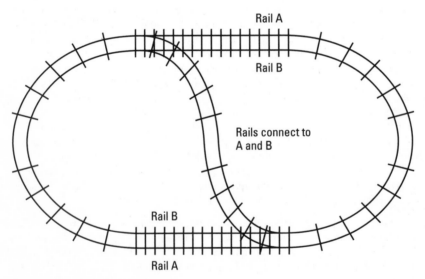

FIGURE **14-16: Switches in a layout**

A combination of gaps and power management solves the problem. Figure 14-17 shows how you can modify the diagram of Figure 14-16 using a Digitrax PM42 Power Management System ($79.95, www.digitrax.com/pm4.htm). Divide the layout into power districts with gaps, then insert the power manager between the booster and the track, configuring two of its four outputs for districts 1 and 2 as short circuit managers, and its third output as an auto-reversing controller for district 3. The gaps prevent changes in the switch positions from creating shorts, while the power manager automatically adapts the power feed to district 3 to match the power fed across a gap by a crossing train.

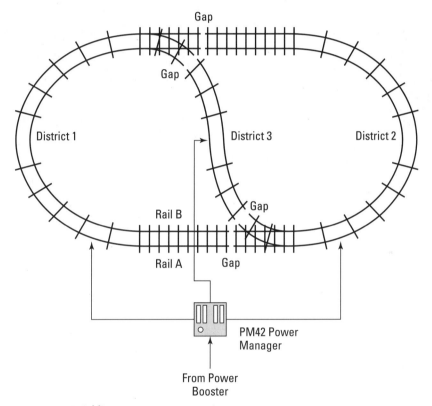

FIGURE 14-17: Adding power management

You need to make some specific settings on the PM42 to work with the lower current capacity of the DCS50. Everything you need to know is on the Digitrax site (www.digitrax.com/pm42_dcs50%20sync.htm).

Operating the Railroad

Once you've handled all the wiring and power management, running your DCC railroad through your PC is simple, because (to use Digitrax's phrase), you run your trains, not the track. Instead of working throttles tied to individual blocks of track, you work throttles tied to the locomotives, no matter where they are on the track. You're the engineer.

The first step in configuring the Railroad & Co. TrainController software is identifying the connected DCC system. Choose Digitrax LocoNet and the serial port you've used for the MS100 cable, with the result as shown in Figure 14-18.

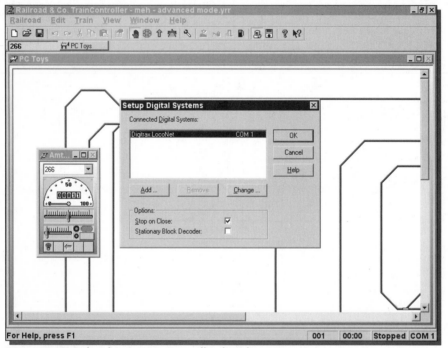

FIGURE 14-18: Railroad & Co. TrainController digital system setup

Figure 14-18 shows two other windows. The larger one in the background is the track layout, useful once you've tied your switches in to DCC and defined their controls into TrainController. The smallest one is an engine control window, in this case for the Walthers 266 locomotive we modified earlier. You set up the engine by creating a new train window, then modifying its properties using the Engine dialog box. The General tab in the Engine dialog box lets you name the engine — that's where we set the name to 266.

You set the key initial parameters in the Connection and Functions tabs, shown in Figures 14-19 and 14-20, respectively. Use the Connection tab (see Figure 14-19) to set the digital system to the Digitrax LocoNet and enter the decoder address. We've set the address to 3, reflecting the default setting of the decoder. You'd set up the transponder built into the DH163D decoder here too if you'd installed detection devices on your layout. Don't forget to enable the transponder's CV if you plan to use it.

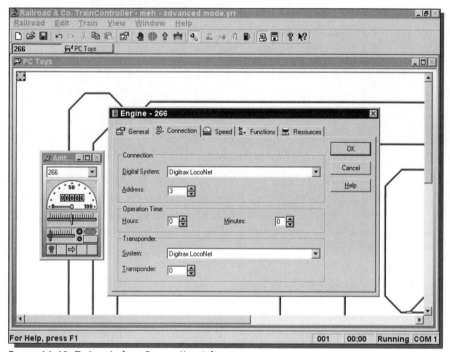

FIGURE 14-19: Train window Connection tab

Set up function F0 (which includes F0F and F0R, the front and rear lamps) in the Functions tab (see Figure 14-20). We chose to define it as an on/off switch so we wouldn't have to hold it down to keep the lights on. Defining the function results in the lamp symbol on the left button of the row of five on the bottom of the train window; pushing the button turns the front/rear lamps on and off.

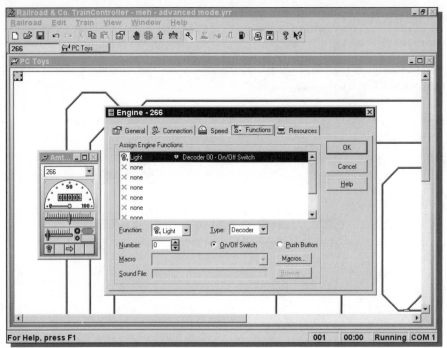

FIGURE **14-20**: Train window Functions tab

When it's hooked up with the TrainController software and MS100 cable, your PC looks like another throttle controller on the LocoNet to the DCS50. You can switch control of any locomotive between the DCS50 and the PC; once you take control of an engine with the PC, the train window controls become usable to control speed, direction, braking, and any functions you've set up. You can control multiple engines from your PC simply by creating a train window for each one.

Building and Using Your Train Controls to Your Own Design

This chapter covers only the basics of DCC, but there's a lot more you can do with the technology. Some of the more interesting applications are ganging multiple engine units together, tracking the position of your trains on the layout, adding your switches and signals to the digital system, and using your old DC power packs as DCC throttles.

Multiple Units

Railroads use the word *consist* as a noun to refer to the number and specific identity of individual units making up a train, and at times use the term to refer to a consist incorporating more than one locomotive to increase the total horsepower (and therefore pulling power). DCC lets you coordinate locomotives into a consist, slaving the operation of the locomotives to the master unit. You define multiple locomotives into a consist by setting CVs in the decoders.

Tracking Position with Transponders

DCC itself doesn't yet define standards for transponders, but Digitrax has embedded transponders into many of its decoders, and offers a variety of transponder detectors. A layout equipped with transponders on the rolling stock and transponder detectors around the track can sense what trains are where on the layout, display position on your PC, use position and train identity to trigger switches and signals, and generate sound effects unique to the specific train.

Converting Signals to DCC

The DH163D decoder in this chapter is a *mobile* decoder, meaning it's intended for installation into a locomotive. You can also get *stationary* decoders, such as the Digitrax DS54 Quad Stationary Decoder, which lets you operate up to four switches of the motor or solenoid type. It also has eight inputs you can use for local switch control, switch position feedback, block occupancy detection, or anything else you can think of. You can also use the CML Electronics DAC10 to control switches and signals (www.cmlelectronics.co.uk/products/dac10.htm), or their DSC8 signal controller (www.cmlelectronics.co.uk/products/dsc8.htm) for advanced signal light operation.

Automated Christmas Trains

At Christmas time, you could wire one of the sensors on a DS54 to an X10 Powerflash module, and then (between HomeSeer and TrainController) start the trains running when someone comes into the room.

Use Your Old DC Throttles with DCC

The ability to control multiple trains on your layout DCC gives you is perfect for sharing operations with friends, but to do that you'll need a throttle for each of your guests. The DCS50 is unique among the DCC controllers in that it provides two *jump ports* that let you reuse your old DC throttles to control DCC trains. Simply wire the DC outputs to Jump 1 or Jump 2 and ground, then use the DCS keypad to assign each jump throttle a DCC address.

Summary

Figure 14-21 shows why you'd want DCC on your railroad — you can do more with your trains, and do it more realistically, after you convert to digital control. You can run multiple trains, coordinate operations between your signals, trains, switches, and throttles, and do it all with simpler wiring. Your PC adds the intelligence to coordinate all the elements of your railroad, adding a level of realism not previously possible.

FIGURE **14-21: On the main line**

Inventing Your Own PC Toys

To invent, you need a good imagination and a pile of junk.

~Thomas A. Edison

The creation of every PC toy in this book followed the same sequence of steps:

1. Have an idea.

2. Structure your approach.

3. Find the parts you need.

4. Build and test the project.

For some, having the idea in the first place is the biggest challenge in creating their own projects. For others, structuring the approach and finding parts is the hard part. This chapter suggests more projects, and approaches to building them, and looks at some of the factors that make them difficult. The projects in this chapter are:

➤ Making a Grandparents' Screen Saver

➤ Using Your Camera as Handy Copier

➤ Setting Up an Automated Watering System

➤ Running Indoor/Outdoor Christmas Decorations

➤ Making Your Own X10 Interfaces

➤ Monitoring Your Telephone Answering Machine and Caller ID

➤ Tracking Cell Phone Minutes Used

➤ Watching for eBay Auctions

Where Do These Ideas Come From?

Our experience is that project ideas are everywhere. Finding them isn't a matter of pounding your head until ideas fall out; it's a matter of thinking about things you experience with a view toward automation. If you look back at the list of projects in this book, or at the ideas in this chapter, you'll see that daily activities can be made more convenient with better information or with automation. There's little in this book you couldn't do by hand; what the PC toys do is make things easier or more fun.

Look at the grandparents' screen saver idea as an example. Most grandparents want photos of their grandchildren in order to watch them growing up; many people feel a sense of guilt at not doing more to give their parents what they want. Printing and mailing photographs isn't something you can do just any time you think of it, however. A combination of digital cameras, PCs, and the Internet can be combined into a solution. Grandma and Grandpa may not be very skilled with a computer, so any approach you invent must be one they can benefit from without hassle and frustration.

The next five sections contain ideas for projects that you can build with your PC. All of them address tasks people do every day; applying PCs, software, and some specialized interfaces make those tasks easier or do them better. Some projects are harder than others, but every one is doable today with products now on the market.

Grandparents' Screen Saver

Some years back Ceiva introduced a Digital Photo Receiver (`www.ceiva.com/public/all_about_ceiva.jsp`), which at $142.49, is an LCD in a picture frame. The unit dials up the Internet nightly and downloads any pictures sent to it through the Ceiva service, which itself costs a little under $10 per month. The picture frame rotates during the day through the images it has loaded. Because it completes the path from digital camera to grandparent, the Digital Photo Receiver is a simple answer to the problem of keeping current photos on hand.

If your child's grandparents have a computer, or if you have an unused one you can install for them, you can build much the same capability. Here are the basic steps:

1. Use your digital camera to take pictures, and download them to your PC.

2. Crop the photos so they look as good as possible, and fix exposure problems with software of your choice. We like Photoshop (or its simpler version, Photoshop Elements). Save the photos compressed as JPEG files, probably with medium level compression (try a JPEG compression index of 5 or 6).

3. Find and set up a screen saver on the grandparents' computer that rotates through an image library. Windows XP has one built in, but there are ones available in the software libraries on the Internet, too (for example, we found a number of them searching for *photo screen saver* on `download.cnet.com`).

4. All that's left is to get the images from your computer to theirs. The Windows task scheduler will let you run programs at specified times, so if you use an FTP client at one end (one comes built into Windows) and an FTP server at the other (we like WFTPD at `www.wftpd.com`) with scripts to drive them both, you can dial up an Internet connection in the middle of the night and move files automatically. Any time the grandparents' computer is on and the screen saver kicks in, they get a slide show of the photo library you've uploaded.

If you're a programmer, you could automate the transfers in a single, integrated program that includes automatic Internet dial-up. Either way, making the operation reliable and automatic is your goal.

Camera as Handy Copier

Have you ever needed a quick copy of a page, but had no copier handy? Or been at the library and needed a few pages for reference, but not had the stack of quarters you needed to feed the copy machine?

No problem. Even if you don't have a digital camera today, a search on www.shopper.com turned up a small (albeit low-resolution) no-name camera for under $50. Carry one around with you and you can take a picture of a printed page any time you need. Download the images to your computer when you're back at home and print them, and your copies are both complete and archived on your computer.

Automated Watering System

How often have you driven past a lawn being watered in a full rainstorm, stepped in a small bog of mud left over from too much watering, or shaken your head in frustration over that one dry spot on the grass you can't keep up with? Doesn't that sound like a PC Toy opportunity?

A trip to the sprinkler department at Home Depot or the like reveals a small wall full of automated sprinkler controllers, which are nothing more than fixed-function microcomputers programmed to turn on relays that activate your sprinkler valves at specified times. You can get sensors to solve the rainstorm problem, but not the wet or dry spots — the duration each valve stays on is fixed unless you remember to go out and adjust the program yourself.

Right. We don't keep up with it either.

Have you ever seen the watering meters in the garden shop, the ones that indicate how wet the soil is? Suppose you hooked up several of the same sort of sensors to your PC along with a bank of relays to control individual sprinkler circuits. Software could monitor the soil moisture levels and control watering times appropriately. You can find an X10 compatible controller at www.wgldesigns.com/rain8.html, but sensors are more of a problem due to cost. The WaterBug sensor (www.smarthome.com/7160.html) is one possibility.

Running Indoor/Outdoor Christmas Decorations

Are you so paranoid about Christmas tree lights left on burning down the house that you rarely turn them on? Your PC can solve the problem with the same X10 technology you saw in Chapter 3. Use a motion sensor to detect when someone's in the room where the tree is, and HomeSeer software to both light up the tree and shut it down when everyone has left the room. If the tree is in a room with lots of walk-through traffic, you could delay the turn on event until motion occurs for at least one minute.

We usually use a heavyweight extension cord with lots of outlets to tie all the lighting strings together, but that doesn't account for the other powered displays — the skaters on a lake, a train, and whatnot. You could build an X10-controlled extension cord to solve that problem, putting a pair of X10-controlled wall outlet devices in a two-gang electrical box to replace the head of a conventional extension cord. Don't forget to secure the cord mechanically where it enters the electrical box to protect against connections getting torn apart.

Outdoor lighting is another Christmas light nuisance, requiring that you either remember to turn the lights on and off yourself or arrange time clocks or other devices to do it for you. We used to use a combination of time clocks and photocell sensors, but we always had the problem that the different light strings went on or off at slightly different times, leaving the house partly lit and partly dark until all the strings switched. Instead of a kludge like that, you could use X10 appliance modules (the lamp modules don't handle enough power, and you don't need the dimming function) and HomeSeer software. HomeSeer running on your PC knows what time sunset occurs and gives you the option to trigger an event a specified number of minutes after sunset. You could wait a while after sunset, say an hour or two, then turn on all the appliance modules, and turn them all off at a specified time.

If those lighting ideas are too tame, consider using your PC to sequence your outdoor Christmas lighting strings in a flashing display. All you need to get started are the X10 controllers, plus some specialized software — Dasher, at www.christmascave.com/software.htm. The X10 technology limits the speed with which you can flash the strings to about one action per second, and if that's not fast enough for what you want to do, look at the animated lighting controllers at www.animatedlighting.com/products/default.asp.

Finally, in the Halloween vein, www.smarthome.com offers some noncomputer-controlled (and questionably tasteful) ideas — www.smarthome.com/hw0276.html was certainly an eye-opener. More reasonable would be to use motion sensors to turn fog machines on and off when people approach, or trigger sound effects and special elements in your lighting.

Running Outdoor/Indoor Lights While You're on Vacation

Home security is a concern for a lot of people. The surveillance system in Chapter 6 can help you find out what happened after the fact, but using lighting for active defense can help fend off break-ins. The old ploy of putting a light on a timer isn't very sophisticated, because there's no variation in what's happening, and not likely to deter anyone with any determination.

One good approach is to write a "script" for X10 home-automation software, such as the HomeSeer software used in this book, creating events at specific times that turn devices on and off. Some events can be set to happen only on specific days, keeping the sequence from looking too consistent from night to night. You can use the scripts to turn the television or stereo on and off, and to turn lights on and off to mimic people entering and leaving rooms, but it's going to be tedious to create that script on your own.

Another approach would be to use the event log that HomeSeer records as a basis for the script. You can write the script by hand, generating the events with the usual HomeSeer dialog boxes based on what's in the log, or if you're a programmer, you can write software to do it for you. That's because the HomeSeer data files use a standard called XML, and include their format definition as the initial part of the file, so it's possible to parse the file without knowing too much about HomeSeer. Commercial products exists to help you get going, such as tools to create C++ code from XML (www.roguewave.com/products/xol/codesamples.cfm) or to support Visual Basic (www.shoutsoft.net/feature.asp?productid=1).

How Do You Figure Out the Approach?

The need for a soil moisture sensor in the automated watering project above, the limited number of choices we found on the Internet, and the relatively high cost of the ones we did find, all combine to the make the project difficult. Finding sensors — the devices that let your PC know what's happening — is often the most difficult part of the approach. You can search for sensors directly through Google, but may also find what you want at www.findasensor.com and www.sensorsportal.com. Don't overlook www.smarthome.com, either.

When all else fails, you (or an electronics-savvy friend) might need to resort to creating your own designs.

Advanced X10 — Making Your Own Interfaces

The automated watering project is a perfect example of why you might want to think about creating your own design:

- You don't really care about the actual soil moisture content, so you don't need a laboratory-grade sensor. You just want to know if the soil is wet or dry at a specific depth.

- You can go to the garden shop and get a small, inexpensive probe you shove into the ground that reports moisture levels on a built-in meter. If you could interface the circuits in that meter to your PC, you'd have as good a sensor as you need.

There's no shortage of ways in which to build sensor interfaces. One interesting method (because it's so versatile) is the Basic Stamp, a dedicated microcomputer with interface circuits that runs the Basic programming language. You can find an overview of the different versions of the Basic Stamp at www.parallax.com/html_pages/resources/start/getting_started_main.asp, and a catalog at www.parallax.com/html_pages/products/basicstamps/basic_stamps.asp. By itself, a Basic Stamp will interface to a PC serial port. Add a two-way X10 interface module such as the X10 model TW523 (www.smarthome.com/1135.html) and you can remote the Basic Stamp over power lines.

The Basic Stamp is overkill for converting a single garden shop soil moisture probe — the probe simply drives a voltage into the meter, so all you really need is a voltage comparator to check when the voltage is above or below a threshold. The NTE1434 voltage comparator (www.nteinc.com/specs/1400to1499/pdf/nte1434.pdf) should do the job, and has the advantages of working from a single voltage source and being able to drive a relay directly. Use a simple voltage regulator (such as a Zener diode) and a small potentiometer to set the reference voltage for the comparator. Add a small reed relay and you can control an X10 Powerflash module to signal that the voltage is above or below threshold. A four-wire cable out to the sensor should be sufficient — two for the supply voltage, derived from a small wall brick DC transformer, and two for the relay tied to the Powerflash.

If you have more than one moisture sensor you want to handle, you need to get fancier. One possibility is the I/O Linc, which can look like up to four Powerflash modules (www.smarthome.com/1624.html). Another is a more complex X10 controller, the Ocelot (www.smarthome.com/73101.html) plus a multi-input expansion module (www.smarthome.com/73111.html); a third is a Basic Stamp remoted with the TW523 interface.

Telephone Answering Machine/Caller ID

Caller ID on your telephone line is a wonderful thing, because while unfortunately it can't reliably tell you when a telemarketer is on the line (why yes, we'd love to invest in stocks or refinance our home with someone who has nothing better to do than make cold calls), it can tell you someone you care about is calling or has called. Caller ID monitoring devices are so cheap there's no reason to bring your PC into the loop just to monitor caller ID, but if your modem has the right capabilities already, a PC opens up other options:

- **Answering machine.** Your PC can serve as both a caller ID monitor and answering machine, and with the right software, could provide Web access to the phone logs and messages.

- **TV display.** A caller ID unit across the room from where everyone watches TV isn't very convenient. If you're using your PC as a personal video recorder (PVR) already (Chapter 1), you could a program to pop up a display window with the caller information.

The software is the trick. We can write our own software, but our approach is nearly always to look for existing software first. We started searching with Google for *"caller id" modem windows software*, and found over 22,000 hits. Top results included the following:

- **ActiveCaller** (www.modem-software.com/ac_callerid_features.htm), a complete call center package. Probably overkill.

- **YAC: Yet Another Caller ID Program** (www.sunflowerhead.com/software/yac). This one looked like a clear winner — it does pop-ups on screen in Windows, can interface with a (hacked) TiVo to display caller ID information through that PVR, and can send caller ID notifications through your home network to a listener on the machine on which you're running the PVR software from Chapter 1. YAC can send text messages to other computers too, meaning you have the opportunity to interface the program to your home automation.

- **AnswerMyPhone** (www.pppindia.com/answer/), which provides caller ID and answering machine functionality.

We haven't evaluated any of these programs; our point is that the right first step in looking for software for your project is to search the Internet. We tend to look broadly, with Google, before we search the specialist software download sites, but if you can find what you need on a download site you'll have the advantage of reviews and comments from previous users.

Track Cell Phone Minutes Used

Going over your minutes limit on your cell phone billing plan can be horribly expensive, and there's not much you can do once it's happened. Many phones let you track minutes but may not differentiate between evening/weekend minutes and daytime minutes with those counters, plus you have to remember to check. Few people we know are that disciplined — cell phones are supposed to make life more convenient, not add another chore to remember.

However, many cellular service providers report current usage on their Web sites. Checking that information is easier than remembering to set up your cell phone every month but is still easy to forget. Clearly, this is another job for your PC. The easiest approach is to use a Windows scheduled task to bring up the cellular provider's site periodically — say once a week — as a reminder for you to log in and check minutes.

You can do even better. Languages like C++ can be hard to learn, but it's not too hard to do straightforward tasks in some common scripting languages. If you wrote a script in ActivePerl (`www.activestate.com/Products/ActivePerl`) you could automatically log into the provider's site, navigate to the page reporting your minutes, extract the value, and append both it and the date to a file. You could then compute how far the date is into the month and, if your usage is more than the fraction of the month elapsed times your monthly minutes, pop up a warning window. You could launch the program to check your usage one of several ways:

- Nightly, using the Windows scheduler, if you leave your computer on and connected to the Internet

- Each time you boot the computer if you prefer to turn your computer off at night and have an always-on Internet connection

- Every time you connect to the Internet if you use dial-up

Watch for eBay Auctions

Bidding at the last second on eBay is a proven way to win a higher proportion of the items you bid on, but only works when you know the auction exists. Spending all your waking hours searching for new listings can be hard on your social life.

Once again, your PC can help, and can do so with the same scripting approach we recommended to track cell phone usage. A Perl script could connect to eBay periodically — say every few hours — and using search terms you've predefined, crawl through the search response listings to find new auctions. If a new auction pops up that's ending soon, the script could email you a link to the page, while a new one that's closing some days off could be listed in a popup you get in the evening.

Summary

Every project in this book starts with an idea for doing something useful. Once you have the idea, you have to figure out three elements:

- The information you need, where to get it, and how to get it into your PC

- The processing and storage you need on your PC, and either where to get software that does what you need, or how to write it yourself

- The results you want and how to create those results in the real world

You're likely to find resources to build all three elements of your project on the Internet, far more likely than in stores near you. Remember that Google is your friend.

Appendix A
Working with
Your PC—
Software

in this appendix

☑ Reliability

☑ Simplicity

☑ Security

☑ Don't get fancy

I want to be alone.

~Greta Garbo in *Grand Hotel*

Important as the ideas in this appendix are—serve you well, they will—nothing we can tell you is as important as this one idea: If you want to keep a computer up all day, don't play with it.

The number one cause of computer crashes is using them, so if you want your computer to stay running, leave it alone. Pick a machine to run your PC Toys, and let that be its only job.

That said, on to the rest of what you need to know.

Basics

We based all the projects in this book on Windows to reach the biggest audience—an enormous number of people know how to work with Windows. Many of the PC Toys operate continuously, however, so your Windows installation needs to be stable and reliable. That's probably a foreign idea to many readers, but in our experience, a stable and reliable installation is achievable. We typically leave some of our Windows computers on all the time and don't reboot them for months on end. This appendix will show you how we do that.

Which Version of Windows

The first decision you need to make is which version of Windows you'll run on your PC Toys computer. From our point of view, you have only three choices—Windows 98, Windows 2000, or Windows XP. Most of the software you'd use to run the PC Toys won't run under Windows 3.1 or earlier, and there's no longer any excuse for running Windows 95, because Windows 98 Second Edition (Win98 SE) is more stable and adds USB support.

Our bias is to run Windows 2000. Windows XP is technically superior to Windows 2000, with some very nice added features, but we choose not to deal with Microsoft's Windows Product Activation (WPA). We properly license each copy of all software we run — intellectual property is what keeps authors fed — but we've seen enough documented cases of WPA failing and shutting down properly licensed machines that we chose not to deal with it.

The choice between Windows XP and Windows 2000 is technically far less significant than between one of them and Windows 98. Windows 98 retains a mixture of 16- and 32-bit code, is far less secure, and uses the older and less robust VxD device driver model, causing inherent stability problems. Windows Me was no better, and on some computers, worse. Windows XP and Windows 2000 are pure 32-bit code, are more secure, and use Windows Driver Model (WDM) device drivers. They are both much more robust and stable than any version of Windows 9X — 95, 98, or Me — can ever be. Unless you *must* run software that operates only under Windows 98, you should use Windows XP or Windows 2000 for your PC Toys.

Most software that runs under Windows 98 will run under Windows XP or Windows 2000. The only limitation that would prevent you from using the newer operating systems would be if you needed a device driver that the manufacturer provided only as a VxD. If your only option is a VxD, you're stuck with Windows 98.

Rebuild from Scratch

Your second decision is the path you'll take to set up your PC Toys computer. You could use an existing, running machine, but we recommend you wipe out the entire disk contents (delete all the existing partitions) and reinstall the operating system from scratch. You'll lose all the old, accumulated software, files, and registry entries in the process, leading to a slimmer, more stable installation.

Be sure to make a complete backup of the old disk image before you wipe it out, because you're sure to need something from it you didn't foresee. The simplest way to ensure you have a backup is to replace the existing disk with a new one. You'll gain more disk space and will know for sure that you have all your old files.

Using an Old Machine

Many people have old, retired computers lying around, enough so that PC recycling has become a growth industry. Only a few of the PC Toys require more than what an old Pentium III will provide, however, so that old PC gives you a way to dedicate a computer to your PC Toys. You can set up the old warhorse, add network and USB cards or memory if needed, install the application software, start it running, and then leave it alone. Strip it clean first, hardware and software, because with all the junk and detritus removed it will be more stable than you'd expect.

Patches and Updates

Patches and updates to Windows are a fact of life. The best source for updates to your running Windows system is Windows Update (`windowsupdate.microsoft.com`). Most of the fixes you'll find here are security fixes categorized as *Critical Updates*. You'll also find corrections to other problems. We install from Windows Update using the following procedure:

Updating a Windows System Using Windows Update

1. *Connect to the Internet.* A broadband connection is best, because you will be downloading tens or hundreds of megabytes of data.

2. *Connect to Windows Update.* The Windows Update site is `windowsupdate.microsoft.com`. You may have to load some software — a security dialog pops up if so. Do so, because Windows Update can't work without it.

3. *Scan for updates.* Click on the Scan for Updates link to request Windows Update to check your system versions against the servers at Microsoft. The scan progresses in three parts: Critical Updates, OS Updates, and Device Driver Updates.

4. *Deselect Critical Updates as required.* All the Critical Updates are selected in Windows Update by default — you must choose to not load the ones you don't want. Some Critical Updates can only be loaded in isolation, not combined with other updates, and some may be for changes you don't want (for example, we refuse to let Microsoft automatically download updates to our machines, so we won't install the components that support that operation). Click Remove for the Critical Updates you don't want. We typically install most of the Critical Updates and all of the Security Updates.

5. *Select OS Updates.* Review the list of OS updates, and select any that are bug fixes or that specifically address capabilities you want. Otherwise, ignore them.

6. *Ignore device driver updates.* Even though (with a few exceptions) we're going to tell you a few paragraphs from now to avoid third-party device drivers if you can in favor of the drivers shipped with Windows, we've found that installing device drivers from Windows Update doesn't always work. When it fails, we've at times been left with inoperable systems.

7. *Review and install updates.* Once you've finished making your choices, tell Windows Update to install the updates. Once the updates finish, you'll get a list of what worked and what you'll have to retry. You may have to reboot to complete the installation.

8. *Do it again.* You can't assume you're done once you've loaded updates — the fixes you load may themselves need further patching. Cycle through Steps 3 through 7 repeatedly until Windows Update indicates that there are no more useful patches to load.

Third-Party Device Drivers Bad; Beer Good

A large fraction of the crashes in Windows systems happen because of defects in device drivers written by companies other than Microsoft. Errors in sample code originally written by Microsoft is the source of some of those defects, but nevertheless third-party device drivers have a spotty record, which is why Microsoft introduced device driver signing in Windows 2000. Device drivers signed by Microsoft offer some assurance that the code has undergone compatibility and stability testing and therefore that it's reasonably safe to install in your system.

Not that we're saying all third-party drivers are junk. For example, we invariably use the "reference drivers" from the nVidia Web site (`www.nvidia.com/content/drivers/drivers.asp`) for any board using nVidia graphics chips, regardless of the actual board manufacturer. Those drivers are typically significantly faster, more fully featured, and as stable as the drivers included with Windows. If you don't have good, solid experience with a specific vendor's drivers, use the ones packaged with Windows if you can. If that's not possible, search the Internet newsgroups (we use Google at `www.google.com/grphp`) for problems people may have had with the hardware you're trying to install, pour a beer, and think about exchanging the product for something else if your search turns up significant problems.

Anti-Virus with Automatic Updates

You're going to want an Internet connection—preferably an always-on broadband connection—for many of the PC Toys. The Internet is a wonderful source of information and capability, but it's also the hands-down winner in the contest for things likely to attack your computer. Attacks can take the form of viruses, Trojans, spyware, and hacks; you need specific defenses against each.

In the case of viruses, there's no excuse for not running good anti-virus software and for not keeping it continuously up to date. We run McAfee's Virus Scan, and configure it to automatically update the virus definition files from the McAfee servers every week (we schedule it to run early every Sunday morning). Scanning files on access is the minimum functionality you want; be sure you've configured the anti-virus software to scan e-mail if you're ignoring our advice and using the machine to read e-mail.

Don't forget that *every* machine on your network needs to run anti-virus software, because an infected machine can spread the infection to files resident on other machines and bypass the anti-virus protection on the other machine. You'd find out about the infection when you accessed the corrupted files on a protected machine, but by then damage has already been done. Don't leave gaps in your defense.

Defrag

Once we've configured the basic software load—Windows, the Windows patches, and anti-virus—we run the Windows disk defragmenter. Disk drives give you much better performance reading long stretches of contiguous data from the disk in a single pass, but Windows can't schedule those high performance reads if the data resides in multiple fragments on the disk. Program loads, covering hundreds of thousands of megabytes of data, are particularly likely to benefit from defragmentation. Your system won't be more stable for having run defrag, but doing the post-install housekeeping should give you the best possible performance.

LANs and the Internet

In case you missed the other 40,000 times we said it, networks make your computers a lot more convenient and useful. You can get at files on other computers from your PC, share printers, and get to the Internet. Follow our suggestions, and your network will be easy to use and reasonably secure from outside attack.

Networking and Sharing

You make your network easy to use by making everything shared (without access restrictions), by making sure the same network shares are mapped to the same drive letters on every machine, and by keeping your data files on a file server. The file server could double up as your PC Toys machine, because you want to leave the file server alone as well—let it serve files, not run applications for someone at the keyboard. You want to leave it alone for the same reason you want to leave your PC Toys computer alone: you want the file server to be stable.

Here's an example of how we've implemented these ideas:

- Our file server, named llamah, sits in the basement. No one uses it, and we literally never reboot it except when the power fails for longer than the uninterruptible power supply can handle. The E drive on llamah holds all the data files we use on any of our computers, and gets backed up periodically.

- Every other computer on our LAN has `\\llamah\e` mapped to drive letter Q, so no matter where you are, your data files are on `Q:\<path>`.

- Every drive on every computer is shared, with full read-write access for every user.

LANs built to this design are horrifically vulnerable to attack, so connecting one of them directly to the Internet would be a disaster. Instead, you should connect through a router.

Security and Firewalls

You have precisely two objectives in securing your LAN connection to the Internet—keep everyone out, and should something get in (such as a virus, Trojan, or spyware), prevent the rogue program from sending anything out. Beyond the anti-virus software we suggested earlier, you need a combination of two elements to achieve that security:

Hardware Router. As you saw in Chapter 13, a hardware router implements Network Address Translation (NAT) and, in the process, prevents external access to your LAN. You can test your network's security at Web sites including Speed Guide (`www.speedguide.net`) and Gibson Research (`www.grc.com`). Unless you've chosen to open ports on the router to direct specific traffic to one of your computers (see the sidebar "Cable/DSL Router Security and TrackerCam" in Chapter 6), the tests on those Web sites should show no response on any of the common Internet ports. We use a Linksys wireless router, but any of the ones listed in Chapter 13 should do.

Firewall. The hardware routers available at consumer prices aren't sophisticated enough to trap unauthorized outgoing traffic (which might occur if you've fallen victim to spyware), but firewall software on each PC can. Zone Alarm, which is free and well designed, is a product of Zone Labs. You can download it from `download.com.com/3000-2092-10196007.html`. Any time a program you haven't already approved tries to open a connection from your PC to the Internet, Zone Alarm pops up and asks if you want to block the connection. It's a little tedious until you get your standard programs set up, but runs reliably after that.

Set Up E-mail and Web Servers

Some of the PC Toys in this book, such as those using the HomeSeer or TrackerCam surveillance software, can alert you to conditions through e-mail. HomeSeer can be controlled by e-mail, too. We've found that these capabilities are a lot easier to use if you create a separate e-mail account specifically for the PC Toys instead of trying to share your existing e-mail accounts. Using a separate account for the PC Toys avoids the problem of multiple e-mail reader programs accessing one account. Many ISPs now provide multiple e-mail accounts with your subscription, so you might not incur any additional monthly costs.

You might want to set up a Web server with more than one of your projects, such as those with HomeSeer and TrackerCam. You don't need multiple computers; you just need the servers to run on distinct TCP/IP ports. HomeSeer runs on port 80 by default, which is the standard Web server port, while the default for TrackerCam is port 8090. That means that you can run both Web servers on the same PC at once.

Should you need to run other Web servers on that PC, you simply need to keep the port numbers separate. Both HomeSeer and TrackerCam permit you to change port numbers, so the only problem you might have is making sure the client Web browsers use the right port number.

Applications

No matter how hard you try, we guarantee that you will have to reboot your PC Toys computer now and then, if for no other reason than long-term power failures. You want to make sure that your software runs when the computer starts up again, so you should create shortcuts in the Windows Startup folder to launch each program that must run continuously. You may also want to protect the PC from short power failures with an uninterruptible power supply (UPS). We use ones from American Power Conversion (`www.apc.com`); a small UPS capable of handling a 350 watt load can be had for $50 and up.

We keep an archive on our file server of nearly everything we download, which guarantees that we have the files we need should we have to reinstall or to rebuild the computer, regardless of any changes companies may have made on their Web sites. We've been doing that for many years, so our archive has grown to over 6GB. You can argue that that's too much and that the old material ought to be pruned, but none of our installation files ever turn up missing.

We strongly recommend that, when you're installing new software you've not used before, you limit installations to one every few days of active use. In this way, you can discover whether the new installation causes stability problems. If you install multiple programs you are not familiar with all at once, you'll have no chance to figure out which program is at fault should the machine become unstable. Even if you install them one at a time, however you can't assume that the program that crashes is the one responsible for the problem. For example, we once had the problem of Windows Explorer crashing on a previously stable machine. The only recent change had been to upgrade to version 6 of Internet Explorer, making it a likely candidate. What we found, however, was that the installation of Roxio's EZ-CD Creator on that machine had compatibility problems with both programs, and that uninstalling EZ-CD Creator was required before we could restore both Windows Explorer and Internet Explorer to proper operation.

You're going to need a way to unpack compressed files you download from the Internet. If you're running Windows XP, the ability to open and extract from the ubiquitous ZIP files is built into the operating system. For other operating systems, or if you're looking for stronger features under Windows XP, we recommend WinZip (www.winzip.com).

In line with your other efforts to control viruses, Trojans, and other hostile programs, you'll want to protect your computer from spyware. There are several good scanning and removal tools; we use AdAware from LavaSoft (www.lavasoft.de). The paid versions of AdAware include good features such as continuous, online scanning for spyware, but the freeware versions at www.lavasoft.de/support/download include a good scanner that should do if you run it periodically. Assuming you're using Internet Explorer, you can also improve your defenses against spyware by relegating their home Web sites to the restricted zone (In Internet Explorer, look under Tools, Internet Options, Security). We've done that to Gator, for example, by adding *.gator.com to the restricted zone sites list.

Summary

The key to software for your PC Toys computer is keeping stability and security foremost. We recommend wiping the computer clean and rebuilding Windows from scratch, then installing only the software you really need. The more software you install, the better your chances of coming up against bugs, so resist the temptation to install lots of utilities, tools, and other packages. Protect your LAN with a hardware router and software firewall.

Using quality hardware and following the guidelines in this chapter should result in a machine that runs well and never crashes. It's hard to ask for more from a PC.

Appendix B
Working with Your PC— Hardware

The most likely way for the world to be destroyed, most experts agree, is by accident. That's where we come in; we're computer professionals. We cause accidents.

~Nathaniel Borenstein, in *Programming as if People Mattered: Friendly Programs, Software Engineering and other Noble Delusions* (Princeton University Press, Princeton, NJ, 1991)

More than anything, when you're working with a PC's hardware you don't want any surprises. You want everything to be simple and to proceed smoothly, from the point when you remove the first screw to when you button it up, power it on, and marvel that everything works. A few solid techniques and guidelines will help you achieve that objective.

Control Static Electricity

Transistors are the tiny devices, made from silicon, that nearly all electronic devices are made from. The first transistor radios marketed in the early 1960s contained only a few transistors. The processor and graphics chips in your computer now contain tens of millions of transistors (see Figure B-1), and Intel has published many articles about its path to chips containing a billion transistors. The size of each transistor has shrunk proportionately in the intervening 40 years, which means the transistors in computers today are fantastically small. Most transistors in a computer do nothing more than switch on and off, letting electricity flow when they're on and blocking the flow when they're off. In that sense, switching transistors are much like tiny water valves.

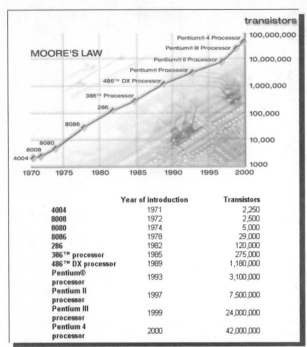

Figure B-1: Numbers of transistors in Intel processors
Source: Intel Corporation.

A tiny water valve can withstand only a small amount of water pressure before it's destroyed. The analog of water pressure in a computer is voltage, and it's precisely correct that the microscopically small transistors in a computer can withstand only a small voltage before they're destroyed. In the most recent chips packing the most transistors, the absolute maximum voltage they can withstand is less than three (or sometimes two) volts.

You, however, being somewhat bigger than a transistor, can't even feel 2 or 3 volts. If your skin's dry, you can't feel 12 volts from your car battery. You usually notice nothing below 30 volts, ten times what it takes to destroy transistors in your computer. That means voltages you're incapable of sensing can puncture holes in transistors and damage critical chips in your computer beyond repair. Static electricity (also called electrostatic discharge, or ESD) at the level that sparks as it jumps from you to a metal surface carries thousands of volts, the equivalent of a flash flood to your computer. Your feet scuffing on the floor or clothes rubbing on each other are generating enough power to create major problems. Figure B-2 shows the kind of damage ESD can create inside a chip.

You're not likely to have problems when your computer box is closed up, because unless you touch a pin on a connecting cable before you touch a grounded surface, the static charge can't reach anything vulnerable. Most cable connections are somewhat protected (however, see the sidebar "Be Careful How You Handle Ethernet Cables"), but it's good practice to avoid touching the contacts.

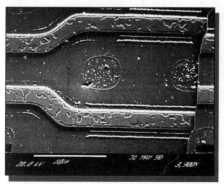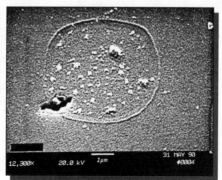

FIGURE B-2: Electrostatic discharge damage to an integrated circuit

Be Careful How You Handle Ethernet Cables

The RJ-45 modular connectors you find on 10/100Base-T Ethernet cables are potential static electricity problems. If you have one end plugged into a computer or switch, but the other end isn't connected, that open end is a direct path for static electricity to the sensitive electronics at the other end. The cable jacket is always insulated, so it doesn't drain away the static charge. However, if you pick up the cable and even brush against the exposed contacts, any built-up charge goes straight down the cable. We've seen many switch ports fail from just this sort of accident, so pay attention when you're connecting and disconnecting Ethernets.

We're well aware that millions of people have opened their PCs, inserted or removed components, closed them up, and had nothing untoward happen (or, latent damage being what it is, nothing happen right then). Nevertheless, we're not making this up, and we're not alone in what we say. Consider the following:

- Intel advises its customers about ESD at www.intel.com/design/packtech/ch_06.pdf (among others; search the Intel Web site for ESD).

- Gateway Computers warns about ESD and offers guidelines on how to prevent damage at support.gateway.com/s/Mobile/SHARED/SoloESD.shtml.

- The United States Marine Corps Aviation Training Branch training on ESD is at www.tecom.usmc.mil/atb/MATMEP/MS%20Word%20Lesson%20guide%20PDF%20files/Lg13.pdf.

- NASA provides a general description of their ESD protection requirements at workmanship.nasa.gov/lib/insp/2%20books/links/sections/11-01%20General%20Requirements.html.

- www.esda.org/ is the web site of the Electrostatic Discharge Association (ESDA).

- Enough people care about ESD to make a magazine devoted to the subject worthwhile; see *ESD Journal* at www.esdjournal.com.

It's not that hard to prevent ESD damage—all you really have to do is to make sure to minimize the potential sources and ground the sources you can't eliminate. At a minimum, touch metal before touching your computer when you're working on it, and avoid moving your feet around. Far better is to wear an anti-static wrist strap ($4.99 at Radio Shack, see catalog number 276-2397 at `www.radioshack.com`), connecting the alligator clip at the end either to a cold water pipe or the metal chassis on the computer. However,

UNPLUG THE COMPUTER FROM THE WALL BEFORE CLIPPING ON YOUR GROUND STRAP.

There are some very bad recommendations in books and on the Internet that say you should leave your computer plugged in while you work on it so the ground line in the power cord can help drain off static electricity. It's a good idea only on the surface, because computer power supplies no longer really turn off when you shut down the computer. Instead, a small auxiliary power line remains active to run the circuits that actually turn on the computer when you push the power switch, when a LAN message arrives, or when the modem needs to answer the phone. Therefore, if there's a short in the power supply, you could be electrocuted. Always unplug your computer before you open it up.

You should also be careful about the surfaces on which you work. Wood and metal are good, but plastic and carpet (which build up static charges) are very bad. The anti-static bags that electronic devices are sometimes packaged in (look for the anti-static label on the bag) are good for storing circuit cards, but don't close them with cellophane or adhesive tape. (Peel tape off plastic in absolute dark, after letting your eyes adjust, and watch the light show from the static sparks. Every one is a death warrant for unprotected electronics.)

Finally, avoid touching other people while you're working on exposed electronics. They likely won't be grounded, and the spark that jumps from them to you won't stop until it passes through you, through the electronics in your computer, and dissipates into ground.

Use the Right Tools

Yeah, we know there's nothing you can't do with a vise grip, a hammer, and a screwdriver. Nevertheless, you might want a slightly more comprehensive tool kit for working on your computer. We suggest this list:

- Screwdrivers (both slotted and Phillips) in a range of sizes from small to medium. Magnetic screwdrivers are good because they help keep screws from falling where they're hard to retrieve. The magnetic field isn't strong enough to cause damage to disk drives, although you should keep it away from floppy disks. We used a really tiny watchmaker's screwdriver once to make an adjustment that fixed read errors on the DVD drive in a Sony Playstation 2, but it's rare to need a screwdriver that small.

- Socket (hex head) drivers in 3/16, 7/32, and 1/4 inch sizes.

- Pliers, including a pair of very long needle-nose pliers.

- Flashlight. We have both a regular flashlight and another with a bright halogen bulb at the end of a stiff but flexible extension.

- Mirror, preferably one on a long handle that can pivot.

A multimeter (even a cheap one) is useful for testing power supply levels. It's been years since we needed a soldering iron to fix a problem in a computer, but if you do need to solder around tiny electronics, make sure you're using a small, low power iron, not a butane torch and not the branding iron the family patriarch used to make tin cans after the Civil War. You can get complete kits (see Figure B-3) with sets of tools sized for what you'll be doing.

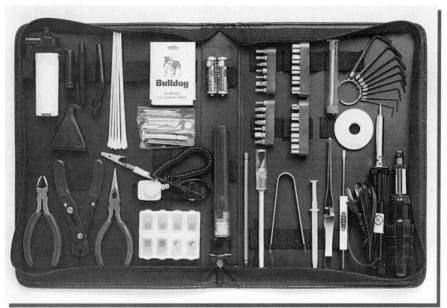

FIGURE B-3: Computer repair tool kit
Courtesy of Belkin Corporation

Keep Track of What You Do

Usually, when friends show up at our door with a bucket of computer parts and a sheepish grin, the first thing they say is "Oops." This happens more than you might suspect. The very next thing they say, without fail, is "We couldn't figure out how this goes back together."

Unless you know enough about the insides of your computer to figure out how it goes back together, make drawings or print pictures to refer to later. Be sure to record the location and orientation of connectors (such as from the front panel), and of the striped wire (pin one on the connector) for all the ribbon cables. Power connectors are almost always keyed, but be sure to note which way they're turned. Keep track of screws you remove and put them back where they were—some disk drives have restrictions on screw depth in certain locations, and if you put too long a screw back in the wrong hole, you'll either short out a circuit card or damage the internal mechanism.

Summary

Even if you've never done it before, working inside your computer isn't very hard. Follow the manufacturer's instructions for the disk or card you're installing, be careful and methodical, guard against static electricity, and use the right tools, and you shouldn't have any problems.

What's on the CD-ROM

A library, to modify the famous metaphor of Socrates, should be the delivery room for the birth of ideas — a place where history comes to life.

~Norman Cousins, American Library Association Bulletin, Oct 54

This appendix provides you with information on system requirements, using the CD, and the contents of the CD that accompanies this book. The most current information will be in the ReadMe file located at the root of the CD.

System Requirements

Make sure that your computer meets the minimum system requirements listed in this section. If your computer doesn't match most of these requirements, you may have a problem using the contents of the CD. Your PC must meet the minimum requirements for the version of Windows you're running in order to operate the CD. Individual programs on the CD have varying requirements; see the relevant chapters in the book or ReadMe files with each program.

The CD should work with Windows 9x (preferably Windows 98 or later), Windows 2000, and Windows XP. It may work with Windows NT.

Using the CD with Windows

To install the items from the CD to your hard drive, follow these steps:

1. Insert the CD into your computer's CD-ROM drive.

2. A window will appear that gives you the following options: Install, Browse, eBook, Links, and Exit.

   Install. Gives you the option to install software from the CD-ROM.

   Browse. Allows you to view the contents of the CD-ROM in its directory structure.

   eBook. Allows you to view an electronic version of the book.

   Links. Opens a hyperlinked page of Web sites.

   Exit. Closes the autorun window.

If you do not have autorun enabled or if the autorun window does not appear, follow the steps below to access the CD.

1. Click Start ➔ Run.

2. In the dialog box that appears, type **d:\setup.exe**, where *d* is the letter of your CD-ROM drive. This will bring up the autorun window described above.

3. Choose the Install, Browse, eBook, Links, or Exit option from the menu. (See Step 2 in the preceding list for a description of these options.)

What's on the CD

The following sections provide a summary of the software and other materials you'll find on the CD.

Applications

The following applications are on the CD.

Shareware programs are fully functional, trial versions of copyrighted programs. If you like particular programs, register with their authors for a nominal fee and receive licenses, enhanced versions, and technical support. *Freeware programs* are copyrighted games, applications, and utilities that are free for personal use. Unlike shareware, these programs do not require a fee or provide technical support. *GNU software* is governed by its own license, which is included inside the folder of the GNU product. See the GNU license for more details.

Trial, demo, or evaluation versions are usually limited either by time or functionality (for example, some will not allow you to save projects). Some trial versions are very sensitive to system date changes. If you alter your computer's date, the programs will "time out" and no longer be functional.

Acrobat Reader, from Adobe Systems Inc.

Acrobat Reader is the free Portable Document Format (PDF) reader version for Windows. You'll need to install Acrobat Reader to view the eBook of *PC Toys* included on this CD-ROM.

GoldWave, from GoldWave Inc.

GoldWave (www.goldwave.com) is a terrific sound file editor, able to play, edit, mix, and analyze audio; apply special effects; improve recordings with noise reduction and pop/click filters; record audio through your sound card line-in port; make copies of audio CD tracks and save them in MP3, WMA, or Vorbis files; and convert among file formats, including WAV, MP3, OGG, AIFF, AU, and VOX.

The shareware version of GoldWave on the CD-ROM requires Windows ME, Windows 2000, or Windows XP. Windows 98 works, but is not officially supported. Windows NT/95 are not supported and will not work. System requirements include a 700MHz processor,

256MB RAM, 1GB free hard drive space, an accelerated video card, and a DirectX compatible sound card driver with DirectX 8 or later installed.

HomeSeer, from HomeSeer Technologies LLC

The CD-ROM includes a 30-day trial version of HomeSeer, the home automation software used in Chapters 3, 6, and 7. You can find more information and purchasing details on HomeSeer's Web site (www.homeseer.com). HomeSeer runs on Microsoft Windows XP, Windows 2000, Windows NT, Windows 98, and Windows 95.

Nero Burning ROM, from Ahead Software AG

Ahead Software's Nero Burning ROM (www.nero.com) is the CD-ROM/DVD burning software we use, because it's straightforward and reliable. The demonstration version on the CD-ROM includes Nero Express, a wizard to simplify making CD-ROMs and DVDs. Nero runs on Microsoft Windows NT 4.0, Windows 2000, Windows XP, Windows 95, Windows 98, and Windows Me, and against a wide variety of recorders.

Pinnacle Studio, from Pinnacle Systems Inc.

We use Pinnacle Studio (www.pinnaclesys.com) to make DVDs of recordings from our Personal Video Recorder, and have found it easy to use and dependable. A trial version of Studio on the CD-ROM is capable of running on Microsoft Windows 98SE, Windows Me, Windows 2000, and Windows XP.

Railroad & Co. TrainController, from Freiwald Software

TrainController (www.railroadandco.com) gives you the ability to control your computer-controlled model railroad from your PC. The trial version on the CD-ROM is limited in some of its functions and in how long it will run without restarting. TrainController runs on Microsoft Windows XP, Windows 98, Windows 2000, Windows NT or Windows 95.

SocketWatch, from Robomagic Corporation

SocketWatch (www.locutuscodeware.com/index.htm) is a shareware utility that keeps your computer's time synchronized to time servers on the Internet. Time synchronization is particularly important on computers used for telescope control (see Chapter 4). SocketWatch is compatible with all versions of Windows 9x, Windows NT, Windows 2000, and Windows XP.

TrackerCam, from Eagletron Inc.

TrackerCam is the pedestal control and motion tracking software supporting the TrackerPod in Chapter 6. The CD-ROM contains an evaluation version; the full version comes with the TrackerPod (www.trackercam.com). The software supports Windows 98SE, Windows Me, Windows 2000, and Windows XP. Windows 95 and NT are not supported.

Unreal Tournament 2003, from Epic Games

Unreal Tournament 2003 is a fast, first person multiplayer shooter that's perfect for LAN parties (Chapter 13). The free demo is on the CD-ROM, and runs on Windows 98, Windows ME, Windows 2000, or Windows XP. You'll need a 1 GHz or faster CPU and a robust video card to play; much less to host a server. The web site is www.unrealtournament.com.

VisualGPS, from VGPS

VisualGPS gives you insight into the operation of the GPS receiver you've connected to your PC, as described in Chapter 10. The version on the CD-ROM is freeware; an extended version (VisualGPSXP) is available for purchase on the Web site (www.visualgps.net). The software runs on Microsoft Windows 9x, Windows NT4.0, or later.

WinZip, from WinZip Computing, Inc.

WinZip is the definitive file compression tool suite, providing a standalone application, integration into Windows Explorer, and a wizard to coach new users through making and using ZIP archives. The version on the CD-ROM is shareware; full details on purchase options are on the Web site (www.winzip.com). WinZip runs on all versions of Microsoft Windows 9x, Windows NT, Windows 2000, and Windows XP.

WXSIM Weather Simulator, from Thomas J. Ehrensperger

WXSIM is the freeware weather simulation software you'll use in Chapter 11 to create weather forecasts from data you collect with your weather station. Tom Ehrensperger's WXSIM page (members.aol.com/eburger/wxsim.html) contains the full details on the program, and contains details on how to purchase a version customized to simulate your exact location. The customized version is also available at Weather Graphics (www.weathergraphics.com/wxsim/index.htm).

eBook version of PC Toys

The complete text of this book is on the CD in Adobe's PDF format. You can read and search through the file with the Adobe Acrobat Reader (also included on the CD).

Web Links

There are nearly 300 Web links in PC Toys to connect you to sources for products and information. The CD-ROM includes all those links, organized by chapter, so you can simply point and click rather than typing each URL into your browser. Web links break when people and companies change the linked sites. If you find a broken link, check the PC Toys web site at www.wiley.com/extremetech for updates. If we've not found and fixed the problem, try either looking at the base web site (so from www.wiley.com/extremetech you'd move to www.wiley.com) or searching the site with the site's built in search or with Google if the site doesn't offer search."

Troubleshooting

If you have difficulty installing or using any of the materials on the companion CD, try the following solutions:

- **Turn off any anti-virus software that you may have running.** Installers sometimes mimic virus activity and can make your computer incorrectly believe that a virus is trying to infect it. Be sure to turn the anti-virus software back on after you've finished the installation.

- **Close all running programs.** The more programs you're running, the less memory is available to other programs. Installers also typically update files and programs; if you keep other programs running, installation may not work properly.

- **Check the ReadMe:** Please refer to the ReadMe file located at the root of the CD-ROM for the latest product information at the time of publication.

If you still have trouble with the CD-ROM, please call the Wiley Product Technical Support phone number: (800) 762-2974. Outside the United States, call 1(317) 572-3994. You can also contact Wiley Product Technical Support at www.wiley.com/techsupport. Wiley Publishing will provide technical support only for installation and other general quality control items; for technical support on the applications themselves, consult the program's vendor or author.

To place additional orders or to request information about other Wiley products, please call (800) 225-5945.

Index

Continued

Continued

Continued